TWAYNE'S WORLD AUTHORS SERIES

A Survey of the World's Literature

GERMANY

Ulrich Weisstein, Indiana University

EDITOR

Heinrich Böll

TWAS 622

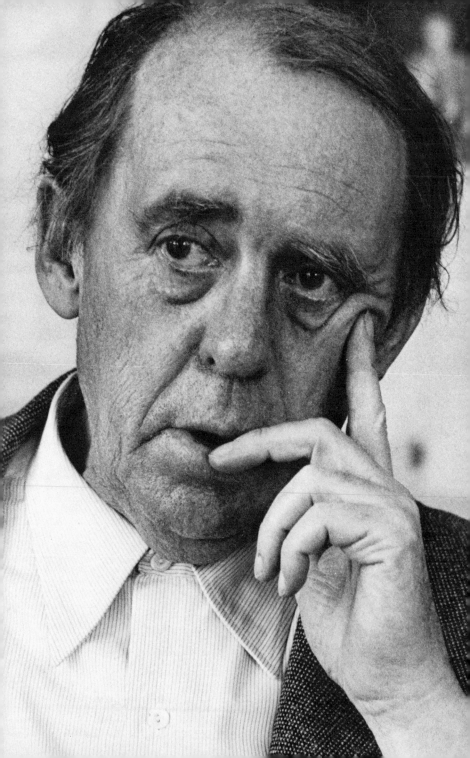

HEINRICH BÖLL

By ROBERT C. CONARD

University of Dayton

TWAYNE PUBLISHERS

A DIVISION OF G. K. HALL & CO., BOSTON

Published in 1981 by Twayne Publishers,
A Division of G. K. Hall & Co.
All Rights Reserved

Printed on permanent/durable acid-free paper and bound
in the United States of America

First Printing   ·

Frontispiece photo of Heinrich Böll
© by Isolde Ohlbaum

Library of Congress Cataloging in Publication Data

Conard, Robert C., 1933–
Heinrich Böll.

(Twayne's world authors series ; TWAS 622. Germany)
Bibliography: pp. 217–25
Includes index.
1. Böll, Heinrich, 1917–   . 2. Authors, German
—20th century—Biography. I. Title. II. Series:
Twayne's world authors series ; TWAS 622. III. Series:
Twayne's world authors series. Germany.
PT2603.0394Z596   833'.914 [B]   81–2419
ISBN 0–8057–6464–X   AACR2

To

Guy Stern

Contents

About the Author

Robert C. Conard was born in 1933 in Cincinnati, Ohio. In 1956–1957, he studied at the University of Vienna and in 1966 at the University of Munich. Shortly before receiving the Ph.D. from the University of Cincinnati in 1969, he accepted a position at the University of Dayton, where he is currently Professor of German Language and Literature. The recipient of several research fellowships from the University of Dayton, he has also received National Educational Act and National Endowment for the Humanities grants, including one for study at Yale University in 1978.

During his years at the University of Dayton, Professor Conard has published many translations of essays, poetry, fiction, and dramatic works. The plays *Highwater* by Günter Grass and *The Bakery* by Bertolt Brecht received their U.S. premier performances at the University of Dayton in his translations. In collaboration with Ralph Ley of Rutgers University, Professor Conard is also the American translator of Heinrich Böll's poetry. Other works translated by Dr. Conard include fiction by Wolfgang Hildesheimer and poems by Nelly Sachs.

Numerous essays on Hermann Hesse, Adalbert Stifter, Jonathan Swift as well as Brecht and Böll comprise Professor Conard's contributions to criticism of German and comparative literature. These articles, along with reviews, have appeared in such professional journals as the *German Quarterly, Monatshefte, Brecht-Jahrbuch, Michigan Academician, University of Dayton Review, Modern Languages Journal, Germanic Notes, New German Critique,* and *German Studies Review.*

Preface

In this monograph I treat the life and major works of Heinrich Böll, discussing all the novels and novellas published before 1978 as well as most of the important short stories. I omit discussion of Böll's two outstanding satires, "Nicht nur zur Weihnachtszeit" [Christmas Everyday] and "Der Wegwerfer" [The Thrower-away], because my interpretations of these stories have already appeared elsewhere in scholarly journals. I also exclude treatment of Böll's plays, essays, and poetry although I refer to his works in these genres when references to them enhance my interpretations of the fiction. These limitations are appropriate in this series, for Böll's international reputation rests primarily on his novels and short stories.

In these two genres Böll demonstrates not only his considerable talents as an artist but also his deep political and religious convictions. Despite the public reaction to the political content of his work, Böll's impetus to write seldom derives from political considerations. In an interview in 1976 with René Wintzen, Böll concluded: "I am of the conviction that what comes to one from outside does not change one very much.... Everything history throws at one's feet, war, peace, Nazis, communists, the bourgeois, is really secondary. What counts is a thorough-going, I would almost say, mythological-theological problematic that is always present.... There are authors whose immediate impulse to write is political. Mine was not" (*Werke: Interviews*, pp. 516, 519).

This apparent political disclaimer does not, however, remove the obvious social criticism from Böll's works. He remains a critical realist, a writer who tells his romantic stories in a manner which challenges the society he lives in. When Böll says his novels would be essentially the same without war and without Nazis, without Germany's economic recovery—works about marriage and the church, or as he expressed it in an interview with Marcel Reich-Ranicki in 1967, about love and religion—he is not denying his social commitment or the political aspect of his work, only emphasizing that for him theme is more important than setting.

In analyzing the theme and setting of Böll's work, I draw freely on contemporary theology and German politics to support my interpretations. In choosing this approach, I offer no new method, but carry on a well-established tradition in Böll criticism—the most fruitful one to date.

The translations used in this book are my own unless otherwise stated, and throughout the book, in referring to titles, I have given the date of the German publication.

ROBERT C. CONARD

University of Dayton

Acknowledgments

It is a pleasant task to record my gratitude to those persons and institutions that most helped me in this work. I am most indebted to Ralph Ley of Rutgers University and Jeffrey Sammons of Yale University, who generously read the typescript of this monograph and from whose wise counsel and invaluable suggestions I have drawn encouragement and profit.

I also wish to thank the staff of the University of Dayton Library for procuring the necessary research materials for me, the University of Dayton Research Council for a summer grant to begin this project; the Mugar Library of Boston University for opening its holding in the Heinrich Böll Archive to me; especially the National Endowment for the Humanities for making available a summer seminar at Yale University, where I was able to complete the first draft of this book; and finally Mrs. Sue Kirtley-Dyer, who, often from poor copy, patiently and conscientiously typed the manuscript for me.

Chronology

1917 21 December: Heinrich Böll born in Cologne to Viktor and Maria (née Hermanns) Böll.

1924– Begins his formal education at a Catholic elementary
1927 school in Cologne.

1928– Attends Kaiser Wilhelm Gymnasium in Cologne.
1937

1932 Member of a Catholic youth club, gives up membership when the club begins to support the Nazi program.

1933 1 May: Observes the first Nazi march in Cologne; realizes the seriousness of the political situation.

1938 Becomes an apprentice to a book dealer in Bonn; commutes daily from Cologne; in spring gives up the apprenticeship.

1939 Summer: enrolls at the University of Cologne to study German and classics.

1939– July: inducted into the *Wehrmacht* as an infantryman.
1945

1942 Becomes interpreter for the German staff in a small French coastal village; while on leave marries Annemarie Cech, an English teacher.

1947 Publishes first short stories.

1949 Signs contract with Middelhauve and publishes first book, the novella *The Train Was on Time*.

1950 *Wanderer kommst du nach Spa...*, collection of twenty-five short stories (all contained in *Children Are Civilians Too*).

1951 Receives the prize of "Group 47" for the short story "The Black Sheep"; publishes first novel, *Adam, Where Art Thou*. Middelhauve cancels his contract because of few sales.

1952 Receives the René Schickele Prize; signs new contract

with Kiepenheuer & Witsch; publishes the satire *Christmas Every Day*.

1953 *Acquainted with the Night*; receives the German Critics Prize and the Southern German Radio's Writers Prize for the radio play "Mönch und Räuber"; made a member of the German Academy for Language and Literature.

1954 *Tomorrow and Yesterday*; receives the prize of the *Tribune de Paris* for the best foreign novel.

1955 *The Bread of Those Early Years*; takes first trip to Ireland; receives the Cultural Prize of German Industry.

1956 *Unberechenbare Gäste* [*Uninvited Guests*], a collection of satires; takes second trip to Ireland.

1957 *Irish Journal; In the Valley of the Thundering Hooves*; visits East Germany and Poland.

1958 Receives the Honor Award of the Bavarian Academy of the Arts and the Edward von der Heydt Prize of the city of Wupperthal; publishes *Doktor Murkes gesammeltes Schweigen*, a collection of satires.

1959 *Billiards at Half-past Nine*; receives the Grand Art Prize of North Rhineland and Westphalia.

1960 Cofounds and coedits the Christian-Socialist periodical *Labyrinth*; receives the Charles Veillon Prize.

1961 *Erzählungen, Hörspiele, Aufsätze*; receives the Literature Prize of the City of Cologne.

1963 *The Clown.*

1964 *Absent without Leave*; summer: becomes guest lecturer for poetics at the University of Frankfurt.

1966 *End of a Mission; Frankfurter Vorlesungen.*

1967 *Aufsätze, Kritiken, Reden*, essays, criticism, and speeches from 1952–1967; receives the George Büchner Prize; becomes seriously ill with hepatitis, diabetes, and inflammation of the liver.

1968 August: witnesses the Warsaw Pact's invasion of Czechoslovakia while visiting Czech writers in Prague.

1969 Elected president of the West German PEN club; receives the Literature Prize of the City of Cologne for the second time; moves to Hülchrather Strasse 7 in the old section of Cologne.

1971 *Group Portrait with Lady*; September 13: elected president of the International PEN club, serves till May 1974; makes first visit to the United States to read from his works at American universities.

1972 10 January: publishes in *Der Spiegel* the essay "Will Ulrike Gnade oder freies Geleit," appealing for compassion for radicals hunted by the police. Receives the Nobel Prize for literature; publishes *Gedichte*, first volume of poetry; *Erzählungen 1950–1970*.

1973 *Neue politische und literarische Schriften*, essays from 1967–1972; takes second trip to the United States for the publication of *Group Portrait*.

1974 *The Lost Honor of Katharina Blum*; receives the Carl von Ossietzky Medal from the International League of Human Rights; made honorary member of the American Academy of Art and Literature and of the American National Institute of Art and Literature; gives Soviet Nobel laureate Alexander Solzhenitsyn his first refuge in the West.

1975 *Berichte zur Gesinnungslage der Nation*.

1977 *Einmischung erwünscht*, essays from 1971–1976; *Heinrich Böll Werke*, 5 vols., novels and stories from 1947–1977.

1978 *Heinrich Böll Werke*, 5 vols., radio plays, dramas, film texts, poems, essays, reviews, speeches, commentaries, interviews, and sundry writings from 1952–1978.

1979 *Fürsorgliche Belagerung*.

CHAPTER 1

Introduction

HEINRICH Böll's life and work bear the mark of a man who experienced before he was thirty years of age an empire, a republic, a dictatorship, a military occupation, and a second republic. Böll is as old as the Russian revolution and would be the same age as John F. Kennedy if Kennedy were alive today. He was born in the city of Cologne 21 December 1917 as the eighth child of Viktor and Maria (née Hermanns) Böll. In the short biographical sketch "Über mich selbst" (1958) Böll reveals the experiences which have become the subject of his fiction: hunger and poverty, Nazism, war, and the liquidation of the Jews. His earliest experience with poverty was the inflation after World War I when the first pocket money the young Böll received was ironically a "bill which bore a figure to honor Rockefeller's account: one billion marks" (EHA, p. 397); with it he bought a stick of candy. The inflation was so intense that his father hauled money from the bank in a truck to pay the workers in his shop. Unemployment and hunger were so widespread that his school comrades begged bread from him at recess. Less momentous, but still important for Böll's literary development, were his father's woodworking shop with its smells of wood, glue, shellac, and stains; the parks and gardens of Cologne; the Teutonic names of the streets where he lived; the Rhine; the barges on which he played; and his mother's coffee. This hot and friendly drink was offered to every visitor in the Böll house as a token of hospitality. The offered cup recurs throughout Böll's work as a symbol of simple human pleasure and shared brotherhood.

Böll's moral response to the events of history was shaped in his childhood by devout Catholic parents who reared their children with respect for Christian teachings as embodied in The Sermon on the Mount and Christ's command to love one's neighbor as oneself, but with a critical attitude to the church as an institution. Böll's mother was descended from a long line of German Catholic farmers and brewers, and his father's family, as Böll states, "came centuries ago from the British Isles—Catholics who preferred emigration to the state religion of Henry VIII" (*EHA*, p. 396). These early immigrant forbears who eventually settled in the Rhineland were skilled craftsmen, and through the centuries the Böll's have remained in the artisan class. Böll's father was a cabinetmaker, trained in the old tradition of ornamental wood sculpture. Upon his death, Böll's older brother, Alois, took over the family workshop. After World War II, before finding work with the city of Cologne in its statistical office and before publishing his early stories, Böll too worked briefly in the family carpentry shop.

Böll's childhood was not, as is often the case with prominent artists, an unhappy one. Böll has written very little autobiography, but in "Interview mit mir selbst" (1965) he praises his mother as a "wonderful great woman"[1] and in the essay, entitled after that part of the Rhineland where he grew up, "Raderberg, Raderthal" (1965), he writes of a happy childhood although his family was forced by the inflation of the 1920s and the depression of the 1930s to move several times to various quarters in and near Cologne. Despite the hard times, his parents treated their children with exceptional understanding. They were not swayed by public sentiment, were confident enough in their political and religious convictions to permit their children to associate with the Socialists in their neighborhood. They "never . . . thought to do what the professors, attorneys, architects, and bank directors did: forbid their children to play with the 'reds'" (*AKR*, p. 184).

This free atmosphere of the parents' home taught the children that people were to be judged by their character, not by shibboleths. Böll traces his favorable attitude to socialism to his family's liberal Catholic tradition. Although his father was a solid supporter of the Catholic Center party ("black to the marrow"[2]), his mother, though nonideological in her thinking, was a "real and true Catholic leftist in comparison to whom all other Catholic leftists paled."[3] Böll also gives credit for his rejection of fascism to his parents, his brothers and sisters, and countless friends and their friends, as well as a few teachers who protected him from becoming a Nazi.[4] The East German critic Günter Wirth states simply: "Böll's humanism . . . would be unthinkable without his Catholic background."[5]

At the age of six Böll began to attend a Catholic elementary school. Three years later he left the denominational institution for a college preparatory high school (*Gymnasium*). He was surprised that none of the children of his Socialist neighbors went to the *Gymnasium* with him. He liked the preparatory school "but could not understand why the others, the 'reds' and the 'not so good Catholics'" could not go with him ("Raderberg, Raderthal," *AKR*, p. 187). With this last remark Böll complains of the social conditions in Germany which, then and now, make it difficult for many children from working-class backgrounds to prepare for the university.

While attending the *Gymnasium* in the closing days of the Weimar Republic, Böll saw how the National Socialists brought the strikes, riots, and unemployment caused by the depression of the 1930s under control. He observed how "the unemployed were given work as policemen, soldiers, executioners, and armament workers—and how the rest went to concentration camps" ("Über mich selbst," *EHA*, p. 397). He condemns the bogus prosperity of the early Nazi years and acknowledges, without accepting the idea of collective guilt, the German responsibility for the Nazi crimes: "The statistics balanced, the Reichsmark flowed in streams, the bill was paid later by us, as we, in the meantime, unaware, became men and tried to comprehend the evil but could not find the formula; the sum of suffering was too great for the few who were obviously guilty; there remains a residue of guilt which today has not yet been apportioned" (*EHA*, pp. 397–98).

After graduation from the *Gymnasium* in 1937 Böll became an apprentice book clerk in Bonn, to which city he commuted daily from Cologne. Here he catalogued the book collections which his employer purchased and sent out lists of the dealer's holdings. For his labors he received ten marks a month. But the job brought him into contact with books difficult to come by in Nazi Germany.

In the winter of 1938–39 he was called to compulsory labor service and was required to dig irrigation ditches and to do forestry work. After completion of his labor service he wanted to study German philology and literature at the University of Cologne, but his refusal to become a party member made enrollment difficult. However, shortly after matriculation in 1939 he was called into military service for an eight-week training course. He felt then that Hitler was set on war and that the short training period would last much longer. When the war broke out in September, he was already in the army. His military service lasted the full six years of the war. Through this entire period Böll never stopped hoping for the defeat of his country and liberation from National Socialism.

In 1940 he was garrisoned in Poland. In Bydgoszcz (Bromberg) he witnessed for the first time the cruelty of the SS to the suppressed people in the occupied territories. At the end of June 1940 he was sent to France, where the war was already over. Near Amiens he became sick with dysentery and had to be returned to Germany. After his recovery he guarded supply depots in Cologne and the surrounding Rhineland. In 1942 he was returned to France and stationed on the Atlantic Wall between Abbeville and Dieppe. In France he read whenever possible, especially the passionate French Catholic Léon Bloy, to whose writings he had first been introduced as a student in the *Gymnasium* and to whose work his own writing bears an affinity.[6]

On leave in 1942 he married Annemarie Cech, his boyhood sweetheart, now a teacher of English. He sensed if he were to survive the war and retain his mental and moral balance, he would need the help of this woman. His wife has since borne him three sons and works with him in translating American and English literature. During the remainder of the war they wrote daily letters to each other. (None has ever been published.)

In the summer of 1943 Böll was transferred to the eastern front, but before the train crossed the French frontier it struck a mine laid by the Maquis. Böll was injured on the right hand and again returned to Germany. This reprieve from the terrors of the war in the East lasted only two weeks. He was then sent to the Crimea, where he was wounded in the leg. But the injury was not serious enough for him to be shipped home. Shortly afterward a grenade fragment struck him in the head and necessitated his being sent to a field hospital in Odessa. When he recovered, the front was approaching the city. He was transferred to Iasi (Jassy) in Rumania, where eight days later he was wounded again, this time seriously, in the back. Until August 1944 he remained in a field hospital in Hungary. Böll, who previously had often tried to avoid military activities by malingering, now made more serious attempts to escape the war. Because of the growing confusion of the imminent German defeat, he was able to return to his regimental headquarters in Metz with forged papers. Here he managed to obtain a legitimate pass to visit home by claiming a death in the family.[7] On this visit, he and his wife conspired to keep him out of the war by dangerous intravenous injections used against syphilis. The resulting high fever kept him in the hospital until February 1945, after which time the injections no longer had their desired effect. When this ruse failed, Böll deserted and took his wife to a small village outside of Cologne. Because desertion meant immediate execution, Böll forged his own papers to return to his regiment near Mannheim. Here he was able to procure a pass to return home. In these final desperate days of the war, survival was the only sensible plan of action. When his pass expired, he deserted again, hoping for a speedy Allied liberation from his fellow Germans. When the American army approached, he found a gun that would not shoot, joined a troop in the area, and pretended to fight the enemy for fourteen days until he was taken prisoner on 9 April 1945. In 1964 Böll wrote: "I was released on 15 September 1945, but from German imprisonment" ("Stichworte," *AKR*, p. 170). After six years in the service he had reached the rank of lance corporal—customarily most graduates from the *Gymnasium* became officers upon induction—an indication of his contempt for the military.

Although the policies of the National Socialist regime had led to the deaths of 20 million Russians, 6 million Jews, and several million other combatants and civilians in the occupied countries, in the Allied nations, and in Germany itself, Böll's experiences in the Hitler years led him to reject the concept of collective guilt.[8] He witnessed too many individual acts of humaneness by Germans to condemn his compatriots outright. For example, there was the young lieutenant who did not report him for falling asleep and forgetting the password while on sentry duty,[9] an offense which near the end of the war was most often punished by death; he also singles out the Nazi functionary who eliminated his mother's name from a Gestapo list of those who had publicly denounced Hitler (Interestingly, the informant who reported his mother for her traitorous remarks made in an air-raid shelter in 1940 was not a party member and after the war ran for political office as a Christian Democrat with a "clean political past"); then too there were the Germans he knew who had hidden Jews and secretly fed Poles and Russians ("Hierzulande," *EHA*, p. 434).

Böll sees, however, another kind of common culpability in West Germany: "If there is a beginning of collective guilt in this country, then it starts with the 'currency reform' when this nation sold out its pain, sorrow, and memory" ("Hierzulande," *EHA*, p. 437). Böll's critical attitude toward the currency reform and the resulting "economic miracle" is an essential point to grasp. The currency reform, designed by Ludwig Erhard and Adenauer's Christian Democratic party, and supported by billions of dollars of U.S. aid and investment, was a triumph to stagger the popular imagination. Germany's present prosperity can be traced to it. Its success kept the Christian Democrats in power for two decades, until the victory of the Social Democratic party under Willy Brandt in 1969.

Böll's objection to the currency reform of 1948 rests on two counts. The first is moral. The lessons so painfully learned during twelve years of National Socialism were forgotten in a brief time with the new prosperity—greed quickly replaced remorse. Böll's second objection to the currency reform is economic. The reform favored most those who controlled the means of production, and least those who had to work for a living. Ralph Ley's summary of this historic event is terse and accurate: "Overnight the market was flooded with hoarded goods, and the farmers began rushing the foodstuffs they had hidden to the city markets. Although it was hard on the 'little man', the value of whose bank account or savings was reduced by more than ninety percent, the reform favored the capitalist. His resources in factories, real estate, and stocks were left intact and his debts were generally reduced by nine-tenths."[10] As a critic of this "German salvation" Böll is an outsider in his own country.

Since the war and its aftermath represent the central experiences in Böll's life and work, it is important to understand how Germans were living on 15 September 1945, the day Böll returned to Cologne, to a city and a nation in hunger and in ruin, finally freed from what he considered twelve years of "German imprisonment" ("Stichworte," *AKR*, p. 170). Until 1945 Germans thought of the Thirty Years War (1618–1648) as their greatest period of suffering and death. During those years about half of the German population succumbed to war and plague, but after World War II the Germans could measure disaster from a new personal point of reference. Every large city lay in ruins. Three and a half million soldiers had died in the war; millions more were in prison camps, and very few Germans had adequate shelter. There was no industry to give jobs, and there were no incomes to buy the little food or clothing available. The nation was reduced to a barter economy with a thriving black market. Without heat, light, or water Germany was exposed, in the winters of 1945–1946 and 1946–1947, to the worst cold in fifty years. Besides the high loss of life in the war, there were a million and a half wounded, of whom half were 50 percent disabled; there were nearly a million widows, 250,000 orphans, a million and a quarter half-orphans and a female population double the male population. But for Böll's generation who had fought the war, those born about 1917, the ratio was much worse.[11] Two-thirds of the males in this age group were dead by 1945, and there were at the end of the war 80 percent more women aged twenty-eight than men. Most of the German population was very young or very old.

Food, however, remained the worst problem. The official ration was 1,500 calories per day; whereas United Nations experts calculated 2,650 calories per day were necessary to maintain health, most Germans were lucky to receive 900. By January 1948 the daily ration was two potatoes (not always available), three slices of bread, a tablespoon of cheese (if available), 2.8 ounces of lard, and a small quantity of malt coffee. There was also a monthly ration of seven ounces of meat, a pound of flour, and a pound of sugar. Böll writes of this period: "Everyone possessed his naked life and besides that only what he could get his hands on: coal, wood, books, building materials. Everyone was guilty of theft. Whoever did not freeze to death in the destroyed large cities must have stolen his coal, and whoever did not die of hunger had procured his food in an illegal manner" ("Heimat und keine," *AKR*, p. 204).

When Böll returned in 1945 from the relative security of an American POW camp to the destruction and chaos of Cologne, one of his immediate concerns was to procure a ration card. To do this he had to have an occupation. He enrolled at the University of Cologne and with his student status and ration card began the integration process into a new Germany, temporarily at least a nearly classless society. Although he had no need of de-Nazification and accepted Germany's defeat and economic collapse as a necessity, he has never completely reconciled himself to the form of democracy and economics which has developed in the Federal Republic. He had high hopes for a "new Germany," for a democracy built on the concept of humaneness derived from the common experience of the nation's guilt, sorrow, and collective suffering. His hope was rooted in the reality of brotherhood which existed after the war in those brief years before the currency reform ushered in the new prosperity, aroused greed, and revived the old class system. But Germany was not able to build a nation on the principle of shared political and economic need. The near "utopia" born of deprivation dissolved with the advent of the "economic miracle."

Böll's first job after the war was in the family carpentry shop, now run by his brother, but he soon found employment with the statistical office of the city of Cologne; still, the financial basis of his life was his wife's income as a teacher. During this time he wrote continually and in 1947 published two outstanding short stories: "Die Botschaft" [Breaking the News] and "Kumpel mit dem langen Haar" [My Pal with the Long Hair] in the periodical *Karussell*.[12] Both stories had as their themes the psychological and physical deprivation of the immediate postwar years and called for love and compassion as the prerequisites for survival. Böll had been writing, however, long before 1945, and had completed possibly six novels before the war,[13] all of which were destroyed in the bombing of Cologne. By 1950 about sixty short stories by Böll had found their way into various newspapers and periodicals. Although in the late 1940s Böll was not a known writer, he was an experienced one. Writing had been his lifelong practice: "I had always wanted to write; I tried it at an early age but found the words only later" ("Über mich selbst," *EHA*, p. 398), and on another occasion he claimed: "Vocation and avocation have been clear to me since my seventeenth birthday: writer" ("Stichworte," *AKR*, p. 171).

The two stories in *Karussell* attracted the attention of a technical publishing house, Middelhauve, which wanted to expand into fiction. Middelhauve signed Böll to a contract and offered him sufficient income to devote more time to writing. In 1949 Middelhauve published his first book, *Der Zug war pünktlich* [The Train Was on Time]. A year later Middlehauve brought out *Wanderer, kommst du nach Spa . . .*, a collection of twenty-five short stories (all contained in *Children Are Civilians Too*), treating the war and the hunger years. Many of these tales have become classics of postwar German literature. In 1951 Middelhauve released Böll's first novel *Wo warst du, Adam?* [Adam, Where Were You?]. A single chapter of the book, recounting the murder of a young Catholic Jewish woman in a concentration camp, established Böll as a powerful master of postwar German prose.

In the same year, Group 47[14] awarded Böll his first literary prize for the story "Die schwarzen Schafe" [Black Sheep], a humorous tale of how a family's black sheep makes good in a hostile bourgeois world. After the award Middelhauve published the story in a limited edition. Although Böll's works were generally well received by the critics, praised for their effective literary use of the language of the people, their uncompromising attitude to the senseless criminality of the war, their sympathetic, compassionate presentation of the sufferings of the 'little man,' they were not financially successful for Böll's publisher. In 1951, after he had just published some of the best literature to appear in the German language since the war, Böll was released from his contract by his publisher, whose main interest was still in technical publication, not fiction. Interest in and appreciation for Böll's work, nonetheless, did exist. In 1952 his present publisher, Kiepenheuer & Witsch, signed him to a new contract and in 1953 published his first major success, the novel *Und sagte kein einziges Wort* [Acquainted with the Night]. Ralph Ley calls it "one of [Böll's] best . . . a work which may someday be regarded as the finest Christian novel of post-war Germany."[15]

Böll's success was not related solely, however, to the quality of the latest novel, but also to his new publisher's understanding of the operations of the literary market. Kiepenheuer & Witsch permitted the work to appear in the influential *Frankfurter All-gemeine Zeitung* in April before its publication. They also sent out over 500 review copies to major media and to small news-papers and launched a publicity campaign for the new author whose talents had already been tested. Middelhauve in contrast had been sending out only 150 review copies and had, probably because its traditions were in scientific publication, never used prepublication techniques and employed very little publicity. By the end of 1953 *Acquainted with the Night* was already in its second printing and a best seller.

In 1954 Böll, now an established author with a secure income, was able to take his first of many trips to Ireland, the land of Swift, Joyce, and Behan. Four years later the simple attractions of this island—its fervent Catholicism, its antimaterialism, its be-lief that poverty is no humiliation and wealth no distinction—induced him to purchase a small piece of property in the village of Dugar on an island off the west coast of Ireland where he could spend long months in writing and relaxation. Böll has long since given up these frequent vacations in Ireland as the responsibilities of a successful author and prominent public figure have required more of his time in Germany and traveling to foreign countries.

After *Acquainted with the Night* Böll published at short in-tervals several major works: *Haus ohne Hüter* [Tomorrow and Yesterday, 1954], *Das Brot der frühen Jahre* [The Bread of Those Early Years, 1955], *Irisches Tagebuch* [Irish Journal, 1957], *Bil-lards um halbzehn* [Billards at Half-past Nine, 1959]. Mean-while he was also rapidly writing stories, satires, essays, and plays, so that in 1963 when *Ansichten eines Clowns* [The Clown] appeared, Böll had in the first decade of his contract with Kiepen-heuer & Witsch published five novels and several stories which established him as one of Germany's leading prose writers and his country's best satirist, while his numerous impassioned essays made him an eminent liberal spokesman on political, moral, and church-related issues. In 1966, 1971, and 1974 his latest novels, *Ende einer Dienstfahrt* [End of a Mission], *Gruppenbild mit Dame* [Group Portrait with Lady], and *Die verlorene Ehre der Katharina Blum* [The Lost Honor of Katharina Blum] appeared. In 1971 he was elected president of the international PEN Club. It was the first time since the founding of the organization in

1921 that a German was chosen as its head. The following year he received literature's highest award, the Nobel Prize. In his acceptance speech in Stockholm, Böll made clear in a direct and simple manner that the award was not a distinction for him alone but in a broad sense for all of his compatriots: "I thank the Swedish Academy, your Majesty, and the Swedish nation for this honor, which is not for me, but for the language in which I express myself and the country whose citizen I am" (*NPLS*, p. 282).

CHAPTER 2

The Short Stories 1947-1950

WHEN the war ended in 1945 and the writers returned from the POW camps to the bombed-out cities, they found their homes unfit for habitation and their language not ready for literary use. The corrupting idiom of the Nazi propagandists and the bureaucratic jargon of the government had poisoned the German vocabulary with the taint of death. A great literary language was rendered temporarily useless by linguistic perversion and twelve years of isolation from renewing influences. The simple vocabulary of daily living had become so polluted with associations of terror and ideology that the connotative meaning of words became more powerful than their denotative ones. It was impossible to write even simple words: "camp," "injection," "smoke," "loyalty," "honor," "fatherland," "heart," "pain," etc., without conjuring up unintended visions of the Third Reich. Euphemisms, for example, evoked more powerful associations than the words they replaced. To say "murder" or "killing" for *Sonderbehandlung* ("Special handling") missed the point of bureaucratic horror. A man murders his wife; a woman kills her lover, but a state cannot "kill" or "murder" millions—another word must be found. The best words to express such deeds became the words which the system itself created. *Endlösung* ("final solution") is today the only word which fits the crime. Even the word crime must be replaced because it falls short of the mark. One cannot equate armed robbery with the *Endlösung*.

In the Third Reich property was confiscated under words like *Judenvermögensabgabe* and *Reichsfluchtsteuer*; euthanasia took place in *Heilerziehungsanstalten* and was carried out by organizations like the *Gemeinnützige Stiftung für Anstaltspflege* and the *Gemeinnützige Krankentransport A.G.*, while the anni-

28

hilation of races was controlled and administered by the *Reichs-sicherheitshauptamt*. Under such linguistic conditions what happens to words, their meanings, and their uses? Euphemisms become more pregnant than the actual words which depict the criminal acts and processes leading to death. If, as in the words above, *Heil* ("health") refers to euthanasia, if *krank* ("sick") means dead, if *Abgabe* ("surrender") is confiscation, how can one communicate any longer in such a language? When an everyday word arouses the human fantasy to the horror of recent reality, what happens to the language of literature? How should a writer use the words *Reich, Sicherheit* ("safety"), *Haupt* (in compound words: "main"), and *Amt* ("office") when these words became the means of death for millions? What associations do these words now have in simple sentences: He was paid in *Reichsmark*; He pinned his shirt with a *Sicherheitsnadel* ("safety pin"); He works for the *Postamt* ("post office"); Where is the *Hauptstrasse* ("main street")? Can one speak any more of paying his gas bill, or have Germans been trying to do just that since the war?

These were some of the linguistic problems which writers faced after the war. Böll's single sentence seems to sum up the problem fairly well: "It was a difficult and hard beginning to write in 1945, considering the depravity and untruthfulness of the German language at that time" ("Jahrgang 1922," *Ee*, p. 314).[1] Böll and his contemporaries had to overcome these problems and restore the literary quality of their mother tongue.

"German postwar literature as a whole has been the literature of finding language," Böll maintained in his *Frankfurter Vorlesungen* (p. 56). He insisted that "people have not yet understood what it meant in 1945 to write just a half page of German prose" (*FV*, p. 49) and to find a way through the "darkness which our language had gotten into in the course of our history" (*FV*, p. 13). The linguistic problems were further complicated by the death of German literary tradition. The new writers knew that the image of man which the older generation and its predecessors had inherited could not be revived. They knew that the tradition extending from Goethe to Expressionism was destroyed. Nineteen forty-five was their *Stunde Null*, the point from which the marking of time was started anew. The war had produced a leveling of the cities and the Nazi spirit produced a *Kahlschlag*, a clearing across the terrain of German literature. In his interview with Horst Bienek, Böll expressed the young writer's problem: "In Germany after 1945 it was, I believe, especially difficult because there was no real tradition present, that is, there was actually three traditions: the literature of emigration, that of the inner emigration, and thirdly the literature that had pleased the censor, in general the so-called 'Blut-und-Boden literature,' which I would like to call the 'unbroken literature of war.' "[2]

Two ways seemed open to authors in the late 1940s: a return to the ABCs of vocabulary and syntax, to the power of primitive expression or a conscious playing on the perverted meaning of words. One of the finest examples of the first method is Günter Eich's poem "Inventory," written about life in a POW camp. In the poem the simplicity of language is used to parallel the elemental human conditions in the camp and to reduce language to a rudimentary level to avoid unwanted connotations. When one recalls that Eich's prewar poetry was exclusively of a literary-philosophical nature, a type of poetry now no longer possible in Germany, the piece is even more illustrative of the immediate postwar problem of finding language. The first stanza of Eich's "Inventory" suffices as an example:

> This is my cap,
> this my coat,
> here my shaving things
> in a linen pouch.[3]

The opening paragraph of Böll's satirical story "Mein teures Bein" [My Expensive Leg] exemplifies his use of this method:

They were now giving me a chance. They sent me a card, I was to come to the office, and I went to the office. At the office they were very nice. A man took out my file and said: "Hm." I said: "Hm," too.
"Which leg," the man asked.
"The right."
"All of it?"
"All of it."
"Hm," he said again. (*47–51*, p. 377)

The elemental, repetitive vocabulary and syntax are effectively appropriate for the narrator protesting the unimaginative, one-dimensional, indifferent attitude of a bureaucrat to the problems of a war amputee in a reviving postwar economy. This exchange of dialogue is also paradigmatic of the beginning of many of Böll's early stories contained in the collection *Wanderer kommst du Nach Spa . . .* (1950). Theodore Ziolkowski's observations on the opening lines of one of the stories in this collection, "Auch Kinder sind Zivilisten" [Children Are Civilians Too, 1950], are to the point: "Here we have many of the elements of a typical Böll story: idiomatic dialogue, a style economical to the point of understatement, first person narrative [twenty-two of the twenty-five stories are in the first person], war experience—and the characteristic ironic twist showing the underdog in mild rebellion against 'the system.' "[4]

The second method of playing on the perverted meaning of words left behind by the Nazis—so well exemplified by Günter Grass in the novel *Dog Years*, by Peter Weiss in the word plays of his early works and his later documentary dramas, and by Nelly Sachs in her poems about dust, smoke, and chimneys—is also employed by Böll in the years 1947–1950 to create some of the contemporary classics of short German fiction. His "Wanderer kommst du nach Spa..." [Stranger, Bear Word to the Spartans We..., 1950] effectively debunks the humanistic standards of value furthered by the classical *Gymnasium*. The wounded narrator, as he is carried, mutilated, back to his high school—now a field hospital—evaluates the school's representations of Western tradition—reproductions of Medea; The Boy With the Thorn in His Foot; the Parthenon frieze; statues of Zeus and Hermes; a Greek hoplite; busts of Caesar, Cicero, Marcus Aurelius; pictures of the Great Elector and Frederick the Great—by juxtaposing them to the war memorial with the great gilded Iron cross and the stone laurel wreath. Böll demonstrates by this comparison how the weight of educational tradition, because of its latent martial content, has led to war, not humanism. The semidelirious narrator, not yet aware of his loss of both arms and right leg, remains unconvinced that he is in his old school; to him the familiar motifs are "no proof" for "it is the same in all schools."

In "Unsere gute, alte Renée" [Dear Old Renée, 1950] Böll goes further and reduces patriotism to a pejorative attribute: "The girl in the picture didn't look at all likable, she was young and pretty, but cold, and she had the same patriotic mouth as the man [in uniform] . . . in the picture over the bar. It would be terrible if she had patriotic hands too." In 1950, German literature was the only literature in the West in which such sentences could be written. The unnatural use of the adjective "patriotic" to modify the nouns "mouth" and "hands" makes it only too clear that in the context "patriotic" is an attribute worse than ugliness; it reveals the death of the soul. Böll's irony is nowhere more biting, his skepticism nowhere more pervading than in this story, for the "pretty, young girl" in the picture is not German but French. And as late as 1962 Böll was still using this method of reductionism to question traditional values.

In "Als der Krieg zu Ende war" [As the War Ended] the narrator discusses with a fellow POW the fate of national virtues: "For three months he had tried to explain that a nationalist was no Nazi, that the words honor, loyalty, fatherland, propriety could never lose their worth—and to his flow of language I just kept repeating five words: Wilhelm II, Papen, Hindenburg, Blomberg, Keitel; and it made him furious that I never mentioned Hitler." The passage reveals that besides jingoism all of twentieth-century German history had after World War II lost its meaning.

As important as the concept of *Stunde Null* is for understanding postwar German literature, it is not a perfectly accurate description of the postwar literary situation;[5] for it is psychologically impossible for a generation of writers to forget the literature they had read in their youth and studied in school. Despite the desire on the part of younger West German writers to remove their work from the continuum of prewar literature, they were not able to do so. In East Germany, writers were not affected by this phenomenon, but consciously adhered to the traditions of prewar Socialist literature and Socialist Realism. In the West the attempt to start a national literature from scratch, to ignore literary tradition, naturally failed; Böll, in fact, did not always try to write as if there were no literary antecedents.

There are several examples of Böll's use of literary tradition, especially in his later work, but even in 1950 an example can be found. The story "Stranger, Bear Word to the Spartans We . . ."

follows the structure of Schiller's elegiac poem "Der Spazier-gang."[6] In mock irony of Schiller's narrator strolling leisurely up a mountain and contemplating the state of civilization, Böll's narrator is carried up a series of stairs as he dwells on the horror of his personal situation. Where Schiller manifests a classical optimism, averring faith in Western man, Böll calls into question a mechanized modern society, expressing fear and suspicion of the state of the world. Böll's title for his story also appears in "Der Spaziergang." Where Schiller uses the famous epitaph from the tomb of Leonidas in a clearly positive manner, praising the brave Spartans for saving Western civilization from the Persian invasion, Böll employs the quotation in a fragmentary form to reveal both a broken world and a disdain for the German-Spartan military tradition. In both works, external objects guide the thoughts of the two narrators as they begin the ascent to their destinations. Schiller appropriately refers to nature; mountain, summit, sun, field, trees, branches, forest, etc., and Böll to mechanical objects and machines: car, motor, light bulb, ceiling, socket, wire filaments, etc. As Schiller's narrator reaches the summit of the mountain, the poem ends in a majestic Rousseauian vision in which civilization's wounds are healed. Conversely, Böll's story concludes on the top floor of a school in an operating room with a focus on the senseless misery, suffering, and death of a young man, implying that civilization may not be able to heal its wounds. What Böll attempts in this parodistic treatment of a classic elegy is not humor or ridicule, but the disclosure that the idealism and optimism of the past is inappropriate and unacceptable in a post-Auschwitz age.

In his early struggle for language, Böll found help in foreign literature: "I knew why I often preferred to translate rather than write myself," he says, "to bring something from a foreign terrain into my own language as a way of getting ground under my feet" (*FV*, p. 56). Among the foreign influences which Böll absorbed after the war was the traditional form of the American short story developed by Bret Harte and O'Henry and made familiar again in the Germany of the 1940s in Hemingway's terse style. This form—characterized by a quick tempo, a plunge *in medias res*, a lack of denouement (of the twenty-five stories in *Wanderer*, nineteen conclude with an unfinished sentence), use of contemporary subject matter, little consciousness of events anterior to the present time of the story, no anticipation of the future, concentration on a single event which becomes the focal point of the story, a lack of moralism, and a design appropriate for a public with little time to read—penetrated German literature quickly after 1945 due to the catastrophe of the war, the powerful American influence in Europe, the prevailing uncertainty of the times, the changing circumstances inherent in the construction of a new nation (a factor which also contributed to its popularity in the United States), and the twelve years of cultural isolation and deprivation which gave Germans a taste for things new and a desire to leap headlong into the mainstream of modern literature. Although foreign influences of all kinds imploded in West Germany after the war, the borrowed form of the story rapidly became a completely German genre by its concentration entirely on German subject matter in a distinctly German idiom.

Prior to Böll, Wolfgang Borchert had experimented with the new form, using it with traces of Expressionism to relate the horror of war and its attendant suffering. It was with conscious effort that Böll continued Borchert's experiment with colloquial dialogue and emulated Hemingway's device of expressing inner reality through external objects. One of the most important stories in *Wanderer*, "Der Mann mit den Messern" [The Man with the Knives, 1948], clearly illustrates this technique. Between 1945–1948 there were many who survived the war without surviving the peace. Starvation was only an anticlimax to life in this period of hunger. The narrator of the story is a day laborer who cleans bricks at the rate of three-fourths of a loaf of bread for every seventy-five bricks, and who, in the course of the story, exchanges a deadly way of life for a merely dangerous job. The final sentence sums up the narrator's position: "But I only understood it an hour later that I now had a real profession, a profession, where I only had to stand for a while and dream. Twelve to twenty seconds. I was the man at whom knives are thrown. . . ." His inner fear, despair, and indifference are conquered. Life has a new meaning for him. It is true the change does not alter the nature of fear in his life; he does not live in perfect safety and security, but he does live with meaning: fear has become incorporated into his work; he is now paid for it, and it becomes at least the means of exchange for goods. The forty marks a night he now shares with his partner means he no longer has to labor most of the day for a part of a loaf of bread. He even has a sense of security in the skill of his friend, a feeling he did not know while at the mercy of an indifferent world. He also experiences hope and trust as they are expressed in the smile of his knife-throwing comrade. To be sure, there is still danger in his existence, but it now has a purpose.

In addition to their indebtedness to Borchert and Hemingway, Böll's stories in *Wanderer* show a marked affinity with the works of Albert Camus. His tales parallel Camus's existential concern for human suffering and have, as often as do the Frenchman's, an outsider as hero, i.e., a protagonist who is not reconciled with the world, who is a metaphysical rebel (though often nonintellectual by nature), who does not accept the unjust order of things. Such a person is the speaker of Böll's story "Die Botschaft" [Breaking the News, 1947]. After returning from a POW camp, the narrator seeks out the wife of a friend to inform her of her husband's death. When discovering the wife has taken a lover, he finds no moral fault with her. The guilt, he concludes, is part of the times. As she begs: "Don't despise me," he realizes that "These words struck fear into my heart—my God, did I look like a judge? And before she could prevent it, I kissed her small, soft hand; it was the first time in my life that I kissed a woman's hand."

This early publication of Böll's deserves analysis because it reveals themes and attitudes that have characterized his oeuvre through the years. The wife asks the narrator:

"Where did it happen? In the East?"
"No . . . in the West, in a prisoner-of-war camp . . . there were more than a hundred thousand of us . . ."
"And when?" Her face looked punished, but strangely young—as if her life depended on my answer.
"In July '45," I said softly. She appeared a moment to consider and then she smiled—completely pure and innocent, and I knew why she smiled.

The war, its aftermath and misery, its demythologizing, compassion for the little man in history—in this case an "adulteress"—

a subtle combination of realistic detail and romantic aura (rich sentiment and a tendency to idealization of characters), and a concern for moral problems[7] are characteristics of this story. Here the moral scrutiny pertains to sexual behavior—the guilt or innocence of the wife. She is, according to Böll's liberal theology, pronounced "pure and innocent." Her husband died before she took the lover—a technicality, no doubt, but an important one to a Catholic—as the reader can assume the wife and narrator are. This interest in the nature of marriage is at the heart of much of Böll's later writing.

The wife's assumption that her husband died on the eastern front, the *locus classicus* of death, is natural on her part, showing a desire to give a patina to his passing, but his death does not have even this questionable "glory" of dying with thousands on the most historic front of the war. His death occurs in the West in an allied POW camp after the war is over—a death conspicuous for its lack of meaning or grandeur.

The affinity between Camus and Böll can be pursued further. Ziolkowski writes: "The list of issues on which Böll and Camus agree in essence and to which they react similarly could be extended almost indefinitely beyond nationalism, resurgent Nazism and religious hypocrisy to the plight of the worker, the horrors of totalitarianism in any form, and the position of the creative artist in our society."[8] But there is one major point in regard to which their existential concerns differ. Whereas Camus's contemplation of the human condition leads him to reject the existence of God and to see meaning only in the heroic acceptance of man's absurd situation in the universe, Böll discovers the divine reaffirmed in the waywardness of life. Whereas Camus reasons from the suffering of man that if God existed He would be responsible for man's plight, and that since an unjust God contradicts the meaning of God, God cannot exist, Böll never seriously considers the question of God's responsibility.

The absurd world reveals itself poignantly in several of the stories in the collection *Wanderer*. In the tale "Mein trauriges Gesicht" [My Sad Face, 1950], a satire on a totalitarian state, a man is arrested for having a sorrowful countenance and is sentenced to ten years imprisonment. He unfortunately was unaware of the new decree demanding happiness because he had just been released from prison after serving five years for smiling on the day of the dictator's death. In "Über die Brücke" [Over the Bridge, 1950], a mother and her daughter wash the windows of their house for two generations on such an unvarying schedule that a train passenger can tell the time of day by which window is being cleaned as his coach passes their house. In "So ein Rummel" [What a Racket, 1950], a mother encourages her children to play the original games "Neanderthal," "Bunker," "Total Disability", and "Refugee." In the first game, the older brother is to tear out the younger's jaw bone for a museum piece, and in the other games houses are set on fire and children have to flee a burning city. In the story "Geschäft ist Geschäft" [Business Is Business, 1950] the absurd point of view is expressed in a Kafkaesque streetcar ride without destination from which the narrator can never alight.

The story, however, that best differentiates Böll's Christian existentialism from Camus's atheistic existentialism is "An der Angel" [On the Hook, 1950]. The narrator of this tale receives a telegram from his girlfriend stating that she is arriving on the 1:20 train. No date is given. He goes every day for three months and four days to the station to meet her. He must give up his job, sell all he owns, sacrifice everything to meet the train. In his desperation he concludes the railway officials are holding the girl captive to torment him. He believes a conspiracy by unknown forces, known only as "they," is directed against him. The anonymous "they" manipulate his life: "They control hope, they control paradise, consolation." It is also these attributes: "hope," "pleasure," "joy," "comfort," "happiness", and "paradise" that the narrator associates with the girl's coming. His sweetheart assumes, then, the role so often assigned to female characters in Böll's work; she becomes the bearer of what is good and humane in the world, like the nun in "Lohengrins Tod" [Lohengrin's Death, 1950], the Russian nurse in "Wiedersehen mit Drüng" [Reunion with Drüng, 1950], and the young girl in "Kumpel mit dem langen Haar" [My Pal with the Long Hair, 1947], to mention only examples from the collection *Wanderer*. Thus the girl's coming is an article of faith for the narrator. From one point of view it is indeed absurd to send a telegram to announce an arrival over three months away, but it is this fact that gives the story its religious dimension: the telegram is akin to a biblical prophecy. The believer accepts its promise and makes the necessary sacrifices. The narrator exclaims: "I must, I must, I must go there." To him a religious compulsion is involved in the waiting. In this sense he is like Beckett's Estragon and Vladimir waiting for Godot and Camus's Sisyphus expecting his stone to remain on the summit of the hill. But Böll's character is significantly different. When their expectations are repeatedly not realized, Camus's and Beckett's heroes necessarily consider suicide as a way out. Estragon asks: "Why don't we hang ourselves?" And Vladimir later replies: "We'll hang ourselves tomorrow unless Godot comes."[9] In Camus's Sisyphus essay,[10] although suicide is rejected, man becomes free only when he accepts the absurdity of life, when he acknowledges the curse of his existence, and learns to live in heroic defiance of meaninglessness. Although Böll's hero also considers suicide in his moment of deepest despair, he still differs from Camus's rebel in his rejection of it because he never accepts the absurdity of his situation even when it seems most unalterable.

In the key passage from which the story derives its title, a metaphor is developed to express the narrator's unpropitious situation. Significantly, at this point the narration changes from the first-person singular to the first-person plural to reveal the lack of uniqueness in the narrator's circumstance, to show his condition to be one of the bulk of mankind: "They keep us on the hook, we always bite, we let ourselves be drawn up to the surface, we breathe for a minute the light, beauty, joy, and then some swine laughs, lets the line loose and we fall again into the dark." Despite this seemingly unfortunate and unvariable state, Böll's hero never loses faith: "I must, I must, I must go there." When his moment of hope has been reduced to a single second, when he has made every sacrifice in good faith, sold his last possession at the railway station to buy a platform ticket, never doubting the girl's arrival, the train pulls in; the girl alights and rushes toward him. Faith is rewarded, a promise redeemed, suffering, fear, and anxiety vanquished. The absurd is abrogated; a meaningless world is never fully accepted. "I laugh at them, I laugh at them because the train has arrived, and before they can reach me, she is resting on my breast, and I possess no more than her and a platform ticket, her and a cancelled platform ticket. . . ."

This concluding sentence gains in meaning when compared to the opening sentence of the story: "I know that it is all foolish. I oughtn't to go any more; it is so senseless, but I live from going there." The narration begins on the ninety-fifth day of waiting, when there seems little sense in going again to the station. In the few minutes the story covers, from 12:30 to 1:20, the background and feverish thoughts of the narrator are revealed through interior monologue. The words "fear," "uncertainty," "life on the razor's edge" characterizes his uneasy existence. Thus, against this introduction, the optimism of the conclusion transforms the story into a religious parable of hope.

Besides the theological-metaphysical meaning, the story also has a social one. In the metaphor from which the title is derived, the unpromising situation of the narrator is not so much a philosophical desperation as it is a physical-social one caused by the powerful forces of society which exploit the little man. The narrator does not claim to understand this process of his reification, but he knows it goes on: "We're supposed to croak, we're supposed to choke, we're supposed to completely despair, have no comfort, we're supposed to sell everything and when we have no more, we're supposed to. . . ." These anonymous forces are simply "they." The narrator knows that in their inhumanity "they" control everything:

Their hard-heartedness takes terrible forms. . . . Their hardness is cruel. They don't even buy anything from me anymore. They don't even want any more of my belongings. Up till now they cried for goods. But their greed has become so dreadful that they now sit on their money and eat it. I believe they eat money. I ask myself why. What do they really want? Why don't they ever give anything up? Money, bread, tobacco, whiskey . . . anything . . . anything. They're driving me to extremes.

In his extremity and ignorance of the social forces he knows only hatred for his oppressors. He contemplates the murder of a lackey of the establishment. He senses his alienation is a result of manipulation by anonymous forces. He realizes he "will have to begin to fight," but does not know how. In this perverted order of things he is aware that the "they" are spared his psychological-philosophical desperation and alienation because they have security and power. There is no limit to their control over the narrator or over his like, the poor in the train station—the only figures presented with compassion, and the only ones who show compassion for the narrator—who, together, form a kind of proletarian solidarity which stands against the anonymous "they." The solidarity of the poor adds in a small way to his hope that the hegemony of the "they" will be broken. The narrator says of the "bum" who gives him the money he needs: "He understands me poorly, but it is beautiful at least to be poorly understood; if I return alive from the battle, I will embrace you, friend." And this optimism is justified as the girl arrives. It is a solution by miracle, no doubt, but the beginning of a social evolutionary stage in Böll's work that leads through the novels and finds its high point in *Group Portrait*.

In the early stages, this union of people, this bridge between despair and hope is love in its various forms—love between man and woman in "On the Hook," "My Pal with the Long Hair," "Aufenthalt in X" [Between Trains in X], and "As the War Ended," love as a bond of friendship in "Wiedersehen in der Allee" [Reunion in the Avenue] and "Reunion with Drüng," and love as family loyalty in "Lohengrin's Death." Later this Böllian concept of love develops within a broader social context in the novels. In *Tomorrow and Yesterday* it expresses itself in the friendship of two boys, one rich and the other poor, in *Billiards at Half-past Nine* it grows into a union of the meek and humble against the violent and powerful, and it culminates in *Group Portrait* in the solidarity of foreign workers, civil servants, businessmen, and intellectuals to save the heroine.

Of the twenty-five stories in *Wanderer* eleven treat the war itself; thirteen deal with the immediate postwar situation and one, "My Sad Face," is a satire on a totalitarian state. The war stories reveal in vivid detail the horror and fear of death and the immediacy and urgency of suffering, and show the devastating and crippling effect on the human spirit of boredom, waste, and senseless destruction. The war stories present the individual in his helplessness, caught in the impersonal machinery of death, characterized in one story as a fearsome beast with a "grimacing face, devouring teeth, and cruel breath."[11] But whatever the specific theme of the stories, they demonstrate at all times a sense of religion which serves as a refuge to the individual. By concentrating on the individual and his fate in the chaos of the times, Böll's attitude toward war differs from much war literature, such as Plivier's *Stalingrad*, which shows the totality of the war machine and the disintegration of whole armies. Böll avoids the presentation of mass death, group fear, or collective suffering. He concentrates instead on the single dying soldier, on personal anxiety and individual pain. Böll does not attempt to explain the war, how it started, why it was fought, who was guilty; his emphasis is always on the common soldier, often nameless in his stories, who represents suffering humanity. These simple men all hate the war, sense its vileness, but do not know how to escape its clutches. They do as they are commanded, which is usually to die. Interestingly, they never receive orders to commit atrocities. They do not hate the enemy. In fact, the Russians, Poles, and Frenchmen in the stories are always presented with sympathy. Böll's soldiers merely report to the front and prepare to die. These characters are often underway to battle or waiting in insignificant villages for trains to take them to their deaths. The stories are frequently about the significance of an unexpected encounter between a German soldier and a Hungarian, Russian, or French girl, a tavern keeper, or a comrade in uniform.

The private, intimate situations presented are reflected in the personal tone of the stories and the simple language chosen by the author. But it would be a mistake to consider that simplicity a lack of artistry. Even this first collection of tales clearly demonstrates Böll's linguistic dexterity. The stories in *Wanderer* make subtle use of the interior monologue and the *erlebte Rede* ("style indirect libre"), and although some stories reflect the elemental style of *Kahlschlagsliteratur* others are examples of highly sophisticated language. The last paragraph of "Wir Besenbinder" [Broommakers, 1950] will illustrate this point.

The narrator of the story has been a very poor mathematics student. His teacher castigated his slowness by calling him a broommaker; but with all his knowledge of mathematics, he never had the patience to master the art of drawing circles on the blackboard. The chalk skips, producing a series of dots and dashes with the ends never coming together to form a whole, thereby producing a "symbol of painfully torn creation." The narrator, however, possesses the natural grace and inner harmony to make perfect circles effortlessly. Two months after graduation, while the narrator is waiting at the airport in Odessa for his unit to be flown to the Crimea, he sees a broommaker for the first time: a "quiet poor man," smoking a pipe, the essence of "peace and simplicity," who "without haste and loving industry bound his brooms." The narrator, along with his unit, boards the plane to the front and is shot down before reaching the Crimea. The final paragraph reads:

Then came the real shock: I suddenly realized that this sky-splitting fury was in fact a noise; close to my head I heard a strange hiss as of a baleful, swiftly descending hand, felt a moist, hot pain, jumped up with a cry and reached out toward the sky where just then another searing yellow flash blazed up; with my right hand I held on tight to this flailing yellow snake, letting it spin its angry circle, confident that I would be able to complete the circle, for this was the one and only art I had been born to master—so I held it, guided it, the flailing, raging, jerking, chattering snake, held on to it while my breath came hot and my twitching mouth hurt and the moist pain in my head seemed to increase, and as I brought the points together, drawing the glorious round arc of the circle and gazing at it with pride, the spaces between the dots and dashes closed and an immense, hissing short circuit filled the entire circle with light and fire until the whole sky was burning, and the abrupt momentum of the plunging aircraft rent the world in two. All I could see were light and fire, and the mutilated tail of the machine, a jagged tail like the black stump of a broom fit to carry a witch riding off to her sabbath. . . .[12]

The two symbols—the circle and the broom—are at the core of the final paragraph. The flak, bursting around the plane like the dots and dashes of an imperfect circle, illuminate the narrator's broken world. He tries to catch the tail of the "flailing, raging, jerking, chattering snake" of flames in order to gather it around the plane as a protective circle. He is, however, unsuccessful in his personal endeavor to restore psychological and social harmony. In his mind's eye he transforms the dots and dashes of the exploding flak into a "glorious round arc." But as he closes the arc, the plane receives a direct hit—"a short circuit filled the entire circle . . . and rent the world in two." The fiery tail of the plane, like a black witch's broom, carries all on board to their death. The war has perverted all things: the circle—a metaphor of perfection without beginning or end—devolves into a symbol of shattered creation, and the broom, which earlier in the story stood for peace and tranquillity, becomes the vehicle for riding to a witch's sabbath.

Although several die in the crash, the disaster seems personal because of the alienation effect of having the narrator relate his own death. Actually this device is used in several of the war stories: "Stranger, Bear Word to the Spartans We . . . ," "Reunion with Drüng," "Die Essenholer", [The Ration Runners], and "Reunion in the Avenue." The war stands as an unexplained, abstract power in relation to which the individual is a helpless victim, fraught with fear and burdened with pain, doomed to a violent death that he senses as absurd, but which he does not rise to question. Böll is no Brecht who attempts an historic or economic explication of the causes of war.

Although lyrical passages similar to the one concluding "Broommakers" are not common in the early stories, Böll does not romanticize or mythologize war in the manner of Ernst Jünger or even Gerd Gaiser. Nor does he deceive the reader with inaccurate reportage of the carnage of war. His soldiers die in shocking realism, their bodies blown in half, their remains lying in latrines, and their brains oozing from a hole in the skull. It is not sweet to die for one's country in Böll's stories, but death itself, the passing from this world to the next, offers a religious comfort. If Böll can be said to adhere to an ideology, in a broad sense it would be the theology of Roman Catholicism. As Drüng and his narrator friend lie dead at the end of "Reunion with Drüng," they imagine the figure of a Russian nurse, represented as an angel, coming toward them through a closed door to conduct their souls to a peaceful, better world: "And we knew that we could smile now, and took her outstretched hand and followed her. . . ." Böll's early stories clearly imply happiness beyond death where loneliness and separation end. "Reunion with

Drüng," "Reunion in the Avenue," and "The Ration Runners"
all offer to the problems of this world a conventional religious
solution which Böll abandons in his later works.

The war stories actually constitute the minority of the tales
in the first collection. The majority of the twenty-five narratives
treat the postwar period. These stories deal almost exclusively
with returning veterans who eke out a living as black marketeers or workers and who never share in the growing prosperity
that sets in after the currency reform of 1948. Those characters
who are not black marketeers or laborers find peculiar occupations: one makes candles and distributes them himself as a traveling salesman, but discovers that after 1948 there is no longer a
market for simple, excellently made candles, not even in the devo-
tional industry, now dominated by a preference for ornamental
kitsch. He realizes it makes more sense to burn his wares before a
statue of the Virgin than to try to sell them: "Kerzen für Maria"
[Candles for the Madonna]. One veteran counts people crossing
a bridge for a statistical office, but never counts his girlfriend
in order to preserve, in his own way, her humanity in a society
that seeks to reduce everyone to a number. Of course, his noble
gesture is futile; the experts calculate a percentage of error into
his figures. Thus their number is the same whether she is
counted or not. Every citizen is "statisticalized" and victimized
even without his knowledge. There is no escape from the machinery of bureaucracy. While on one level the narrator's suppression functions as a true but unsuccessful act of quiet protest for humanity, on another it unexpectedly succeeds. With
irony typical of Böll, the narrator's lack of concern for accuracy
is rewarded; his miscount is so slight that he is promoted to
the simpler task of counting horse-drawn vehicles of which there
are only a few each day: "An der Brücke" [On the Bridge]. Another protagonist becomes a cashier for a carnival after a dis-
tracting interview with his employer, The Woman with Half a
Body ("What a Racket"). And one man, as we have seen, becomes the target of a knife thrower. Böll's bizarre sense of humor,
manifested even in the miserable conditions of postwar Germany,
becomes more prominent in his later satires, but even in these
early tales one can see "the confrontation of the individual with
a monster of a world."[13]

CHAPTER 3

The Short Stories 1951-1960

IN the stories written after 1950 the occupations of Böll's heroes become even more unusual than those of the protagonists of the collection *Children Are Civilians Too*. One character earns his living as an interviewer for a research institute gathering statistics on such questions as "How do you imagine God?": "Der Zwerg und die Puppe" [The Dwarf and the Doll, 1951]. A professional laugher finds life so serious that a natural laugh never escapes his lips: "Der Lacher" [The Laugher, 1952]. A linguist spends his life mastering an esoteric island language which the natives themselves no longer speak and which has produced no literature: "Im Lande der Rujuks" [In the Land of the Rujuks, 1953]. An eager businessman masters the art of handling thirteen telephones while another works with a phone in each hand, takes notes with a pen in his mouth, and operates a knitting machine with his toes. In a final rebellion against this senseless productivity, the first businessman turns to the occupation of professional mourner because his talent is in looking sad: "Es wird etwas geschehen" [Action Will Be Taken, 1954]. A radio-station employee collects the snips of "dead" air cut from taped programs and relaxes at home listening to the spliced silences: "Dr. Murkes gesammeltes Schweigen" [Murke's Collected Silences, 1955]. Another hero specializes in the scientific sorting and throwing away of junk mail: "Der Wegwerfer" [The Thrower-away, 1957].

All of these eccentric occupations occur in the satires written in the 1950s, Böll's most productive period for the short story. It is also in the satiric genre that Böll has created his most consummate masterpieces.[1] In the satires, Böll replaces the outrage and indignation of the early works with bitter laughter and warns through humor of even more threatening dangers to the human spirit—dangers which have become less tangible, less obvious than the war, and now lurk behind the facade of a prosperous society. Böll's satires mock social pretentiousness, religious and artistic snobbishness, self-satisfied smugness, and criticize greed, social waste, perversion of culture for profit, and the pathological urge of the Germans to forget the Nazi past. They also reveal a society without conscience, obsessed with senseless productivity, whose only gods are money and success. The popularity of these satires is due in part to their applicability to the whole of Western culture.[2]

Besides the characters who expose the contradictions of their milieu and those persons who, like the thrower-away, cleverly exploit the irrationalities of society for their own interest and financial advantage, Böll has created another type of character, who by his very existence condemns Western society even more completely—the dropout who refuses to work at all. These characters are usually men who have never recovered from the war, who are not physically injured, but who are, nevertheless, dead to the postwar spirit of competition and progress. They are sometimes lazy but always lethargic; they lack energy and ambition, exude an aura of malaise and indifference. They are "those who," as Böll says, "came back from the war . . . not angry, not sad, just tired and hungry" ("Mutter Ey," *AKR*, p. 81). They are passive and quiet people, beyond indignation and rage. To them "not even the guilty ones, the few who were to be acknowledged as such, excited anger" (*AKR*, p. 81).

Böll's own confession reveals the essence of these negative heroes:

I don't know why I refused to do what was propagated with new democratic enthusiasm as the first duty of every returning citizen: to get a shovel and pick and start clearing away the rubble. It was not just the feeling of having something better to do and having done enough, it was not just laziness, not just indifference to the desire of reconstruction—a spirit which, by the way, never got articulated. It was, perhaps, the manner in which the people stood around leaning on their shovels and picks, talking of the war, their imprisonment and political mistakes, it reminded me too much of conversations in beer-halls and barracks. ("Stichworte," *AKR*, p. 174)

The characters who represent this attitude of all-embracing passivity become the "Uncle Freds" and "Black Sheep" of Böll's stories of postwar Germany. These lethargic heroes also form the nucleus of a prototypical character who, in varying guises, manifests himself in most of Böll's work. This person, whom Klaus Jeziorkowski calls (taking the phrase from Böll's "The Thrower-away") the "happy asocial individual,"[3] is independent of the social system, its pressures and associations, and totally free to develop according to his or her own inner nature. The passivity of these characters, however, seldom demonstrates outright laziness, but often signifies a protest against the nonhumanist values of a profit society. But the nonhumanist values of society are attacked in a more forceful way in "Murke's Collected Silences."

I "Murke's Collected Silences"

"Collected Silences" (1955) is one of Böll's most highly regarded works. Cesare Cases refers to it as one of the finest works of European literature since World War II,[4] and Walter Jens claims Böll's work culminates in the book *Dr. Murkes gesammeltes Schweigen und andere Satiren.*[5] Such an important story deserves analysis to see what makes it such a remarkable accomplishment. "Collected Silences" has as its main theme the critique of practicing Christianity. Here the satirical object is the changing religious attitude of West Germany since the end of the war.[6] The focus of Böll's attack is the popular guru, Bur-Malottka, who with 2,350,000 copies of his philosophical-religious-cultural-historical books in print, his editorship of three periodicals and two newspapers, and chief readership at a major publishing house stands as a weather vane for the changing sentiment of the nation (*E 50–70*, p. 157). In the person of Bur-Malottke Böll criticizes religion and culture in West Germany, the shallowness and vapidity which resulted from the postwar political-religious accomodation of the nation.

One Monday morning in the mid-1950s, after being troubled by a night of "religious considerations" (*E 50–70*, p. 157), Bur-Malottke awakens to find he has returned to a metaphysical-theological position "which corresponded to the religious attitudes he has espoused prior to 1945" (*E 50–70*, p. 157). He now

wishes to expunge the word "God" from all his works, beginning
with the two public lectures recently recorded for broadcast
later in the week. That is, Bur-Malottke, as representative of
postwar Germany, returns to a state of religiosity current during
the Nazi period. Bur-Malottke rejects the type of Christian concern to which he had "converted during the religious enthusiasm of the year 1945" (*E 50–70*, p. 157). He now finds it necessary to apologize for his political views of the immediate postwar period and feels the need to revise his public statements
from that era: " 'Especially on political topics I permitted myself, due to the enthusiasm of 1945, to express ideas which now
I must thoroughly reconsider and which I can only attribute to
my youth' " (*E 50–70*, p. 170).

In essays and interviews Böll has often referred to the three
years from the war's end to the currency reform of 1948 as a
welcome period of Christian renewal and as a brief Christian
renaissance. To him this renaissance expressed itself also in the
newly formed political parties. In 1947 the Christian Democratic
Union, now West Germany's conservative right-wing capitalist
party, stood as an example of this social-religious awakening. In
that year it proposed a Christian-Socialist platform for the nation called the Ahlen Program, a statement of principles presumably similar to those Bur-Malottke wishes now in the mid-
1950s, as the economic restoration of capitalism is in full swing,
to recant. These ideas are what he calls the political mistakes
of his youth. The Ahlen Program, justified by the CDU as an
"important programmatic expression of Christian social doc-
trine,"[7] proposed the socialization of the coal and steel industries,
suggested laws to prevent monopolies and to limit the power of
big business, advocated a limit to the amount of stock a single
individual could own, advised federal control of banks, lending
institutions and insurance companies, favored the establishment
of the workers' right to *Mitbestimmung* ("codetermination") in
the policy decisions of their employers, argued for a planned
economy, and urged increased power for unions.

However, the winds of change to which Bur-Malottke responds
in the satire were already blowing, if not prevailing, as early as
1949, one year after the currency reform. In that year the CDU,
in its Düsseldorf Program, modified the social concerns expressed

in the Ahlen Program. Although proclaimed as a complement to the 1947 statement, the Düsseldorf Principles, in effect, altered the Christian-Socialist intent of the Ahlen Program. The Principles retracted the previous call for a planned and directed economy, dropped the demand for socialization of basic industries and instead emphasized the need for free enterprise, free trade, a market economy, and the necessity of rewarding competition. The Principles substantially rejected Socialist ideas and opted for the restoration of capitalism. This religious, political, and economic about-face effected by the CDU in 1949 was made by the majority of Germans in the 1950s. This conversion to prewar thinking is the main point of Böll's satire.

Bur-Malottke's old prewar religious mentality which reasserts itself "suddenly overnight" (*E 50–70*, p. 157), like the change in the CDU platform, is reflected in Bur-Malottke's phrase of non-commitment which he substitutes for the word "God." He plans in all future works to use the formulation, "that higher Being Whom we revere" (*jenes höhere Wesen, das wir verehren*), to replace God. Bur-Malottke's grand, but empty language typifies the social adaptation of the nation as it proudly marched from the poverty and simplicity of the late 1940s into the growing wealth and ostentation of the 1950s. But Bur-Malottke's language reveals more: it shows also that the social adaptation of the 1950s went hand in hand with the use of the persuasive techniques of the mass media and the sales pitches of the ad industry.

The use of "we" in the phrase that replaces God is an all-inclusive plural, automatically embracing the listener as well as the speaker. The "we" becomes a selling device to seduce the hearer into "buying" the cultural-religious opinions of the grand master of sounding brass and tinkling cymbal. Bur-Malottke's phrase is the jargon of an ad man, a method of "hidden persuasion" which substitutes psychological motivation for private consideration. The use of this technique is a blasphemous reduction of religion to the level of a consumer item which is peddled like soap via the media. Moreover, the language of the satire indicates that Bur-Malottke's blasphemy tends to self-idolatry, for to effect the substitution in his taped lectures he must first "cut God out" (*E 50–70*, p. 158). His final intention, if only unconscious, is not just to replace the word "God" with an empty phrase, but to replace reverence for God with admiration for "the great Bur-Malottke" (*E 50–70*, p. 157).

Böll adequately conveys the full egocentricity of Bur-Malottke's style in a brief excerpt from one of his lectures: "Wherever, however, whyever, and whenever we begin to speak about the essence of art, we must first look to that higher Being Whom we revere, must bow in respect before that higher Being Whom we revere and must accept art with thanks as a gift from that higher Being Whom we revere" (*E 50–70*, p. 174). The passage can stand without comment. Its pomposity, self-indulgence, and artificial priestly manner contain its own condemnation. It reads like the sermons Böll condemns in other works, especially in *The Clown*, where Prelate Sommerwild's homilies are characterized as pretentious "honeywater concoctions" of Rilke, Hofmannsthal, and Newman,[8] grounded more in egotism than in love, betraying the speaker's competition with God in vying for the hearts and minds of the listeners.

In Bur-Malottke's repeated formula, Böll also parodies the classics. In the second stanza of Goethe's poem "Das Göttliche" [The Divine], the poet salutes the deities: ("Heil den unbekannten/ Höhern Wesen,/ Die wir ahnen!" ("Hail the unknown/ Higher beings/ Whom we perceive!"). Here the similarity in vocabulary and rhythm is unmistakable. Furthermore, in the forty-ninth line of the poem, Goethe too uses the word ("revere"). Böll not only parodies Goethe's lines but also the theme of the poem. Goethe's poem states that man became aware of the boundless grandeur of the "higher beings" through realization of the lesser grandeur of great men called immortals. In the satire Böll replaces the "immortals" of the poem, those men whose intellectual accomplishments on earth indicate the existence of "higher beings," by the self-proclaimed cultural "immortal" Bur-Malottke. The conversation between Bur-Malottke and the station manager supports this interpretation: " 'One day I shall . . . he hesitated because the information he was about to impart to the station manager was too painful for posterity—'One day I shall . . . One day I shall die'; he paused again and gave the station manager an opportunity to appear startled" (*E 50–70*, p. 170). In addition Böll's use of the famous poem draws attention to the parallels between Bur-Malottke and Goethe. In Bur-Malottke's stout figure, egocentric manner, and role as a cultural potentate, the reader easily senses an effigy of the great man of German letters.

Böll's attack is broader, however, than merely one against the state of religion in mid-century West Germany; it is also an assault on Germany's cultural industry. The two (the decline of religion and the quality of art) are, in fact, so intricately linked in the satire that Böll implies that to expose the one is to strip the other. Only one word occurs more frequently in Bur-Malottke's lectures than "God" (27 times): the word "art" (134 times). The frequent coupling of the two even gives Bur-Malottke himself a certain feeling of guilt for what he calls the *religiöse Überlagerung* ("religious overlap") (*E 50–70*, p. 157) in the station's programming.

In the societal microcosm of the radio world, with its various levels of social hierarchy, its variety of people and types of programmed entertainment, art has devolved simply into a matter of good taste, while good taste has become a matter of marketability. In every aspect of the station the disease of "aesthetization" has set in, that is, fashionableness and appearance: pure form takes precedence over substance, purpose, and meaning. The rugs, wallpaper, and prize-winning ashtrays which decorate every floor of the station are examples. The modish ashtrays, costing 258.77 marks each, do not even fulfill their purpose. No one puts ashes or "anything as unaesthetic as cigarette stubs" (*E 50–70*, p. 164) into them. They are, as the narrator[9] claims, "too beautiful" (*E 50–70*, p. 164) or unrecognizable as ashtrays. Here Böll's description is important: "They were . . . made of embossed copper in the form of seashells on an embossed copper stand of original sea growth: knotted seaweed" (*E 50–70*, p. 164). The description not only parodies the style of *art nouveau,* but gives to the radio station an aura of the aesthetic snobbery of that movement. Jost Hermand characterizes the style of *art nouveau* as the art "of lazily nodding gladioli and preciously adorned ashtrays."[10] It was the movement which sought, above all, decoration and marketability in the *objet d'art.* This concern with appearance, good taste, and profit has its parallel in the station's programming. The atmosphere of capitulation to the milieu is everywhere. Not only the theist Bur-Malottke, but the atheists in the satire also surrender their principles and accommodate

themselves to the trend of decadent purism and substanceless
form.

In a radio play being edited for broadcast, a playwright has an
atheist in an empty church call out loudly: "Who will still think
of me when I have become food for worms?" (*E 50–70*, p. 176).
Twelve such questions are asked, followed in the playwright's
text by long silences, but because the effect of so much dead air
is aesthetically unpleasing, the director decides to splice the
words (God) cut from Bur-Malottke's lectures into the pauses
after each question, giving the atheistic drama a new theistic
content. All concerned with the production agree the play has
been improved. The distortion of the meaning concerns no one,
not even the author.

Everywhere in the radio station superficiality triumphs over
meaningful expression. Even the furniture and the interior dec-
orations conform to prescribed standards of appearance. In protest against this noncommitted, depersonalized, standardized
aesthetic of *Form über alles*, Murke attaches a holy card of the
Sacred Heart of Jesus, which he has received from his mother,
to the wall by the office of the director of cultural programming,
the director responsible for the changes in the play. The artistic
affront of the holy card stands in perfect contrast to the deadly
tyranny of vacuous good taste. Within the realm of the visual Böll
has discovered an appropriate gesture of rebellion, for nothing
can better refute the tyranny of fashion than the sincerity of
religious kitsch.

Böll reveals the sterility of the radio station in other ways as
well. The lectures of Bur-Malottke are only one manifestation of a
condition present in every phase of the station's operations. The
program directors bow to the whim of every listener who desires
stories of the souls of animals and seasonal tales of snow in winter and sunshine in summer. Furthermore, the station pays a
corrupt poet handsomely for a debased version of the Book of
Job, and even rewards him for his appropriation of Murke's private reading material, a dictionary of nineteenth-century London
slang, by allowing him to use the work as the basis of two spe-
cials on gutter lyrics. The narrator characterizes the poet as a
person who will "serve up his only grandmother as a feature"
(*E 50–70*, p. 173). But the ultimate corruption is the narcissism

of the directors who alternately feature each other in their programs. In the world of words in which so much is spoken and so little said, Böll employs the ideal oral symbol of protest. He has Murke collect silence.

Murke is, however, not the ideal hero. Because he is a sympathetic young David slaying Goliath, in his victory over Bur-Malottke it is easy to overlook that he too shows the tendency of becoming what he despises, that he too is infected with the evil he tries to combat. Although more likable than his antagonist, he defeats Bur-Malottke with a ruthlessness similar to his adversary's. Without mercy the young man "tortures" (*E 50–70*, p. 162) and humiliates the high priest of culture, whom "it was as good as suicide to contradict" (*E 50–70*, p. 158). Even Murke's friend the technician finds it necessary to warn him: "For God's sake, don't go too far" (*E 50–70*, p. 162).

Murke is particularly well equipped for his role as giant killer. In the sparse information which the narrator provides about him, he is described as a "young, intelligent, likable" honors graduate in phychology (*E 50–70*, pp. 156–57), but also as "arrogant" (*E 50–70*, p. 157) and "cold-blooded" (*E 50–70*, p. 161). Murke's boss, the station manager, considers him an "animal of prey" and an "intellectual beast" (*E 50–70*, p. 158). But it is not with his skill in open debate that Murke defeats Bur-Malottke; it is with cleverness and power—Bur-Malottke's own weapons. Murke is not only capable of hating his enemy, but of destroying him. He therefore "polishes Bur-Malottke off"; he does what his name (from the word *ab-murksen*) suggests he will do. Thus Murke is a new type of hero for Böll; he is not the defenseless victim of previous works, but an aggressive executioner. It is this aspect of hate that permits the reader to see the struggle between Murke and Bur-Malottke as a battle to the death. As Murke stares at Bur-Malottke from his glass booth "he knew suddenly what hate was; he hated this great, fat, handsome man . . . and never considered for a second to conceal it" (*E 50–70*, p. 162). Bur-Malottke accepts the challenge from Murke by returning "a hateful stare" (*E 50–70*, p. 162). While Murke clearly wins the first confrontation in the recording studio, it appears Bur-Malottke will prevail in the conflict. The great man intimidates the station manager into considering the alteration of all his lectures over the past ten years. The acceptance of Bur-Malottke's proposal would mean that the unpleasant task of eliminating the word "God" from 120 hours of tapes would go to Murke.

As Murke splices the tapes, however, he includes the worst recorded versions of the substituted phrases. When the station manager hears the new tapes, especially the badly expressed vocative: "Oh, you higher Being Whom we revere," he decides conclusively not to alter Bur-Malottke's old lectures. It is important that the ultimate decision against Bur-Malottke does not result from the pompous emptiness of the lectures—the content has not changed—but from the manipulated poor quality of the recording. Bur-Malottke, whose success was due to his calculated mastery of form and his understanding of public taste, is ultimately defeated by a careless act forced by Murke's cunning. Erhard Friedrichsmeyer correctly sees this victory over Bur-Malottke as a turning point for Murke. He calls it his "moment of truth."[11] The question now is whether the young rebel will become the new dictator. The course of Murke's development is suggested in his relationship with his girlfriend Rina. In forcing her to record silence for him, he exercises dominance over her. He now has gone far beyond the legitimate symbolic protest of collecting snips of dead air. Rina, in her innocence (the pure one, as her name indicates), recognizes this perversion: "What you are demanding is inhuman. There are men who want immoral things from a girl, but, I believe, what you are asking of me is more immoral than the things other men want from a girl" (*E 50–70*, p. 175).

Murke is not, as stated, the typical Böll hero of the short stories and novels—a loser; he is an aggressive winner. But he still demonstrates, although from a different perspective, Böll's humanist dictum: He who wields power over others, not for their benefit, but for his own, is a dangerous person. Murke's development indicates that one who makes his way upward in a corrupt world is likely not to advance without himself becoming corrupt. However justifiable Murke's action is in terms of revenge on a tyrannical representative of a vile system, he is still an arrogant, cold-blooded intellectual beast of prey capable of ruthlessness to the enemy and dominance over the weak. The narrator underscores these traits by Murke's sharp response in the cafeteria: "Leave me in peace; leave me alone" (*E 50–70*, p. 165) to the good-natured waitress Wulla's friendly suggestion that he take a vacation and stop smoking. But more subtly Böll hints at the relationship between Bur-Malottke and Murke in the similarity of their names. "Murke" is an anagram for "Bur-Malottke." All the letters of Murke's name are in Bur-Malottke's. Although Murke's faults are not identical with Bur-Malottke's—he is no snob and has no pretentions to cultural guruism—he is nonetheless increasing his power in the jungle of the radio station. The "zoo director" (*E 50–70*, p. 158), as the station manager is called, acknowledges that Murke is not one of the "rabbits" or "deer" (*E 50–70*, p. 158), but an "animal of prey," one of the dominant species. Murke's dreams also indicate an acquiescence on his part to exploit the opportunity presented by Bur-Malottke's tapes. In his first dream he climbs to the top of a staircase whose steps are dangerously smeared with soap and which is as high and as steep as the Eiffel Tower. When he reaches the top he hears the station manager call: "Go, Murke, go; show us what you can do!" (*E 50–70*, p. 158).

His dream on the following night is nearly identical. After paying a man, whom he recognizes as the station manager, thirty cents, he climbs to the top of a giant slide. As he reaches it he realizes there is no way back. The meaning of the dreams is obvious. The job of altering Bur-Malottke's tapes is an opportunity, a challenge, which he accepts. The dreams predict his success, for in each he reaches the top of the stairs, but dangers are present, not so much of failure, but of compromise of human principles, of betrayal of his humanity. The price of his ride on the giant slide—thirty cents—a sum reminiscent of Judas' thirty pieces of silver—suggests this betrayal. From the top there is no easy way back. Both of the dreams, furthermore, duplicate the symbol introduced in the opening sentence of the story: the *Paternosteraufzug*, the revolving elevator which goes up, crosses the top and comes down on the other side—the traditional literary emblem of the wheel of fortune. Life, it implies, has a circular logic, illustrated in the career of Bur-Malottke. To adjust himself to this inexorable law, Murke rides the revolving elevator every day over the top and back down. On the mornings after his two dreams, however, as he follows the dangerous course of challenging Bur-Malottke, he has no need of this daily "existential exercise" (*E 50–70*, p. 156), or as he thinks of it, his "breakfast of fear" (*E 50–70*, p. 157). He senses the prediction of the dreams that he will rise high, but fails to perceive that he will also come low. His life, like Bur-Malottke's, begins to exemplify a ride on the wheel of fortune.

Important to the effectiveness of the satire is Böll's skillful manipulation of a wide variety of speech levels ranging from the pretentious perorations of Bur-Malottke to the cool brevity of Murke's responses; from the crass exchanges of the entertainers to the jargon of the station employees: *verfeaturen* ("to feature"), *Abteilung Kulturwort* ("Department of the Cultural Word"); from the important-sounding but shallow conversations of the intellectuals to the simple directness of Wulla's utterances. It is Böll's linguistic talent, his sure feeling for the spoken language, and his remarkable ability to capture the speech patterns of a variety of levels of German society which more than any other skill make him an outstanding writer and which lends all of his works, even the minor and less successful ones, that element of reality and truth which is characteristic of great literature.

The main attack in Böll's satire, as stated, is against West Germany's betrayal of a genuine religious impulse felt at the end of the war and the nation's insistence, during the economic and political restoration of the 1950s, on cutting God out of social considerations. But Böll, as is usual in his satires, has several targets for his arrows: the cultural life of Germany, the aesthetization of taste, the predominance of form over content in the media and the arts, and one of Böll's favorite objects of satire, the role of technology in society.

Bur-Malottke's reliance on technology, his desire to cut and splice the tapes rather than re-record the lectures, causes his own downfall. He could have retaped the two thirty-minute lectures in one hour without error, without dispute over the increased length of the talks, and without conflict with Murke. By relying, however, on technology, on cutting and splicing, Bur-Malottke himself spends one hour on the job because of unforeseen difficulties and causes Murke and the engineer each eight hours of needless labor (six hours on Monday and Tuesday and two on Wednesday). He could also have avoided humiliation and defeat if he had not been ready to exploit the time of others. Murke had, in fact, prior to his assignment of correcting Bur-Malottke's tapes, "never read a single line by him or heard a single lecture by him" (*E 50–70*, p. 158). Thus, before working with the tapes, he had no basis for "hating this great, fat, handsome man" (*E 50–70*, p. 161).

Böll's story, moreover, is even more ironic, for as the title of the story indicates, Murke, too, is a slave of technology. He is no longer capable of a natural protest against the empty world of words, that is, of turning off the sound and retreating into silence. He is conditioned to the symbolic gesture. His saving snips of dead air, although perfect as a metaphoric protest, loses its moral power and becomes double irony when he forces Rina mechanically to produce silence for him. Technology wins out over common sense; absurdity triumphs over reasonableness, irony over symbol.

The absurd world of technology, with all its emphasis on time saving, division of hours into minutes and minutes into seconds, which Böll treats in "The Thrower-away" (1957), is presented also in "Collected Silences": not only in the details of man-hours worked, but also in the statistical account of the number of times the words "God" and "art" occur in Bur-Malottke's two lectures, in the number of hours he has recorded since 1945 (120), in the number of minutes of silence Murke has collected (3), in the number of seconds it takes Bur-Malottke to say God twenty-seven times (20), in the number of seconds it takes him to repeat the replacement phrases (80), and in the length of the run-over time: one minute and thirty seconds on each lecture, etc., etc. It is a world reduced to quantitative analysis—a world in which quality has no meaning besides good taste. Such a society has lost its center. God has been cut out. That is the point of Böll's satire, but ironically Böll gives God the last word: not only in the final scene of the radio play as his name resounds in the empty church visited by a single atheist, but also in the concluding line of the satire as the engineer reads from the holy card of Murke's mother: "I prayed for you in St. James Church."

II The Death of Elsa Baskoleit

The time from 1950 to 1960 was for Böll his most productive period for the short story, not only in quantity (34) but also in quality. Besides the satirical masterpiece "Murke's Collected Silences" several other short works from this period deserve at least brief comment. "Der Tod der Elsa Baskoleit" [The Death of Elsa Baskoleit, 1951] is a subdued, sensitive tale treating the quiet agony of a father's loss of his daughter and man's casual inhumanity to his neighbor. The story takes place entirely in peacetime—in a prewar and postwar setting of a lower-middle-class neighborhood. Sometime during the war the beautiful fairy-like creature Elsa Baskoleit has died or been killed. No specific information about her death is given. Her absence, however, is a severe loss for her father, who in his mourning slips farther and farther away from reality.

The story is told in the first person by a truck driver who recalls the young Elsa dancing at night on her toes, "hovering like a swan" before her window, clad in a green tricot. He remembers also the insults the figure at the window provoked from the neighbors. "Whore" and "disgusting" (*E 50–70*, p. 55) were the epithets heard in the dark courtyard of their apartment building. At that time, the narrator was too young to understand the word "whore" and could not grasp how anything to do with Elsa could be disgusting. After the war, the narrator returns to Baskoleit's grocery store as a delivery man for a produce wholesaler. It is five years since Elsa's death. He finds the old man reduced in circumstances and pathetically mumbling a single phrase: "My daughter has died" (*E 50–70*, p. 57).

Elsa appears in the story less as a character than as a beautiful swan ". . . in a yellow circle of light in the gray courtyard" (*E 50–70*, p. 55), i.e., she appears as a shadowy symbol of an undefined ideal or an unarticulated hope that could have been but will never be. Because of her metaphorical significance, her symbolic rather than actual reality in the narrative, she is not the main character of the story, nor is her father, the kind grocer who, before the war, gave apples to children and defended his daughter against the anonymous detractors in the apartment complex; nor are the two customers or the frightened young boy the central characters.

The narrator, although he provides very little information about himself, is the protagonist of the story. He is the person who learns from the events of Baskoleit's life. After witnessing the deranged condition of the grocer, he returns to his truck to find a fearful street urchin playing with his turn-signals. Instead of chasing the boy away, as the boy expects, the narrator gives him apples. Thus the story concludes with the same gesture with which it began: an adult giving fruit to a child. The story of death and cruelty stands within a frame of kindness which contrasts with the inhumanity that forms the essence of the narrative. The conclusion is a symbolic act of goodwill and brotherhood in a world woefully short of both.

The Baskoleits, father and daughter, are the typical victims of Böll's early narratives. They are the little people, controlled by forces they cannot understand, hurled back and forth in life by the storms of fate. The most significant development in Böll as an artist is his gradual shift away from characters who cannot understand the world they live in to characters who more and more comprehend their environment, who recognize that war does not come like a thunderstorm, that poverty is less a spiritual flower than a social disease, and who come to grasp the economic and political causes of social situations. In this story of 1951 the determinant forces are not suggested as economic or even political, although Baskoleit is a poor man and the war is presumably the cause of Elsa's death. In this tale the decisive forces appear not to be societal, but personal: man's treatment of his fellow man. Both of the Baskoleits appear as childlike victims of the attitudes of their neighbors who cannot tolerate the natural innocence of a dancing young girl or the eccentric behavior of a mumbling old man. The hard, controlling values of the milieu do not let people be themselves, do not let natural goodness grow and develop, but destroy people by forcing them to be what they are not, as in one way or another they prevented Elsa from becoming a dancer, and forced her kindly father to scream curses into the night.

It is difficult to speak of a main event in a story so skillfully characterized by understatement and so masterfully concentrated as is this tale. In four pages Böll covers a timespan of several years and treats the decline of a family and the development of the narrator—enough substance for a novel. Even at this early stage of Böll's work his talent for handling time, compacting events, finding appropriate symbols, and for extracting essences in a few sentences show a master at work. The scene with the two customers in Baskoleit's rundown shop best illustrates these talents. The decaying store serves as the objective correlative of Baskoleit's crumbling life, as the vinegar purchased by the first customer reveals her acid personality. She leaves the store without returning the narrator's greeting, merely nodding in the direction of the old man and tapping her head with her forefinger. The second customer, in contrast to the first, shows compassion as Baskoleit mutters his formula. Both women are neighbors who know of Baskoleit's condition but continue to shop in his grocery: the first presumably for convenience; the second, as an act of retribution. The women, the reader senses, knew Baskoleit and Elsa before the war. The first woman responds to Baskoleit's repeated phrase with the unfeeling comment: "I've known that for five years" (*E 50–70*, p. 57). The second woman's response of tears indicates that she not only remembers the insults in the courtyard but that she recognizes a connection between them and Baskoleit's present state. Thus, the story ends on a note of hope: people can be affected by the plight of others; the witnessing of suffering can cause people to grow in moral awareness of the needs of one's fellow man.

III   The Balek Scales

"Die Waage der Baleks" [The Balek Scales, 1952] has been called a Brechtian *Kalendergeschichte*,[12] a work in which "the fronts of the class conflict are visible,"[13] "a little masterpiece,"[14] but also one of Böll's "weaker efforts."[15] In a Bohemian village at the end of the nineteenth century, the Balek family lives in feudal splendor, controlling the land, the flax works, the village, and the lives of its inhabitants. The Baleks dominate not only the economic base of the community but also the ecclesiastic and legal superstructure of the area. The pastor is indebted to them for his education, and the district chief of police pays court at their house the first of every year. The village has a law, unquestioned for five generations, that forbids anyone from possessing scales except the Baleks. In the Baleks' weighing room all goods sold by the villagers to the Baleks (they can sell nowhere else) are weighed. On the first day of the twentieth century, as the Baleks are to be ennobled by the emperor, twelve-year-old Franz Brücher, the grandfather of the narrator, picks up four quarter-pound bags of coffee, a gift from the Baleks on the occasion of their ennoblement. The young hero unthinkingly places the factory-weighed bags on the scales and is awed to discover the scales inaccurate. When he reveals the inaccuracy to the community, one villager steals the scales and the record book of five generations. The police quickly and violently recover the Balek property and exile the Brücher family, as instigators of the disturbance, to a wandering life of poverty. The power of wealth triumphs over the claim of justice.

The story has been criticized for its lack of probability, i.e., five generations of unquestioning acceptance of an unusual law,[16] and also for its focus on the minor injustice of the scales instead of the major injustice of the system.[17] Although the first criticism seems valid, it fails to take into consideration the fact of history that every age docilely accepts an exploitative system prior to its awakening to class consciousness, and the second criticism does not take into account the details of the story which adequately condemn the entire exploitative Balek system even though the story centers on the false scales. Despite these alleged weaknesses, the story has many aspects which argue in favor of the label "little masterpiece."

The work is an attempt to treat a traditional theme in literature of man's obsession with justice, made most famous in the German language by Heinrich von Kleist's classic *Michael Kohlhaas*. Böll's story even manifests several parallels to this nineteenth-century novella, among them the stubborn hero and the symbolism of the scales. Böll has often cited Kleist as one of the writers he most admires and who has had influence on his work. A detailed comparison of the two stories would prove valuable. The story also provides an additional example of Böll's symbolic use of names. The word Brücher is from *brechen* ("to break") and from *Bruch* ("breach"). Hence the grandfather is a person who breaks with the past at the dawn of a new era by

trying to enlighten the people about a social injustice. He has,
like Kohlhaas, no ideological basis for his action, only the feeling
of indignation and outrage at the discovered unfairness, nor
is he aware of the full significance of his discovery. He does not
consciously attack the system but only a specific inequity.[18] But
his insight is irreversible; it immediately causes more repression
and greater injustice. The authorities kill Franz's little sister
and restrict freedom of expression by forbidding the singing of a
hymn which has become the "Marseillaise" of the community.
Thus it is inevitable that such multiplying oppression will breed
a revolutionary mentality and radicalize a segment of the population. Young Brücher, besides being a harbinger of political
change, is also a David figure who carries a sling and attempts
to slay the mythical giant Bilgan, whom the Baleks have chosen
as the emblem on their coat-of-arms.

One of the most important examples of the unity of form
and content in the story is in the villagers' choice of a hymn
as their rallying cry. The words "The *justice* of this earth, Oh
Lord, hath killed Thee" (*E 50–70*, pp. 79, 80) formulate the
central thesis of the story: it is *justice*, not injustice; it is the
legal system, not the illegal scales, which "murders" (*E 50–70*,
p. 73) the men in the flax works and exploits their labor in the
fields. In this sense, it is the capitalist social order which is guilty
of the inhumanities depicted in the story. Important also is
Böll's reversal of the traditional symbolic meaning of the scales.
Through his manipulation of this traditional symbol of justice,
he shows the Balek system to be unfair and puts the whole concept of bourgeois legality in doubt by showing that those who
make the laws are those who benefit from them. "The Balek
Scales" is an important work in Böll's career. It is the first time
he examines and condemns the economic conditions of society,
and it shows a direction his later works will take.

"Action Will Be Taken" (1954) treats with humorous exaggeration a theme widespread in Böll's work: society's obsession
with productivity, with activity for the sake of activity, with
being busy and looking busy at all times, for ends that are not
always worthy, for purposes not always related to a better quality
of life. "Action Will Be Taken" is similar in this regard to Böll's
"Anekdote zur Senkung der Arbeitsmoral" [Anecdote on the

Decline of the Work Ethic, 1963] in which a tourist, seeing a fisherman dozing in the sun, encourages the man to work harder in order eventually to own a fleet of fishing boats so he can become rich and spend his vacations resting on the beach looking at the sea; whereupon the fisherman reminds him that that is what he is now doing. This anecdote relates the same theme which "Action Will Be Taken" retells satirically.

In "Action" Böll presents the reader with another of his asocial, first-person narrators of the Uncle Fred variety. The narrator, looking for employment, comes to Wundsiedel's factory. He senses that the breakfast being served to the job applicants is a disguised examination. He quickly consumes part of his food, leaving most of it on his plate, so he can impatiently pace the cafeteria floor looking "eager for action" (*handlungsschwanger*) (*E 50–70*, p. 123). On the application form he answers the question "Do you think it right that man has only two arms, legs, eyes, and ears?" (*E 50–70*, p. 123) with equal zeal: "Even four arms, legs and ears would not satisfy my urge for action. Man is miserably equipped" (*E 50–70*, p. 123). To the question "What do you do after work?" (*E 50–70*, p. 123), he replies: "The expression [after work] is not in my vocabulary," and quoting Goethe's *Faust* he adds: "In the beginning was the deed" (*E 50–70*, p. 123). He gets the job and meets a strange assortment of fellow employees, one of whom lives by the slogan "Sleep is sin" (*E 50–70*, p. 124). To get ahead at Wundsiedel's the narrator feigns a love for action; he masters the use of thirteen telephones and practices variations on the phrases which will lead to promotion: "Do something," "Something must be done," "Something will be done," "Something has been done," "Something ought to be done" (*E 50–70*, p. 123). After a short time on the job, his hesitation in giving the prescribed response causes Wundsiedel to collapse dead before him; he informs his immediate superior, who works with a telephone in each hand, takes notes with a pen in his mouth, and operates a knitting machine with his toes, that the owner has died. At Wundsiedel's funeral he discovers his true calling—that of a professional mourner—a job for which "dreaming is a prerequisite and doing nothing a duty" (*E 50–70*, p. 127). At no time does he ever discover what Wundsiedel's factory produces. Only in the last line of the satire does he conclude that: "It must have been soap." Although the story is not great literature—too lighthearted and mild-mannered to cut to the core of a problem as satire should—it is an entertaining diversion deserving its position as one of Böll's most anthologized works.

IV   Unexpected Guests

"Unberechenbare Gäste" [Unexpected Guests, 1954], since its inclusion in the collection *Nicht nur zur Weihnachtszeit: Satiren* (1966), has posed a problem of interpretation. Scholars who try to analyze the story as satire have difficulty identifying the satiric object and answering the questions: What is being criticized? What is Böll protesting? These traditional questions, which must be posed if satire is to be understood as satire, are only tangential to the story.

The eccentric family in the center of the narrative with their excessive kindness is not presented in a negative, but rather in a positive light. The story contains no direct social commentary and makes no references to the state of society. The father of the family narrates the tale about his wife and seven children, who have a soft spot in their hearts for every living creature that comes to their door. Dogs, cats, toads, rabbits, chickens, foxes, birds, pigs, and even a hippopotamus, elephant, camel, and lion have become part of their household. The narrator describes his family: "My wife is a good woman, she turns no one away, neither man nor beast, and for a long time now our children have been ending their night prayers with the embellishment: Lord send us beggars and animals" (*E 50–70*, p. 136). The grinding poverty of the family, however, gives the father concern. Not even the toad, he exclaims, senses the worry that "moves my heart," and like him, his "sole comfort, Bello, the dog, yawns from hunger" (*E 50–70*, p. 137). But he does not permit the oppressing circumstances to get the better of him. He maintains his mental equilibrium—even if somewhat desperately: "I maintain it [my peace of mind (*Ruhe*)] because it is just about the last possession I have" (*E 50–70*, p. 137). To pay debts his wages have been garnisheed, and there is frequently no money in the house for food because his wife has spent the family budget buying household items from peddlers. When the narrator returns from work he sometimes has to go out again selling door to door the soap, razor blades, and buttons which his wife has purchased. On such occasions when he returns late with apples, bread, coffee, and potatoes, there is a "happy" (*E 50–70*, p. 137) family meal: "Satisfied animals, satisfied children surround me, my wife smiles at me, and we leave the door of the living room open so the hippopotamus does not feel left out" (*E 50–70*, p. 137).

The main event of the story is the wife's acceptance of an elephant from an insolvent circus proprietor. The husband warns her it is illegal to conceal property of a bankrupt estate, but she is indifferent to legal realities, preferring fidelity to her nature and her principles: "That doesn't matter to me. . . . I'll not let anything happen to the animal" (*E 50–70*, p. 139). Her response is the key sentence in the story. To her, what is right is above the law; the claim of property is subordinate to decency. She extends to animals and to all things the dignity and respect she accords to people. Neither her own meager means nor the laws of society prevent her from living the communistic ideal of the gospel. She is a typical Böll woman in that she sets the moral tone for her family and determines the person her husband becomes.

Later in the night, the circus owner returns and asks the wife to take in a cat. The narrator awakes to a lion in the kitchen. The final scene culminates with a vision of a contemporary Eden, where the lamb and the lion lie down together in a peaceful paradise: "I let the rabbits into the kitchen where their feed-box stands under the cupboard: the rabbits sniffed the lion and the lion the rabbits. . . . It seemed to me as if the lion was smiling" (*E 50–70*, pp. 140–41). After a few days the elephant and lion are taken away, but the narrator has grown to love the gentle king of beasts: "The quiet, friendly seriousness of the lion had won my heart. . . . I had grown used to him; he was actually the first animal which enjoyed my total sympathy" (*E 50–70*, p. 141).

The conclusion and tone of the story indicate the work is not a satire, but an idyll. The word idyll is used here not for a genre or a form deriving from the pastoral, but for a piece of literature that emphasizes the idyllic—brevity, homely scene, sentimental closeness of man to nature (animals), and the love and happiness of the characters: what Schiller calls poetry which "presents the idea and description of an innocent and happy humanity."[19] In this sense the idyll in no way depends on harmonic, rural, rustic conditions under which the characters live, but mainly on how the characters react to their given conditions. Obviously want and hunger are not usually the essence of peace and contentment, but for these characters, this family, because of their Christian mystical concept of poverty—not verbalized but lived—their life is an idyll. Love and happiness overcome all material opposition because of a religious disposition to life.

The tale also avoids satire by illustrating Böll's concept of humor and by presenting a *mundus inversus*, not a *mundus perversus*, i.e., a world turned upside down, but not perverted. The perspective of the narrator and the intention of the author do not attempt to criticize, but to demonstrate. In the *Frankfurter Vorlesungen* Böll rejects Wilhelm Busch as a model of German humor. He claims Busch's humor is sadistic at its core, for it treats people as garbage (*Abfall*), and, therefore, reveals in its essence a disdain for humanity. Böll suggests, as an alternative model to Busch, Jean Paul, for his humor manifests a love of humanity which never belittles man, never treats a person as a fool, never reduces a human being to refuse, and always reveals man in his nobility. Böll explains this "humane possibility for humor" as the task of "showing sublime that which society declares as waste (*Abfall*), and which society considers as refuse" (*FV*, p. 107).

This theory of humor is what "Unexpected Guests" exemplifies. The narrator's family is society's "poor white trash" (to use an appropriate American expression). The narrator suffers the indignity of having his wages garnisheed and of having his family practice generosity at the price of hunger. The normal dignity accruing from a decent standard of living is denied the family even though the narrator works steadily at a full-time job. It would not be fair or accurate, despite the wife's excesses, to attribute the family's poverty to her extravagant purchasing of shoestrings from peddlers, her taking in of stray animals, or her feeding of beggars. The family's poverty lies in society's failure to provide the narrator as a working man with a humane standard of living. The story implies a criticism of society, but Böll does not focus the story on social judgments, rather on the idyllic quality in human relations. He places in the center of the tale the narrator and his family and shows how they cope with poverty in a Christian and communistic manner. The family is a community which practices in daily life the "Seven Corporal Works of Mercy." They feed the hungry, give drink to the thirsty, and shelter strangers, making no unnecessary distinction between man and beast. The reader can assume that people living by such an ethic would also not fail to comfort the sick, bury the dead, clothe the naked, and visit the imprisoned.[20] In the family's relationship to the things of life—work, food, animals, and their fellow man—Böll reveals the nobility of these "little" people.

Such a view of existence is reminiscent of the one Jean Paul presents in his *Leben des vergnügten Schulmeisterleins Maria Wuz in Auenthal* [Life of the Happy Little Schoolmaster Maria Wuz in Auenthal], where the hero's pleasure in life comes from his single talent of knowing how always to be happy despite hunger, suffering, and poverty. Even the striking fantasy of both works parallel each other in as far as they are the reactions of the protagonists to poverty: Böll's bizarre idea of having his narrator sell at night what his wife purchased from peddlers during the day is not unlike Jean Paul's novel idea of having Wuz write his own library of the classics because he could not afford books.

According to Böll, humor must include along with the comic "a minimum of optimism and at the same time an element of sadness" (*FV*, p. 107), or as he also formulates the thesis: "Humor without sadness is not itself" (*FV*, p. 108). Böll's theory in practice emanates from a mystical Christian concept of poverty. In two separate essays dating from 1960, he proclaims the need to acknowledge the transcendental aspect of suffering. In "Hierzulande" he criticizes Germany as a land in which "poverty is neither mystically at home nor a station in the class struggle" (*EHA*, p. 433), and in "Karl Marx" he criticizes the philosopher (although professing a sympathy for Marx the man and even a halfway acceptance of his sociology) for attributing to poverty only a negative social significance and for disregarding poverty as a "mystical home (*mystische Heimat*) of Christ and all his saints" (*AKR*, p. 87). Of this failure to recognize the human necessity of suffering—for therein lies the mystique of poverty—Böll believes the whole of the Western world—Christian and

Socialist—to be guilty (*AKR*, p. 87). The story "Unexpected Guests" is Böll's testimony to the ideal of living the New Testament message. But the story does not proclaim St. Francis by denying Marx, nor does it maintain religion by discarding sociology or manifest a humane humor by totally forfeiting social criticism. At an early stage of Böll's development, 1954, it shows his interest in people who must live by work and reveals the Christian-humanist basis for all of his social concern.

V   In the Valley of the Thundering Hooves

The tale "Im tal der donnernden Hufe" [In the Valley of the Thundering Hooves, 1957] differs from most of Böll's narratives by its length. It is neither a short story nor a novel, but rather a novella in three chapters. It treats the problems of adolescent sexual awakening seen from the perspective of two fourteen-year-old boys and a girl, but revealed by an omniscient narrator. Thematically the work relates to the novel "Haus ohne Hüter [The Unguarded House, 1954], but in "In the Valley of the Thundering Hooves" the children are three years older than the two boys in the novel. The title of the story refers to the situation of the youths living under the pressure of sexual longing in a repressive society, repressive in that the two boys consider their longing in itself sinful; thus their state of mind represents a perverted understanding of natural sexuality which has been passed on to them through their religious education. It is important that the heroine of the novella is spared the boys' trauma simply by being a nonbeliever.

The story begins just before 5:30 on a Saturday afternoon in summer as Paul, the protagonist, waits in line for confession. He cannot prepare himself spiritually for the sacrament because he is overwrought with sexual desire. He stares at the tiles on the floor of the church, which reflect his inner confusion: "They were red and white, honeycombed, the red ones were speckled with white, the white speckled with red; he could no longer distinguish the white from the red; the tiles ran together, and the dark lines of cement became blurred, the floor swam before his eyes like a gravel path of red and white stones" (*E 50–70*, p. 222). The color symbolism runs throughout the story[21]—red, representing passion, guilt, immorality, damnation, sin, death; white, representing purity, innocence, morality, forgiveness, peace, life. The symbolic red sometimes appears as rust, mahogany, or a dark color shading into black; the symbolic white appears sometimes as brightness, yellow, or light clouds. The symbolic red is most obvious in the plum and cherry jam, the dark mouth of the woman in church, and in the blood over the tennis balls; the white is most obvious in the lamb's fleece, the fuzz of the tennis balls, and the breasts of Mirzova. Because a glimpse of a woman's arm, a girl's voice, or the sound of high heels on the church tiles creates in Paul unabating "sinful" longing, he leaves the church without confessing.

The use of the confessional scene was not new to Böll in 1957. He had used it in the short story "Das Abenteuer" [The Adventure] in 1951 and in the novel *Acquainted with the Night* in 1953. In each case the confessional experience produced a social awareness on the part of the penitent. In "The Adventure" the protagonist discovers the adultery he confesses to be less serious than his cooperation in deceptive business practices. He recognizes that social transgressions are more serious than private ones. In the novel, a woman who confesses her loathing of hypocritical community leaders and of priests accustomed to luxury discovers that her confessor shares the same abhorrence of social privilege, thus justifying in part her enmity toward people who claim class rights. In each incident, and here as well, the confessional scene offers sociological insight. Paul intuitively rebels against a social and religious system which makes him feel guilty for his natural physical development. Since neither he nor his friend Griff can verbalize the rebellion they feel, they act it out in the destruction of the symbols of the oppressive order: the jam jars of the parental world which preserves things in a nonchanging state and the tennis balls of the sports world in which all activity proceeds by rule.

Paul's suffering and moral anguish are a result of the prevailing sexual morality of the Catholic Rhineland. However, the depicted sexual mores of the Rhenish world have a supraregional, suprareligious validity. Here, as so often, Böll in his geographic province achieves a level of local realism which exposes social relationships of a larger world. He tries to show that the oppressive sexual attitudes in the Rhineland originate in the school, church, and home. Hence the youths' problem is socioreligious, not biological, and therefore a problem which calls for the possible (a change in society), not for the impossible (a change in nature).

After leaving church, Paul visits his friend Griff. He, too, sees no escape from their dilemma of desire but sin or death. While their parents and most members of the community are attending the city's annual regatta on the river, the boys in their frustration throw jars of jam against the walls of Griff's room and contemplate suicide. The second chapter begins at 5:50 on the same Saturday as Paul leaves his friend's room to fetch his father's pistol, a World War II souvenir. The gun acquires phallic significance as Paul recalls his father's Saturday-evening cleaning ritual: "Here was celebrated the cult of an instrument which in such an open and terrifying way resembled his sex (*Geschlecht*)" (*E 50–70*, p. 224). Curt Hohoff correctly sees in this ritual another aspect—the identification of the older generation (*Geschlecht*) not only with sexual repression but also with war, militarism, and death.[22] Hohoff's interpretation receives further support in that it is the history teacher Drönsch who makes sexual advances to the heroine, Mirzova, and who also works to revive the reputation of Admiral Tirpitz (1849–1930), the First World War advocate of unrestrictive submarine warfare. The phallic symbolism runs throughout the novella but is most pronounced in the background description of the scene in which Mirzova permits Paul to see her breasts: "The picture was still hanging there on the wall, the one he [Paul] had not seen for a long time, the one he thought about sometimes: factory chimneys with red smoke rising up from them, smoke pouring out and joining together in the sky forming a bloody cloud" (*E 50–70*, p. 244). Characteristic of this story, even more than usual for Böll, is the use of symbols. The weighty symbolism, however, is fitting in this work because the story treats a topic which society does not (or at least did not in the 1950s) discuss openly. Thus the author is justified in his choice of symbolic communications, the shorthand of inference, to suggest the latent and concealed tension behind society's conspiracy of silence. Böll prevents the awesome cargo of symbolism in the story from shifting weight and sinking the ship of art by keeping a tautness on the lines between the plot and the moral quality of the narration.

Paul promises Griff that he will return with his father's pistol by 6:15. Whether they will then commit suicide or not is uncertain. As Paul enters his house, he is seen by his neighbor and classmate Mirzova. Through a pair of binoculars she witnesses Paul's taking of the gun. When he leaves the house she calls him to her. Because she is beautiful and physically mature for her age, she is the object of sexual advances from adults and the victim of slanderous rumors from her peers. Mirzova's mother has locked her in her room to wait for the 7:10 train, which will take her to her father, in Vienna. Mirzova is an outsider not only by dint of her ruined reputation, but also because of her Communist father and her apostate mother. Mirzova has, however, gained as well as suffered from her social ostracism: as an outsider she has become wise about human relations and as a nonbeliever acquired insight into Christianity more profound than that of most believers. As a victim of society's hypocritical attitudes and perverted sexual values, she understands Paul's suffering better than he. Although she exclaims to him: "I am not your Jerusalem" (*E 50–70*, p. 242), she nevertheless becomes the boy's "holy city" (*E 50–70*, p. 242). She prevents his suicide, ameliorates his sexual anxiety through her natural chastity, and even instructs him in religion:

"I know it is the most serious sin to kill yourself. . . . With my own ears I heard the priest say: we must not throw the gift of life at the feet of God."

"Gift of life," he [Paul] said bitterly, "and besides God has no feet."

"Doesn't he?" she said quietly. "If he doesn't have feet, what did they pierce then?"

He was silent, flushed and said softly: "I know." (*E 50–70*, p. 245)

Mirzova's arguments are not strictly logical, but they are effective in changing Paul's life. He now rejects suicide, not so much because it will end his existence, but because it will be his spiritual death.[23] Prior to his conversation with Mirzova he sought in suicide only avoidance of sin and release from his sexual anxieties—in his own mind faithfulness to the tradition of the saints who preferred death to sin. Here Paul's intellectual confusion is most obvious as is the danger to youth of a false conception of human sexuality transmitted to children in terms of sin by society's institutions of authority. Mirzova's remark "What a pity that you are so Catholic" is a sharp indictment of Paul's religious training. She continues: "Otherwise, I'd show you my breasts" (*E 50–70*, p. 247). Paul intuitively understands her offer as a chaste gesture, made to release his frustrations and to restore his psychological balance. The chastity of Mirzova's action is underscored at this point by her question "Why do you call me by this name [Mirzova]? My name is Katharina Mirzov"[24] (*E 50–70*, p. 247), i.e., she is pure like St. Catherine, the patroness of maidens. The result of her action verifies her chaste intention: "He looked at them [her breasts] closely, did not touch her, just shook his head, and laughter rose up in him" (*E 50–70*, p. 249).

Often in Böll's works, the motivation of his characters proceeds on an irrational level. Not the mind but the emotions decide things, as illustrated by the frequency of love at first sight in his plots. This pattern of irrationality is particularly noticeable when good is victorious over evil, as in this story. Instead of discussing with Paul his problem, Mirzova takes the less intellectual, but more dramatic and effective, course of exposing her breasts. When evil is victorious over good, as in the case of the Nettlingers and Hoysers of this world in the novels *Billiards* and *Group Portrait*, the motivation of the representatives of evil is extremely cerebral, even transparently so. The result is that in Böll's work evil is often associated with the calculating and the intellectual and good with the intuitive and the instinctive.

The laughter which wells up in Paul as he sees Mirzova's breasts signals his release, the end of his torment. In a theological sense it is a blessing, a bestowal of grace. It is common in Böll's work that the saving act, the redeeming physical and spiritual deed, lies outside the bounds of what society and the church deem as moral conduct. In Böll's first longer story, *The Train Was on Time* (1949), the hero finds his spiritual renewal in a brothel; in the novels *Group Portrait* and *The Lost Honor of Katharina Blum*, the heroines see their lives revitalized by love that is sanctioned by no sacred or secular authority.[25] This Christian existential-situational theology in Böll's work is in no way new; it has a long tradition running through the works of many Catholic writers of the *renouveau catholique:* Bloy, Bernanos, Greene, le Fort, Claudel, Mauriac, and Andres, among others.

Also typical for Böll, as indicated in the discussion of "Unexpected Guests," is the presentation of female characters who are stronger than their male associates,[26] more certain of their nature, at one with themselves, undivided in personality, and who determine the course of the male's life.[27] This pattern remains unaltered until 1971, when Böll begins placing female characters in the center of his novels. Along with this shift, the direction of influence reverses itself; it becomes the man who influences the life of the woman: Boris-Leni, Ludwig Götten-Katharina Blum.

Mirzova's intuitive wisdom reveals itself again as she suggests Paul and Griff use the pistol to shoot at tennis balls and jam jars, objects which Paul and Griff have already recognized as symbols of petty regulation and the status quo. As Paul departs, he agrees to fire a salute into the air at the railroad crossing when Mirzova's train passes, taking her to her exile in Vienna. Chapter 2 concludes at 7:13 with Mirzova shouting from the passing train the word "Jerusalem." Griff neither understands the word nor comprehends its meaning. He has no Jerusalem to dwell in.

In chapter 3, Paul and Griff shoot at the agreed-upon targets, but they are unsuccessful: " 'We haven't hit a thing.' 'Lies,' said Griff, 'all lies' " (*E 50–70*, p. 258). They cannot destroy the sexual mores of the community which lie about the sexual nature of man. Paul, at least, through Mirzova, has learned to live chastely with himself despite the perverted values he has acquired through the social system. Griff is not as fortunate. He cannot return to his parents and to his ruined room. He plans to run away to the Baltic Sea and work in his uncle's cannery. Before he leaves for the station, they agree on a last target: the beer sign in the shape of a weapon on the house where Drönsch lives. At eight o'clock, as Griff rushes to the station, Paul vents his anger at the lecherous, militarist Drönsch and destroys (what Griff could not do) one of the aggressive symbols of oppression and repression, one of the symbols of the power of the parental generation. When a policeman asks Paul where he lives, he first responds: "In the valley of the thundering hooves" and then corrects his answer: "I live in Jerusalem" (*E 50–70*, p. 262).

The story has a relationship to much of what Böll has written. The language is dominated by Christian motifs. Mirzova is subjected to the epithet "whore" and the ruination of her reputation because of alleged sexual behavior, as are the characters Elsa Baskoleit and later Leni Pfeifer and Katharina Blum. She is a nonbeliever with a Catholic education who like Hans Schnier comprehends Christianity more fully than the believers. And in the reduction of the time of the narrative to two and a half hours (five-thirty to eight o'clock), Böll continues a narrative technique which has fascinated him since the early 1950s. He explains this technical aspect of his work in an interview with Horst Bienek: "Ideally, I would say, a novel ought to take place in one minute. I can only indicate through this exaggeration what I am trying to do in my treatment of time."[28]

VI Irish Journal

In 1957 Böll published his *Irish Journal*, the result of two visits to Ireland in 1955 and 1956. The book reflects his favorable attitude to things Irish: the religion of the island, the kindness of the people to strangers, their accommodation to a hard life, and their concern for the present rather than for the past or future. The title of the work, *Irisches Tagebuch*, however, is misleading. The book is neither a journal nor a diary, but a collection of eighteen stories connected by recurring themes, motifs, and linguistic patterns. It is not a question of whether the characters in the stories, anecdotes, and vignettes are real people whom Böll actually met or if their dialogue is accurately reported. Wolfdietrich Rasch comes to the point: "The *Irish Journal*, since it is entirely constructed as a narrative, excludes by its form the question of factuality. Its authenticity does not rest on provable facts (which it contains), but what is more important, on Böll's transformation of a personally observed and experienced reality into a linguistic work of art which presents the uniqueness and humanity, the charm and sorrow of the island."[29]

Critics have praised the slim volume for its "cultivated style,"[30] calling it "a little literacy delicacy,"[31] "a unique poetic creation,"[32] and a "beautiful, linguistically . . . rich contemporary travel book."[33] Wilhelm Schwarz is typical of these critics when he claims to recognize in the work a new, "more mature Böll of considerable stylistic concentration."[34] Other critics (usually those who like Böll best when he is most critical) point negatively to the work's excursion into the idyllic.[35] Both of these groups are right and both wrong. The *Irish Journal* is different in content but not in theme from the earlier work; it is idyllic but still critical. The commentators who point to a change away from the language of soldiers and the lower strata of society would be more accurate to state merely that there are no soldiers, black marketeers, circus performers, etc., in the stories. They are wrong in claiming that the language and style of the *Irish Journal* are different from that of earlier works. In fact, they are remarkably similar to that of Böll's previous stories. If the *Irish Journal* is couched in a cultivated style and in a beautifully rich language, then it must be recognized that some of the earlier works were also. The *Irish Journal* is not significantly different in word choice and sentence structure from some of the stories in the collection *Wanderer, kommst du nach Spa . . .* (1950) or from the novella *The Train Was on Time* (1949). Böll's style simply had not changed in the meantime. There was still the simple vocabulary of colloquial usage, key words repeated for emotional and aural effect, and rhythmic structuring of sentences. A brief example (as much as a mere two sentences can justifiably represent a style) will illustrate the point:

Als ich an Bord des Dampfers ging, sah ich, hörte und roch ich, dass ich eine Grenze überschritten hatte. . . . Ich war nicht der einzige, der ausstieg; eine alte Frau mit einem grossen braunen Paket entstieg dem Abteil neben mir. . . .

As I boarded the steamer, I saw, heard, and smelled that I had crossed a frontier. . . . I was not the only one to alight; an old woman with a large brown package got out of the compartment next to me. . . .

Although the two sentences seem to be related, they are not even from the same work; the first sentence is recognizably the

opening of the *Irish Journal*; the second is an excerpt from the
first sentence of the second paragraph of Böll's early short story,
"Die Botschaft" [Breaking the News, 1947]. The simple vocabulary (*ging, sah, hörte, roch, ausstieg, entstieg*) and the short,
rhythmic sentence patterns are stylistically the same. Furthermore the quoted fragments are from much longer periods, broken
into short, sentencelike cola by commas, semicolons, and other
means of punctuation—a technique which distorts (stylizes)
traditional grammar (a mannerism still characteristic of Böll's
most recent work). Rasch is correct when he asserts: "Böll's word
choice [in the *Irish Journal*] . . . is exact and avoids every 'select'
pretentious word; it is the simple vocabulary of daily communica-
tion."[36] What Rasch does not mention is that this description is
also appropriate for most of the works prior to, as well as after,
the *Irish Journal*. Although the language of the *Journal* is simple
and exact, it nevertheless tends to mythologize Ireland by presenting a one-dimensional view of the life of the island. It is important to emphasize here, however, that the idyllic, romantic, and
sentimental qualities in the *Irish Journal* serve a critical purpose;
they are meant to enhance the narrative's criticism of Germany
by implying a contrast between the Ireland of the journal and the
Federal Republic.

Although Böll mythologizes, i.e., presents a one-sided view of
Ireland in the *Irish Journal,* he does not idealize the country. He
only emphasizes in his tales the positive aspects of things Irish.
Ireland's poverty and drinking, its restrictive religion, and the
people's predilection for gab, for example, appear as appealing.
Böll shows how poverty teaches pleasures in primal things, how
drinking manifests sociability and friendliness, how the gift of
gab is the ability to entertain by telling a good story, and how
Irish Catholicism produces Irish chastity and humanity.

Just as present in the book, along with Böll's "old" style and his
"old" themes, are his criticisms of Germany. Germany lurks behind every page and sometimes even emerges from the narrative.
One example occurs in an inn where the Böll family meets the
traveler, Dermot, an Irishman knowledgeable about the Bible
and skillful at playing cards, telling stories, drinking whiskey,
making tea, and warming toast over an open hearth, i.e., a good
Irishman in the Böllian mold. Dermot was in a German POW

camp during the war, learned a little German and told the Böll children how he dug graves in the frozen earth to bury gypsy children who had died during the evacuation of the concentration camp Stuthof.

> "But why did they have to die?" one of the children asked.
> "Because they were gypsies."
> "But that's no reason—that's no reason to have to die."
> "No," said Dermot, "That's no reason, that's no reason to have to die." (*IT*, p. 84)

In this episode, the moralist Böll is still in the forefront. He is once again holding the mirror of conscience up to the German people lest they forget their past; he conjures up the recent German horrors even in an account of Ireland.

Also in the *Journal* Böll emphasizes his constant message that the important pleasures in life are the simple ones; in this regard the pleasures of the Irish are the pleasures of all of Böll's heroes: going to movies, eating bread, smoking and drinking (here whiskey and tea instead of schnaps and coffee). Even the character traits of the Irish are those of Böll's heroes: natural piety and chastity, respect for the religious dimension in life, recognition of the Christian aspect of poverty. Furthermore, the *Irish Journal* is similar in tone to Böll's Rhineland essays of the same year, 1957. In "Grosseltern gesucht" the passages on childhood in the provinces and in "Im Ruhrgebiet" his use of statistics to stimulate his imagination are reminiscent of the *Journal*.

Everywhere the comparison between Ireland and Germany can be noticed, even when Germany is never mentioned. Ireland exports priests, nuns, and children; Germany technology and industrial goods. The Irish are happier with less, the Germans discontent with more. In all the implied comparisons, Ireland fares better than Germany. Its appeal for Böll is obvious. The country and its people closely resemble the idyllic worlds and positive characters he had already created in such works as "The Black Sheep," "Unexpected Guests," and in the Bietenhahn episode at the end of the novel *The Unguarded House*, i.e., worlds and characters natural to Ireland but exceptional to Germany.

Why does Böll mythologize this little republic? Why doesn't

he see what is wrong with Ireland as he does so clearly with Germany, the reader may ask. The answer is simple. Böll is a German citizen; he lives in the Rhineland. He is a guest, a visitor in Ireland and, therefore, chooses to see the island with a friendly eye. Still Böll does not avoid in his journal the sorrow of the Irish although, like a polite guest, he chooses to ignore the people's shortcomings. In the episode entitled "The Ninth Child of Mrs. D.," the misfortune of having too little of this world's material goods is recounted with controlled passion—neither romanticizing nor idyllizing the poverty of the D. family. From the statistic that two-thirds of Ireland's population must emigrate, therefore, five or six of Mrs. D.'s nine children, Böll envisions the time which the family refuses to face. Concerning Mrs. D.'s youngest child, he writes:

In fourteen years, in the year 1970, on October 1 or April 1, when he is fourteen years old, with his cardboard box in his hand, with holy medals pinned to his undershirt and with an extra package of especially good sandwiches, little Pius will be embraced by his sobbing mother at the busstop, ready to start his great journey to Cleveland, Ohio, Manchester, Liverpool, London, or Sidney, to an uncle, a cousin, perhaps a brother, who has promised to care for the boy and do something for him. . . . The future departure and tears have not yet begun for the D. family. None of the children has yet had to pack his cardboard box, and ask the indulgence of the bus driver, so the parting can be prolonged, and no one is thinking about it because here the present weighs more than the future; but this preponderance of the present whose consequence is improvisation instead of planning, will be paid for with tears. (*IT*, pp. 125, 127)

Whether the reader responds to this passage as sentiment or sentimentality is his choice. But it certainly does not ignore the greatest of Ireland's problems, the one that troubled Swift: the inability of the island to provide for its people. Böll's emphasis, however, differs from Swift's; it is not on the economic, political, or sociological, but rather on the human and the individual elements of life which have the power of fate. The circumstances of the D. family are beyond their control, accepted as the inevitable, therefore, not thought about or analyzed and certainly not considered alterable—hence the scene has the power of tragedy:

destiny reaching its ordained end, it has nothing of the socialist call for reform.

The charge of sentimentality is more likely to arise in the concluding episode of the *Irish Journal* in which Böll captures his final hour on the island. In the chapter "Farewell," the author's eye catches that of "a young woman," and the last line of the book reads: "She smiled at me, and I smiled back." The smiling young woman is another typical Böll figure, reminiscent especially of the girl in the short-order restaurant who plays such a prominant role in *Acquainted with the Night*. Henri Plard has characterized these figures of smiling women who populate Böll's world as angelic messengers of hope.[37] Thus, from the first line to the last there is little new in the *Irish Journal*: the same style, the same qualities, the same themes, the same characters, the same commitment, and the same criticisms of Germany.

CHAPTER 4

The Short Stories After 1960

ALTHOUGH some of Böll's short stories after 1960 go over material treated in the collection *Wanderer kommst du nach Spa* . . . as do the 1961 and 1962 stories "Als der Kreig ausbrach" [When the War Started] and "Als der Krieg zu Ende war" [When the War Ended], still the 1960s represent in Böll's work a period of postmodernist, formal experimentation. In his search for new literary forms, Böll was part of a worldwide movement to find new literary ways to express old realities. Böll experimented with mythological themes, tried the epilogue as a story form, and in the work "Warum ich kurze Prosa wie Jakob Maria Hermes und Heinrich Knecht schreibe" [The Seventh Trunk, 1965] attempted to explain in narrative style the craft of writing fiction, i.e., chose a theme more appropriate for an essay to handle in the guise of a story.[1]

In 1933 the narrator of "The Seventh Trunk" read an installment of a tale by Jakob Maria Hermes in an obscure, small-town newspaper. For political reasons the periodical had to cease publication with that issue, and ever since the narrator has been trying to find the conclusion to the Hermes fragment. For thirty-two years he has been looking for the final installment of "the best short story I had ever read" (*E 50–70*, p. 390). In his search he discovers that Hermes is really the writer Heinrich Knecht, the author of the pamphlet "The Secret of the Seventh Trunk: Or How I Write Short Fiction." He later discovers, however, that the name Knecht is also a pseudonym.

The secret of writing, according to Knecht's pamphlet, is to have the essence of a tale rise naturally from the seventh trunk at the conclusion of the story. Each trunk is a separate bit of narrative material or factual information which is smaller, more detailed, than the preceding one; thus the seventh and final trunk is the smallest bit of information and contains the nucleus of the narrative. According to Knecht's theory, life is *not put* into the seventh trunk, i.e., into literature, but *originates* inside the trunk and springs alive into the consciousness of the reader.

The story "The Seventh Trunk" can be read as a model of Böll's artistic theory which tenders that every work of art will contain some element defying explanation, analysis, and understanding. The essence of art is, then, as Böll maintains in the essay "Kunst und Religion," a "secret" (*EHA*, p. 403).

The story, however, reveals more of Böll's art by symbolic implication than by prescriptive theory. Hermes, the name of the first author, is also the name of the god of invention, imagination, and fantasy. He is the proper god of Böll's work, more so than Apollo, the god of beauty and the sublime. Furthermore, the full name Jakob Maria Hermes evokes the name of the author Johann Peter Hebel, a writer whose calendar stories Böll much admires and whose work reveals an economy of means and a tolerant love of humanity parallel to Böll's.[2] The pseudonym Heinrich Knecht indicates the other side of Böll's artistic ideal. A *Knecht* is someone who serves, i.e., the name Heinrich Knecht indicates the social function of literature, suggests that literature must relate to society, must be *engagé* and corresponds to Böll's statement: "For me commitment (*Engagement*) is a prerequisite; it is the foundation, and what I build on this foundation is that which I understand as art."[3] The name Heinrich Knecht also evokes the writer Heinrich von Kleist who, along with Hebel, represents the other major influence on his work. In the reference to Hermes and Knecht, Böll acknowledges in his cryptic fashion that art must have the fantasy and invention of a Hermes, the craftsmanship of a Hebel and a Kleist, and the commitment of a *Knecht*.

"The Seventh Trunk" has a unique place in Böll's oeuvre, for it is in its way a study for the novel *Group Portrait*. The inchoate story by Hermes tells of a girl nine years old in 1933 who is educated by a sensual nun thought crazy by her fellow religious and by other students, i.e., Hermes' fragment is one of the trunks for the life story of Leni Pfeiffer, who is also nine years old in 1933, educated by an eccentric nun, and who emerges living from the seventh trunk of the novel *Group Portrait with Lady.*

In 1968 and 1970 Böll wrote two stories uniquely different from any he had previously produced. Each work illustrates his increased interest in literary sources. The first, "Er kam als Bierfahrer" [He Came as a Driver of a Beer Truck], is a modern version of the mythological story of Taurus and Europa. Böll presents Taurus as a Zorba-like Greek *Gastarbeiter* traveling only with the clothes on his back, with a bottle of wine in his hand, a piece of bread and a chunk of cheese in one pocket and tobacco and matches in the other, ordering in restaurants only food he can eat with his hands, appearing as a hobo in the first-class compartments of trains, and revealing his divinity by curing a cripple. After taking employment as a driver of a beer truck in order to criss-cross the country, he finds his Europa in a liberated teenager. Despite the new mythological theme, characteristics of Böll's previous work are still obvious: the working man as hero and the symbolic use of bread, wine, and cigarettes to represent the essential sacraments of the living.

In this tale, too, there is much to remind the reader of the novel *Group Portrait.* Europa is a fifteen-year-old girl, educated by nuns, innately talented, but too nonconformist to succeed in school or desire to. Because she is sexually free, she leaves school to live with an electrician employed in a paper factory. To him she remains faithful until Taurus appears. Her liaison with the electrician begins with his advances in a parking lot when she says: "Not here . . . in the woods . . . far, far away from automobiles" (*E 50–70*, p. 423). Europa is a clear omen of the heroines to come: Leni Pfeiffer and Margret Schlömer. She has Leni's nonconformism, her Catholic education, and Margret's sexual compassion and her capacity for love. Europa's schoolmaster summarizes her life in a phrase equally appropriate for Leni and Margret: she represents, he says, "a new architectonic dimension of a renewed Christianity" (*E 50–70*, p. 424).

I *Epilogue to Stifter's* Indian Summer

Böll's second short story based on a literary source, "Epilog zu Stifters *Nachsommer*" [Epilogue to Stifter's *Indian Summer,*

1970], is one of his best works after 1960. Although written as an entertaining spoof, it reveals, as all satire does, a serious side of its author. The satire is not easily understood, however, without knowing the book on which it is based, "the greatest of totally unread novels,"[4] as one critic calls *Der Nachsommer*, and without knowing something of Böll's attitude to Adalbert Stifter prior to 1970.

Stifter's *Der Nachsommer* (1857) is a utopian *Entwicklungs-* and *Bildungsroman*, a first-person narrative of Heinrich Drendorf, son of a wealthy businessman, lifelong student of nature, art, and literature, an ideal human being and perfect spouse of a perfect young woman of sensibility, beauty, intelligence, and modest charm. The work is a culmination of the German romantic-classical tradition of bourgeois humanism: showing respect for life, art, nature, and people, illustrated by self-control, confidence in friendship, patience with one's emotions, and resignation to a world as it is. Restraint is the characteristic trait of the narrative. The book moves unhurriedly, harmoniously, and tranquilly through the stages of Drendorf's life. Only near the very end of the novel does Heinrich reveal his own name and Natalie's (his fiancée's) family name. The characters of the novel live in an intimate world of friendship and family, where children always strive to please their parents and friends are always considerate of one another. It is a private world of perfection in which the passage of years is measured less by the calendar than by growth of intellect and character, a world in which time is spent immersed in art, nature, and the beautiful. The narration concerns detailed descriptions of flowers, cacti, paintings, dramas, statues, furniture, and stone collections. The novel's pace is set by sentences that come in slow rhythmic breaths. The mood is always quiet, calm, mild, peaceful, gentle, humane, civil. Goethe's *Wilhelm Meister* and Novalis's *Heinrich von Ofterdingen* hover over the book like protecting angels. The youthful lovers, Heinrich and Natalie, live in total submission to the will of their parents; there is no generation gap. Parents and adults represent the noble image in which the children are formed. Love is abundant but sex absent from this bourgeois utopia. Even in the engagement scene in which Heinrich and Natalie profess their eternal devotion to one another, sexual delight does not enter the minds and hearts of the characters. They even agree never to see one another again if any elder objects to their union. On the day of Heinrich and Natalie's wedding, the joy of the bride and groom is to witness the blooming of the rare cactus *cereus peruvianus*, the symbol of the uniqueness and beauty of their love and marriage. It is a novel of perfection and purity, the ideal utopian dream of Stifter's *sanftes Gesetz* ("mild law").[5]

In his summer lectures of 1964 at the University of Frankfurt, in which he attempts to develop an aesthetic of the humane, Böll praises *Der Nachsommer* as the "grandest model for living in German literature" (*FV*, p. 51). In the course of the third lecture Böll contrasts a long passage from *Der Nachsommer* describing beautiful inlaid furniture to the poem "Inventory" by Günter Eich (see p. 30) in order to illustrate the inability of postwar German literature to find roots in the traditional values of home and family. A nostalgia runs through Böll's lectures for the soundness of a civilized, pre-Auschwitz past. However, he in no way advocates an escapist literature of inwardness. Because of his double longing for a healthy world and a committed literature, Böll has mixed feelings about the unreal quality of Stifter's masterpiece. He calls it a "desperate dream of permanence, learning, and living" (*FV*, p. 72); yet, he concludes:

The only person after Goethe who found continuity was Stifter. It is from his work, as from Jean Paul's, that one can glean an aesthetic of the humane. . . . My profit from my occupation with Stifter consists in the rediscovery of his hidden fullness and modernity under his prudish language—which means to me actuality of means. I believe he could become the father of a new humane realism, could stand as sponsor for attempts, not at closing the chasm between statistical reality and reality as described in literature, not at bridging the chasm, but perhaps at slowly filling it in. (*FV*, p. 96)

As the 1960s progressed, Böll became more concerned with current German politics. Inherent in this interest was a growing sensitivity to socialist criticism and a growing awareness of a socialist economic point of view against which, in 1970, he reevaluated Stifter's *Der Nachsommer*.

Der Nachsommer appeared in 1857 nearly a decade after the revolutionary events of 1848. The action of the novel, however, despite all of Stifter's attempts at timelessness,[6] takes place, as he states in a letter of 1857, "not in our time, but over thirty years ago,"[7] i.e., in the 1820s. Thus the action of the novel predates, and the writing of the novel postdates, the March Revolution of 1848. Although the novel takes place in the period prior to the uprisings of the middle of the century, nowhere in the work are the problems which caused the revolutions: industrialization, expanding capitalism, and the frustrated longings of the middle class for political equality touched upon by Stifter. They are deliberately disregarded in his dream world of the leisure life in which persons seek self-fulfillment, unfettered by a profession, unhindered by work, unhampered by material worries. Despite the enormous expense in pursuing a life such as Heinrich Drendorf and his friends lead—paying private tutors, enjoying unrestricted travel, investing in scientific studies, building homes and laying out gardens, purchasing jewels, statues, and works of art, supporting servants, buying good food, clothing, and furniture, giving presents, paying generous wages, and treating employees with dignity—nowhere is there any indication that such a life is possible for any but the wealthy few. Stifter's dream of each man developing according to his potential is, under the conditions presented in the book, a false dream for humanity. Stifter's dream is not an ideal based on character or ability. It is merely a social construct for a wealthy elite despite all effort on the part of the author to pass off his vision of education as a possibility for all who seek it. Heinrich's leisurely road to maturity is for those who can live according to the advice of Heinrich's father: *Sei immer deines Grundvermögen sicher* ("Be always certain of your basic investment"), and for those who, like Heinrich, can count on *eine Vermehrung eures Eigentums* ("an increase of wealth") (p. 24).[8]

Heinrich's father justifies the system under which they live with the belief: "We all stand in the hand of God" (p. 24); "God directs the world in such a way that talents are properly distributed, so that every kind of work is done which has to be done on earth, and so that there will never be a time when all men are architects" (p. 12). And Natalie's mother promotes their way of life by instilling in her daughter and in Heinrich a belief in "the highest power that orders every thing that exists" (p. 395). Such a faith is for them not only a religion but a social philosophy. God for them is a protector of a social system rather than a creator of a changing universe. Since religion per se is absent as a theme from the novel, the world that is in order, controlled by God, perfect as it is, is the social order which guarantees the interest on Heinrich's investments and increases the value of his property.

This artificial utopia, this world which hides poverty, exploitation, and evil, ignores sickness, suffering, death, and class struggle, this world which avoids the negative, the harsh, the bitter, this world of distorted ethics is what Böll satirizes in his epilogue.[9]

The manner in which Böll comes to terms with the other side of Stifter's *Der Nachsommer* derives from Böll's considerations of *War and Peace*, especially his considerations of Tolstoi's epilogue, set eight years after the end of the novel.[10] Böll agrees with the critics who judge Tolstoi's final family scene, in which all the main characters are married, have children and have settled into a life of bourgeois responsibility, as a weakening of the artistic structure of the novel, but Böll argues its weakness is not the surprisingly philistine conclusion. It is due, he believes, to the inability of the reader to believe in or trust the artificially happy denouement. Böll feels Tolstoi's entire novel casts doubt on marriage as a happy institution; too many broken and unhappy marriages depicted therein speak against marriage as a happy state. He asserts conjugal fidelity has too often been betrayed for the reader to trust the status of Tolstoi's epilogue: André had loved Natasha while he was married to another; after his wife's death and his engagement to Natasha, she eloped with an attractive scoundrel; Pierre's first marriage was to a woman more courtesan than wife, who provided him with years of misery; André's old father railed frequently against women and marriage. All the unhappiness and suffering which came through marriage is too vivid in the reader's memory, Böll maintains, for him to put much confidence in Tolstoi's epilogue.

Böll wrote his essay on *War and Peace* in 1970, in the same year he wrote the epilogue to Stifter's *Der Nachsommer*. The sociological and aesthetic considerations which he treats in the essay also form the basis of his reevaluation of the Austrian classic. Böll's epilogue does far more than demonstrate the problems in Heinrich and Natalie's marriage and does more than show it to be a union reduced to habit and convention. The epilogue is a fullscale attack on the social values represented by Heinrich Drendorf and embodied in Stifter's novel. In the epilogue, Heinrich, besides becoming an adulterer, is an opportunist, a manipulator, a militarist, and a self-satisfied hypocrite. Böll manages to compact in his nine-page conclusion the sociological aspects of life ignored or minimized by Stifter: economics, politics, class differences, and the danger of conjugal routine. In the epilogue Böll scrutinizes the increase in Heinrich's wealth and the growth of his inheritance since his marriage. He details the disposition of the business of Heinrich's father, refers to Austria's political relations with Russia and Prussia, and comments on the sexless relationship of the wise old Risach with Mathilde, Natalie's mother.

To summarize the lives of several characters in a few pages and to continue Stifter's form of first-person narration, Böll employs in the epilogue a unique temporal structure. Heinrich recounts the events of his last twelve years in a thirty-minute period prior to the beginning of his twelfth wedding anniversary. The first section of the epilogue is an eighteen-minute reverie surveying his own life and the lives of his children, his wife, and his friends during the years that have elapsed since his marriage. The second section is an actual account of the twelve minutes immediately prior to the anniversary celebration, as Heinrich visits the plant house to see once again the blooming *cereus peruvianus* and there becomes involved in a spontaneous adulterous relationship with the gardener's grandchild, ironically named Natalie after his wife. The epilogue concludes with Heinrich returning to his family on the balcony to observe the fireworks opening the anniversary celebration.

The epilogue offers several levels of parody. Heinrich's flashback of the past twelve years has its parallel in the novel in Risach's flashback account of his sad courtship with Natalie's mother. But whereas Risach's reminiscence is a lecture to Heinrich on the wisdom of patience, moderation, self-control, and submissiveness to parents, Heinrich's flashback is a parodistic revelation of his snobbishness, social ambition, and careerism. The parody continues with Natalie's superstitious attachment to the number twelve which Böll uses as a leitmotif in the epilogue (her

six children born at regular two-year intervals, their twelfth anniversary, and Heinrich's unfaithfulness twelve minutes before the
beginning of the anniversary celebration). But the parody is most
effective in the language of the epilogue: at times an accurate
imitation of Stifter's style with the use of his vocabulary, tone,
and sentence structure, but varied with crass modernisms and up-
to-date expressions (*Präzision, Experimenten, Praxis, das Fleischliche, Sensibilitätssystem*, etc.) to indicate the change in Heinrich's character.

In the opening paragraph Böll indicates Heinrich's snobbishness and class attitude with his use of the word *Gesinde* when referring to servants, an expression which evokes the diminutive
form *Gesindel* meaning rabble. The impersonal word *Gesinde* is
not used by Stifter in his novel, instead the servants are referred
to as *Diener* ("servants"), *Mädge* ("maids"), or by their occupation: *Hausverwalter* ("stewards"), *Gärtner* ("gardeners"), etc.,
or most often by name. In the household of Heinrich's father the
servants eat with the family and the employees in the father's
business share the same food and wine as the family. The tone
of Heinrich's epilogue indicates he no longer follows this democratic practice. Although Heinrich's father was a successful and
wealthy businessman, it was clear in the novel that he spent
many hours at work. Heinrich, however, never had to work because of his inheritance; he was granted the leisure to pursue an
"ideal" education of *freie Entfaltung* ("free development"). It is
this "ideal" education made possible by the labor of others which
Böll puts in question. With his knowledge of science and art,
Heinrich has become a cartographer, appropriately an artist-
scientist, but not one who uses his skills and insights to increase
man's knowledge of the earth; his expertise is put at the disposal
of the Kaiser's army. The free unfolding of his talents which was
to satisfy his growing intellect and lead naturally to service of
society does not become a benefit to mankind. Heinrich makes
this adjustment in his education in order to rise socially, to satisfy
his egotism, and to gain aristocratic advantage. As cartographer
on the general staff for military planning, he is appointed colonel,
raised to the nobility, and eventually promoted to general. The
tenor of the epilogue in the section which records these events
is no longer in the language of Stifter, but that of Böll's "Haupt-

städtisches Journal" [Bonn Diary, 1957], in which the militarist Machorka-Muff recounts his political maneuvers, his sexual conquests, and his advancement to general. Also Heinrich's desire for a title of nobility places him in the company of the exploiting Baleks ("The Balek Scales") who, indeed, treat their social inferiors as *Gesindel* and who, like Heinrich, are favored with aristocratic franchisement primarily for their wealth and loyal support of the system.

The key sentence in Böll's satire occurs when Heinrich concludes: "The main subject of my interests and research [will be to investigate] the limits, the domains and the border transgressions between art and artificiality (*Kunst und Künstlichkeit*), or to express it more practically [to investigate] the possibilities of artifice (*Möglichkeiten der Verkünstlichung*)" (*E 50–70*, p. 436). "The possibilities of artifice"—that is the theme of the satire. Böll's epilogue shows the magnificent world of Stifter to be "artificial" and deceptive. In their Indian summer, Risach and Mathilde have "raised [their lives] above the sexual (*Fleischliche*) and the passionate" (*E 50–70*, p. 435); their lives now proceed with such "precision" (*E 50–70*, p. 436) that the narrator compares them to figures in a clockworks; they have ceased to be people and have become "automatons" (*E 50–70*, p. 436). Heinrich's marriage has fared even worse than the union of Risach and Mathilde. In the final chapter of the novel which recounts Heinrich and Natalie's wedding day and their visit to the *cereus peruvianus*, a plant so rare and difficult to cultivate that few Europeans have ever seen it in bloom. This exquisite blossom becomes the symbol of Heinrich and Natalie's marriage. On this twelfth anniversary, Heinrich's present to his wife is not the living blossom, but an expensive porcelain replica in a precious golden case. The real blossom is plucked by the gardener's grandchild, a fraudulent Natalie, and instead of the real flower, the artificial symbol is presented to Heinrich's wife. When Heinrich says: "Between my dear wife and me there was no visible disharmony" (*E 50–70*, p. 435), the important word is visible. The disharmony is there. The marriage has become like the porcelain *cereus peruvianus*, an imitation cased in gold.

Heinrich's life, too, has become a perversion, an artifice of what it was intended to become—a model of human intellectual development which strove first to fulfill itself and thereby serve society. Heinrich's father argues in Stifter's novel against the concept that man must first strive to be useful to others: "Man is not on earth for the sake of society, but for his own sake. And when each person lives the best way he can for himself, then he lives also for society" (p. 12).[11] Böll's epilogue shows how easy it is to deceive oneself, how almost inevitable it is that a person reared in the philosophy of Heinrich's father, a person educated as Heinrich has been, educated to follow his *Neigungen* ("inclinations") in the belief that the fulfillment of self will *automatically* benefit society, will turn out as Heinrich does in the epilogue. Böll's satire reveals how a person educated to pursue all of his intellectual pleasures is likely to become a person who lives selfishly. Heinrich has become in Böll's epilogue what he should not have become according to Stifter's bourgeois theory of liberal education. He has become an adulterer, not a faithful husband; a snob, elitist, and aristocrat, not a benefactor of society; a deceiver of self and others, not an honest man; a self-satisfied egotist, not a modest person. Böll's epilogue in its ironic, satirical manner challenges the premise of Stifter's dream which underlies the novel. It is Böll's reevaluation of Stifter as a model for a humane society. The epilogue indicates that Stifter's *Humanitätsideal* has in it the basis of its opposite: *Inhumanitätsgesellschaft*.

Der Nachsommer was intended by Stifter as a model fulfillment of his "sanftes Gesetz," which he defines in the foreword to *Bunte Steine* as "the law of justice, the law of morality, the law which would that every person be respected and honored, that he stand next to his neighbor without fear, that he be able to pursue his highest human career, that he acquire love and admiration from his fellow man, that he be treated as a precious stone, for every man is a precious stone for all other men" (pp. 7–8).[12] Stifter explains further where this "mild law" most clearly manifests itself: "It lies in the love of spouses for each other . . . in the work which maintains us, [and] in the activity which one does for his circle, for the future, and for mankind . . ." (p. 8).

Böll's epilogue does not question the goal of Stifter's "sanftes Gesetz." It only questions whether the goal is, indeed, realizable according to the conditions presented in *Der Nachsommer.*[13] Böll's epilogue exposes with satiric and ironic means how Heinrich has failed in those spheres of life in which the "sanftes Gesetz" reveals itself best: family, work, and society.

II Reports on the Attitudinal State of the Nation

Böll's continued interest in the political situation in West Germany after his article on the Baader-Meinhof group appeared in *Der Spiegel* (10 January 1972) produced in 1975 the satire *Berichte zur Gesinnungslage der Nation* [Reports on the Attitudinal State of the Nation]. The title derives from the yearly report which the federal chancellor presents to parliament on the state of the nation. The key word in the title is "attitudinal." Böll implies with it (*Gesinnungslage*) that the government, since the approval of the *Radikalenerlass* ("Radical Decrees") in January 1972, has become paranoiacally concerned with discovering the attitudes, views, and opinions of its citizens, not by means of surveys and questionnaires, but by spying on its citizens in both their public and private lives. The *Berichte* is a series of fictional dispatches from undercover agents to three separate and independent unnamed governmental intelligence agencies. The American reader is immediately reminded of the recent revelations in the United States by the investigating subcommittees of the senate that the FBI, CIA, and army have been gathering information, often contrary to their charters and by illegal means, on private citizens who have been neither accused nor suspected of crimes. The process, therefore, which Böll treats is the phenomenon of domestic spying and private snooping on people who do no more than practice their rights guaranteed them in the constitutions of most democracies.

Böll's message in this slim volume of sixty-two pages is clear enough: democracy, one of the proclaimed advantages of Western society with its free exchange of ideas, freedom of speech and press, is being eroded. Böll strengthens this critique of Western democracies in his final chapter, entitled "Confidential Report . . . ," in which the superintendents of the three secret intelligence agencies discuss establishing a research institute to develop techniques to determine the ideas and thoughts of people who refuse to express their opinions in words, but unconsciously reveal them in facial expressions. The tendency in the West, the satire indicates, is toward a totalitarianism similar to that which the West attributes to the East. Böll's subject, then, is of utmost seriousness. Böll's talent, his genius, one might say, of having a finger on the central nervous system of Western society is attested to again with this work, in which, however, the critical question is one of appropriate means. Despite the cleverness of this satire: its remarkable language, its accurate recreation of the idiom of spies and undercover agents, and the jargon and lingo of the Watergate-Nixon era; its presentation of the internal contradictions of the intelligence agencies; spying on themselves, organizing protests and supplying the materials for political demonstrations; and its verification that the really dangerous subversives, i.e., those who act contrary to the Constitution, are the employees of the government—despite all this the work is not a complete artistic success.

The weakness of the work lies not, as one might suspect, in its lighthearted treatment of serious material or in the ironic handling of the substance of social tragedy, but in its choice of strategy. The weakness of the work derives from its mildness, its characterizations which present informers as harmless butts of humor. In the *Berichte* Böll does not follow his theory of humor developed in the *Frankfurter Vorlesungen*; he does not treat as sublime what society has declared as garbage. He does much the opposite; the *Berichte* leaves the reader with the impression that the repressive authorities in society are amusing and inept people, intelligent bunglers who only make fools of themselves, people who, if ignored, will do themselves in. Even in the key point of the establishment of an Institute for the Research of Attitudinal Physiognomy Böll emphasizes less the danger of the social trend than the ridiculousness of the proposal. What this satire lacks is the cutting edge of Swift's "A Modest Proposal," or of Böll's own satires "Christmas Every Day," "The Thrower-away," "Murke's Collected Silences," or of Alfred Andersch's poem "Artikel 3 (3),"[14] which treats the same subject matter as Böll's *Berichte*. The work is more like a satire by Gore Vidal which conveys an aloof view of political problems with a supremely indifferent detachment. Instead of presenting Germany in the winter of its discontent, Böll öffers a picture of Germany in the springtime of its bungling oppression.

Böll deals with the theme of *Berichte* much more accurately and, therefore, artistically in his speech "Plädoyer für den Rechtsstaat" [Appeal for a Nation of Law, 1974].[15] Here Böll argues that to have one's name listed in a government file by a federal snooper is an official denunciation potentially more dangerous than a public one in the press. Böll sees this trend to catalogue and denounce radicals and leftists and to deny them employment as an attempt to frighten the populace into becoming cowering conformists, to create, as Böll claims, "a new generation of hypocrites, toadies, opportunists, cowards, and intimidated individuals who will be more obedient than the Hitler Youth."[16] The trend to denunciation received a legal justification with the signing of the Radical Decrees by Willy Brandt in January 1972.[17] The immediate cause of this turn toward the methods of Germany's past was the legitimate but hysterical fear of social revolutionaries like the Baader-Meinhof group; however, most of the hundreds[18] of people who have suffered under the Radical Decrees are people who have never advocated action or acted contrary to the constitution of the Federal Republic. Böll claims in his speech:

I am fed up. . . . It is quite simple to see the method being used. First the left opposition in all the parties was shot down. . . . Now the left-liberals—to which I count myself—are in line. . . . Next it will be the liberals; they are already beginning to show signs of weakening. . . . Then the conservatives will get their turn. I warn you conservatives and liberals to watch out. It is going step by step, systematically forward. And in all that I say here . . . I beg you not to discover one spark of Rhenish humor. (*Ee*, pp. 183–84)

Böll's fear for all groups, for the end of pluralism, is also reflected in his *Berichte*. One informer uses after his reported list of names a code (rb, sb, bb, rf, Likaki, and Kaki),[19] indicating not only political but also religious attitudes of each subject of investigation, characterizing each one as red or brown, as a believer or nonbeliever.

The *Berichte zur Gesinnungslage der Nation* is divided into nine chapters: two letters each from two agents and three letters from one agent, written to separate contact men from three investigating agencies; one additional chapter is a separate letter from a contact man to one of the agents, and the final chapter is a confidential committee report of a meeting of the three coordinators of the intelligence services. The informers and their contact men report under colorful code names: *Rotgimpel an Rotkopfwürger* ("Red Finch to Red-head Strangler"), *Ackergaul an Stallmeister* ("Field Nag to Stall Master"), *Rotmolch I an Majordomus* ("Red Salamander I to Majordomo"), and they refer to their packets of information with equally inventive terminology: the *Doppeldecker* ("double cover"), *Schleimbeutel* ("slime bag"), and *Flüstertüte* ("whisper sack"). The most colorful figure is the ex-radical Red Finch, a pyro-artist, a creator of "ignition art," and ex-serviceman who learned his skill with explosives while in the army. Field Nag is a civil servant masquerading as a Danish radio journalist preparing a report on postwar cultural developments in West Germany. Red Salamander I is a university co-ed organizing political demonstrations to lure dissidents into antigovernmental intrigues. Each of these agents behaves suspiciously enough to be suspected by the others, and each reports the others' incriminating activities. Field Nag, for example, appears in Red Finch's report as the "Pseudo-Dane" and in Red Salamander I's as the "Viking," while Field Nag calls the suspicious Red Finch "Mendoza." The only political demonstration reported in *Berichte* is that organized by Red Salamander I of blocking traffic with political posters. It is harmless fun for those involved, although leading to the arrest of the innocent printer of the posters. The atmosphere after the demonstration resembles that of a stage premiere, with the director and actors anxiously awaiting the reviews in the press.

Böll acknowledges for the *Berichte* a literary model in the humanists' *Epistolae obscurorum virorum* (1515) written against late scholastic formalism. Even the names of Böll's informers recall the Epistolae's correspondents Mistladerius ("Manure Pile"), Dollenkopfius ("Dumb Head"), and Schlauraff ("Clever Fellow").[20] By choosing this model Böll implies a similarity between the problems of suppression by sixteenth-century church authorities in Cologne and twentieth-century suppression by governmental authority in the Federal Republic. However, the similarity of his *Berichte* is much more with the first part of the *Epistolae*, composed by Crotus Rubeanus, characterized by indirect, non-polemic satire than with the second part, composed by Ulrich von Hutten, characterized by a direct, tendentious attack on intolerant, nonhumanistic theologians. But common to both parts of the *Epistolae* and to the *Berichte* is the self-incrimination of the correspondents. The letters in Böll's *Berichte* are written by representatives of the point of view which the work condemns. The lack of humanistic standard of ethics on the part of the agents of the government in the *Berichte* as of the agents of the church in the *Epistolae* is revealed by the correspondents themselves, not by a narrator writing about them. In this aspect of fictitious personae who unconsciously condemn themselves, lies the real strength of Böll's satire.

Since the publication of *Berichte* in 1975, Böll has continued to publish short stories. Of the four to date which have appeared in the recent *Werke: Romane und Erzählungen*, three have indirectly treated political topics, "Erwünschte Reportage" [A Desired Report, 1975], "Höflichkeit bei verschiedenen unvermeidlichen Gesetzesübertretungen" [Politeness in Varying Unavoidable Transgressions of the Law, 1977], and "Du fährst zu oft nach Heidelberg" [You Go to Heidelberg Too Often, 1977], and one has treated the theme of marriage, "Bis dass der Tod euch scheidet" [Until Death Do You Part, 1976]. Thus the major topics of Böll's work remain constant; only the manner of his treating his material has undergone change. It is unlikely in the 1980s that a new Böll of different interests will appear in the genre of the short story. Even if he again begins to experiment with short fiction, as he did in the 1960s, his themes will continue to be the same.

CHAPTER 5

The War Novels

I The Train was on Time

*T*HE *Train Was on Time* (1949) and *Where Were You, Adam?*
(1951), as well as many of the short stories of this period, treat
from a personalist, existential, religious perspective the tragedy
of the individual in war. In these works, Böll neglects the social
origins of war to present the tragedy of the individual caught up
in the horror of events. In *The Train*, the unity of the novella
is determined by the recurring motif which holds the story tightly
together from first page to last: Andreas's fear of imminent death.
Böll avers in *The Train* that war is superhuman, beyond comprehension and understanding, that it is like a tidal wave that
carries everything away that stands before it, the innocent and
the guilty, the "victims" and the "executioners." Even when Andreas and his girlfriend Olina believe escape is possible, when
they opt to intervene in their own destiny by loving, hoping, and
planning, they only deceive themselves that death can be averted,
and even more decisively bring about their own end. Death at
the conclusion of the story is required by the form of the work
itself. From the words of the first page: "I don't want to die,"
the reader knows death will make its visitation at the appointed
time and place. The very form of the work proclaims man's position in war, the universe of the story, to be existentially hope-
less; love, the author admits, can change the subjective quality
of life but cannot affect the objective reality of existence.

The Train with its religious, mystical point of view reveals
Böll's limited understanding of, his lack of interest in, and his
unwillingness or inability to deal with the social aspects of war
in the period immediately following 1945.[1] This criticism, how-

ever, does not negate the novella's formal achievement or its humanistic, anti-Fascist sentiment. From both the human and aesthetic points of view, the novella deserves its growing reputation as a minor masterpiece. Gert Kalow pronounces the work a "Geniewurf,"[2] and Ziolkowski claims: "Never again has Böll written a story of such closed perfection and inevitability. . . . It is an artistic tour de force."[3] But Ziolkowski wisely warns that it is a type of work "that cannot and should not be repeated."[4]

The opening sentence of the novella introduces the ominous theme of death which dominates the story: "As they walked down through the dark underpass they could hear the train above rolling to the platform, and the sonorous voice in the loudspeaker saying softly: 'The troop train to the front from Paris to Przemysl via. . . .'" The sentence concludes with an ellipsis. Omitted are the coming stations of the hero's passion. The "they," the soldier Andreas and his friend Paul, a priest, descend into the "dark underpass," into the nether world, to begin Andreas's journey into the moral abyss of war. The overhead train serves as his conveyance to the land of death, and the "soft sonorous voice" from the loudspeaker, like "a cloud of slime," reveals the anonymous power which mysteriously manages death by controlling the horrors of war.

In the second paragraph the narrator informs the reader: "It was as always. . . . The train was on time." The ominous tones of death become overwhelming as the hero murmurs four times: "I don't want to die," and Paul betrays an uncanny "fear" for the fate of his friend. As the train arrives, Andreas momentarily looses his composure and exclaims desperately: "I can throw myself under the wheels if I want . . . I can desert . . . I can go crazy . . . as I have a right to do . . . I don't want to die, but the terrible thing is that I will die . . . soon." Still he is in a relative state of calm as he boards the train. All that Andreas asks in the way of consolation is that his friend pray for him.

These first lines present the major themes and motifs of the story. The novella needs only to augment, in the succeeding pages, the fear, anxiety, terror, and the inevitability of death which have been compacted into the opening passages. But also important for the novella, though less obvious at first, are the aspects of love and religion which Paul prefigures in this classically brief exposition. The friendship between Paul and Andreas anticipates the selfless relationship which later develops between Andreas and the Polish prostitute Olina, and the request for prayer which Andreas makes of his friend culminates in the mass which Paul celebrates for Andreas on the last page of the novella at the moment of the latter's death.

Critics have long recognized the similarity of structure between tragic drama and novella. Several classical novellas have been interpreted in terms of dramatic form with exposition, development, turning point, climax, and denouement. This approach has merit in analyzing *The Train Was on Time*. The "acts" are fairly obvious. The succinct exposition has just been mentioned. The development of the plot occurs when Andreas joins the soldiers Willy and the blonde, who are also doomed to share his fate; the turning point in the novella occurs when Andreas contemplates returning home, stepping out of the train and out of the drama in which he is the tragic hero. In fact, each character, for his own reason, contemplates but rejects the idea of abandoning the train. The climax of the drama occurs in the bordello scene when the glow of love momentarily shifts the vision of the characters from dark death to bright life. But the engendered hope that a life of peace and love is possible fades quickly into the explosion of the denouement as the protagonist and his friends die on their way to a new existence.

Because the dramatic structure of the novella is rather obvious, the dramatic approach can penetrate to the artistic essence of the story. The artistry of the novella derives not from any modernity but from the lack of it, from the tale's successful evocation of a timeless archaic world view which fits perfectly the genre of the novella. Although Böll refers to *der Führer*, the years 1943–1944, and lists a series of historical place names prominent in World War II, he removes the story from the realm of political reality by failing to indicate why the side on which Andreas is fighting is not worth fighting for and by demonstrating that the forces opposing the Germans are morally no better than the Nazi armies. Böll categorizes all participants in the war as belonging to only two groups: "victims and executioners" (*47–51*, p. 91). Such an ahistorical point of view is only possible if political realities are ignored and all similar human suffering merits equal concern.

Böll also carefully transfers the story from the historical level to the human plane by recreating the frame of reference of the Bible and Greek tragedy. In the New Testament, for example, the tragic story of Jesus of Nazareth is presented without psychological or sociological explanation, without, in fact, any phenomenological explanation of the behavior of the main characters. It is merely preordained that Jesus will accept his cup of suffering, that Judas will betray Jesus, and that Peter will deny his Lord. It is inevitable in the economy of the narrative that each will play his role. *Why* each plays his role from the psychological or sociological standpoint is unimportant.

The works of Aeschylus and Sophocles are similar in this respect. The lives of their heroes are also preordained. What Walter Kaufmann attributes to these two dramatists is equally appropriate for Böll in his novella: "It is the poet's very point that . . . behavior itself is *accidental* in the sense that it is a mere means to a predetermined conclusion that would have been inescapable, no matter what the hero might have done; and the hero's behavior is *necessary* only in so far as it leads to his undoing."[5] In such an inexorable world, suspense must develop along lines that are nonmodern. There is no room for suspense concerning *what, why,* or *if.* The reader must disregard the desire to anticipate what will happen next, to speculate if the hero will be saved, to question why he must die. The reader simply knows the hero's death is inevitable. Suspense in such dramas of predestination, preordination, or prophecy develops in relationship to the *how.* The only information withheld from the audience from the outset is how the known events will occur: how Jesus will die, how Judas will betray Jesus, how Oedipus will kill his father and marry his mother, how Andreas will meet his end.

From this point of view, *The Train* has more in common with the detective story, adventure yarn, and the Bible and Greek tragedy than with the modern realistic novel. In reading Arthur Conan Doyle the reader does not doubt that Sherlock Holmes will solve the crime, but wonders only how he will do it. In reading Karl May, the reader does not doubt that old Shatter-

hand will escape all dangers, but only wonders how he will survive the ordeal. The role of predestination in the Bible and in
Greek tragedy is replaced in such mystery and adventure stories
by the requirements of the genre, by a known world of characters: those with worldly power and those with the power of
righteousness—so it is in Böll's novella. As the story proceeds,
the certainty of death prophesied on the first page becomes even
more certain. Even when and where death will occur are revealed: "Sunday morning I will die between Lemberg and Czern-
owitz" (*47–51*, p. 26), and later Andreas adds: "Perhaps Paul has
understood and will say a mass for me on Sunday morning, an
hour before or after I am dead" (*47–51*, p. 63). Even which characters belong to which categories, who the victims and who the
executioners are, is never in doubt.

Such an arranged world is the essence of tragedy. And all
tragedy retains, by its nature, something of the sacramental quality of Greek drama and the Bible in that tragedy originates in
ritual. Böll's *The Train* is no exception. As the action of *Hamlet*
and *Macbeth* is propelled by a ghost and witches, *Oedipus* by
prophecy, and the story of Jesus by the foreknowledge that someone will die for the sins of man, so too in *The Train* the action is
driven by Andreas's utterance on the first page: "I will die . . .
soon." Such a conviction brings about the events that would lose
their essential character without Andreas's belief in his imminent
demise, and such certainty creates a suprapsychological aura that
raises the drama beyond mere coincidence. Andreas's belief in his
approaching death generates the numinous atmosphere of awe
and the religious certitude required in the story. Furthermore, the
monotony of the sonorous voices calling out the stations to Andreas's Golgotha, and the routine nature of Andreas's repetitious
prayers function together as a variation of the chorus in Greek
tragedy and reinforce the numinous tension of the novella.

To further achieve the tragic effect, Böll, in the manner of classical tragedy, sets his hero apart from the other figures in the
"drama." But he does so in a different way. Whereas the great
tragic figures of the past are alone because of the dominance of
their active personalities which leads to their misunderstanding
of people and events or to their being misunderstood, Andreas is
a passive figure who finds understanding, love, and acceptance,

especially in his friend Paul and in the prostitute Olina. Here Böll sacrifices the tragic model of the hero's uniqueness to the romantic method of characterization and the romantic creation of a pathetic figure. Böll takes Andreas out of the realm of extraordinary tragic heroes and makes him instead a projection of the author and his readers—a suffering everyman. In this romanticization of character, Böll reveals a pattern of his entire oeuvre, a paradigm which has made his work both great and trivial; he yields to sentimentality. He does so, however, knowingly and intentionally. Although he sets Andreas apart from the crowd by endowing him with the power of empathy, a depth of feeling, and a noble character, Böll has no desire, in *The Train* or in any other of his works, to create a superhero (an Oedipus or Hamlet, much less a Faust or Tamburlaine), a person above his fellow men. He is content with presenting the greatness of simple things and little people. The artistry of *The Train* lies in the creation of a work with a classical world view and a romantic spirit of humanity clothed in the language of realism.

In *The Train*, Böll's first book-length narrative, the author uses time (the attempt to concentrate the entire story, the life of a person, into a few days or hours)[6] as his organizational principle. It is worth analyzing this aspect of the novella because understanding the temporal structure and how it combines with the religious dimension of the story is essential to understanding the work. The exact time Andreas boards the train is impossible to calculate, but it is close to midnight on Wednesday, that is, the story covers Thursday, Friday, and Saturday night until Andreas's death at about six o'clock on Sunday morning, simultaneous to Paul's celebrating mass for his friend. The time of the novella, because it corresponds to the days of Christ's passion and death and concludes with the mass, which in turn symbolically reenacts Christ's final days, cannot be considered accidental. Böll consciously plays on the three most important events of Christ's passion: the last supper, the crucifixion, and the resurrection. On Thursday evening Andreas eats his meal of dry bread and butter. The solitary repast, with its simple ritual and subsequent prayer, takes on the quality of a sacrament: "His hunger greeted it [the bread and butter] with pleasure, and it tasted magnificent . . . afterwards he sensed a dreadful state of well-being and a frighteningly good mood. . . . Now I will pray, he thought, all the prayers which I know by heart. . . . He prayed first the Creed, then the Our Father and the Hail Mary, De Profundis, Come Holy Ghost, and again the Creed because it is so magnificently complete, and then the Good Friday petitions" (*47–51*, p. 32), which he follows by his own prayers for the suffering Jews.

The sacramental quality of Andreas's meals becomes more pronounced on Saturday evening in Lemberg as Andreas and his two friends feast on a dinner of soup, salad, several meat dishes, and vegetables, accompanied throughout with wine, followed by pudding, and finally cheese. Andreas calls it *eine richtig Henkersmahlzeit* ("a proper last meal"), which, indeed, it is—a last supper. Andreas again prays throughout the meal and concludes: "Twelve hours before my death I now realize that life is beautiful . . . I have denied that there is human joy" (*47–51*, p. 69).

Still more subtle parallels exist between Andreas's life and the life of Christ although Andreas is no Christ figure who dies for others. He is characterized as an archetypal victim. Olina, upon first seeing him, recalls: "There are only victims and executioners. As I saw you . . . your back, your neck, your bowed young figure, as if you were many thousand years old, it occurred to me that we murder only the innocent . . . only the innocent" (*47–51*, p. 91).

Even Andreas's relationship with Olina, because it is strikingly nonsexual, hints at Christ's relationship with the prostitute Mary Magdalen. Olina, as is fitting, considers Andreas not a lover, but a brother: "I am two days older than you. I am surely your sister" (*47–51*, p. 80 and again on p. 91).

Appropriately, this love is a benign influence in their lives, inspiring them to escape the world in which there are only "victims and executioners." Olina suggests they steal the car belonging to a general who has come to visit her and flee with it into the mountains. Andreas agrees to the desperate plan on the condition that his two comrades come along. Although Olina believes two more people will make the flight excessively hazardous, she acquiesces in Andreas's act of solidarity. Andreas's attempt to save his friends is fraught with irony; his taking them along leads to their early death. Polish partisans fire upon the general's car, killing the passengers. Before the final explosion, Andreas thinks of Paul starting the Sunday morning mass. He begins even to recite the opening words of the mass: "Introibo [ad altare Dei] . . ." ("I shall go to the altar of God,") (*47–51*, p. 112). At this moment the shell lands, and Andreas is thrown onto the road. His final thought is reminiscent of Christ's in the Garden of Olives: "On my breast lies the weight of the world" (*47–51*, p. 105). He realizes the mystery of selfless love, and his death gives solemn meaning to Olina's words said in the bordello: "Wherever I lead you, there will be life" (*47–51*, p. 106). Seated in the car, it is this promise that Olina repeats to Andreas. Now even the popular song which Olina has played for Andreas on the piano—"I'll dance with you into paradise (*Himmel*)" (*47–51*, p. 100)—takes on the power of prophecy. When the car explodes, Andreas indeed "goes to the altar of God"; he is resurrected to a new, eternal life.

II Where Were You, Adam?

This conclusion of the novella with the death of the hero from an exploding shell is the same conclusion Böll gives to his next work, his first novel, *Where Were You, Adam?* (1951). This story also has the same setting (the eastern front) and is imbued with the same spirit as the novella *The Train*, for the novel, too, proclaims man incapable of changing his circumstances, reveals him at the mercy of events, shows him dying senselessly when the war's outcome is no longer in doubt, when escape seems near, when hope is at its highest. While in *The Train* fate and destiny dominate to make a tragedy of war, in *Adam* chance and accident combine to show its absurdity. Although the structure of the two works varies according to the differing genres, each work tells a similar story: the novella, the deaths of Andreas and Olina; the novel, the deaths of the soldier Feinhals and his sweetheart, the Jewish schoolteacher Ilona.

The novel is divided into episodic chapters related by an omniscient narrator, with peripheral characters from early episodes becoming main characters in later chapters. Except for the reappearance of these characters, the episodes have little relation with one another and could stand alone as independent stories. The chapters relating the life and death of Lieutenant Greck and the building of the bridge at Berczaba are good examples of this episodic independence. In fact, the bridge episode has been performed as a successful radio play.

Because the soldier Feinhals is the narrator's primary concern, his death and tragic love affair with Ilona become the foci of the novel. Böll places their love story in the central fifth chapter of the nine-chapter narrative. Feinhals meets Ilona while he is working in the school where she teaches while it serves as a temporary field hospital for the retreating German army. They have known one another for only three days and have spoken to one another only a few times before they agree to meet after her working hours. The meeting never takes place, however, because Ilona is rounded up by the SS as she returns to the village ghetto. She is transported in a stifling, crowded furniture van to a concentration camp, where she is shot the following morning. Although they never see one another again, their relationship, like that between Andreas and Olina, moves Feinhals to flee the war, the arena of death, and urges him to seek a new life, which he, like Andreas, finds in the explosion of a mortar shell.

Several works of literature, notably Peter Weiss's *Die Ermittlung* [The Investigation] and Rolf Hochhuth's *Der Stellvertreter* [The Deputy], have in recent years presented accurately the horror and evil of the concentration camps. But no work has succeeded as well as Böll's *Adam* in characterizing the type of people who worked in the camps. His characterization reveals a perfect understanding of what Hannah Arendt was later to call "the banality of evil."[7] In the episode of Ilona's death, the main characters are the two drivers of the furniture van and Filskeit, the commandant of the camp.

The drivers, Schröder and Plorin, are merely nonquestioning functionaries of a mechanical military apparatus. They represent servants of a system, not believers in an ideology. Since these men are unwilling to reflect on their actions, their dedication to their work is the same whether it serves a noble or an ignoble cause. They transport innocent people to their death as they would furniture to a warehouse or cattle to slaughter. Their satisfaction comes from a job well done, from performing a good day's work. Schröder is a man who loves his family and delights in showing pictures of his wife and child. Plorin is a conscientious worker whose concern is the smooth functioning of the truck's motor. They are not interested in the contents of their van, only in delivering their freight on schedule. To distract themselves from the noise coming from the back of their truck, they sing sentimental songs of love and of military life which fill them with sadness and move them to tears. When they arrive in the camp after their all-night ride, their first desire is a good sleep.

While Schröder and Plorin are good citizen-soldiers doing the best job they can for the smooth functioning of the war, Commandant Filskeit is an officer with a firm belief in Nazi ideology and with a background in the party. He is intelligent, strict, industrious, and ambitious, known for his exactness and intolerance of sloppiness; he lives by the rules and insists on order. He neither smokes, drinks, nor consorts with women. His special talent is for organization, which he combines with his love for music and his passion for directing choirs.

Böll pictures these men who run the concentration camps as exemplars of bourgeois virtue, as men who accept a system of values which lacks only the primary virtue of charity. These men are bulwarks of bourgeois propriety. They stand for industriousness, cleanliness, honesty, chastity, punctuality, reliability, obedience, and respect for authority. They lack only that virtue which discharges the New Testament imperative, which fulfills the whole law of God and man—the love of God and one's neighbor.

Böll demonstrates in this chapter what men can become who subscribe only to secondary values which have no meaning in themselves. Carl Amery explains the lack of wholeness in the secondary values prevalent in the milieu: "I can be punctual serving the parish or working in the Gestapo-cellar; I can be fastidious in the 'final solution' or in social work; I can wash my hands after a day's work in the field or in the crematorium of a concentration camp."[8]

Commandant Filskeit, however, embodies even more than this perversion of values; he also exemplifies the perversion of art. Filskeit loves music. He is solemn about life, earnest about work, but deadly serious about art. All of his inclination toward correctness, exactness, and intolerance finds its terrifying expression in his career as choir director. The camp provides him with the ultimate opportunity for a technical, sterile choral perfection. Those who can sing well are spared for his choir; those who cannot are doomed. Under such conditions, his bourgeois values have complete reign. In Filskeit's love of art, Böll expresses the final perversion of Nazism, for the first purpose of art is to make man more humane.

In *Where Were You, Adam?* Böll treats the war directly for the last time in his novels, although the war years and the Hitler period continue to loom in the background of his later works. Starting in the 1950s, he begins analyzing in his novels Germany's economic miracle.

CHAPTER 6

Novels of the Economic Restoration

I Acquainted with the Night

IN the war novels Böll explored the alienation of moral men from Fascism and an unjust war. Beginning with *Und sagte kein einziges Wort* (Acquainted with the Night, 1953), he examines the postwar years in the same manner, i.e., by setting a moral person in an immoral situation. In this novel it is Fred Bogner, a married man with a fulltime job in an expanding economy who is unable to earn enough money to provide an acceptable minimum standard of existence for himself and his family. Central to this novel and many of those to follow is the alienation which has not ceased with the end of the war but has actually increased with the peace. The estrangement of Böll's heroes from postwar West German society derives from their disdain of the ethics of restored capitalism (although they never express their alienation in these Marxist terms). In *Acquainted with the Night*, Böll shows that the economic miracle was not an economic recovery for everyone, not even for everyone working for an established employer in a regular job.

The novel relates the dire poverty of the Bogner family as told in alternating first-person narratives by the husband Fred and his wife, Käte. The history of the family is revealed slowly and fragmentarily in flashbacks, interior monologues, and conversations. The narrative time of the story extends from before noon on Saturday to before noon on the following Monday, the weekend of St. Jerome's Day (30 September) 1951. Fred (forty-four years old), married for fifteen years, has been living for the past two months away from his wife (thirty-eight years old) and his three children (Clemens, thirteen; Clara, eleven; and an infant son). During this time Käte and Fred have continued to meet one another in cheap hotels. The noise, crowded conditions, and pressures of five people living in one small room have driven Fred to beat his children. To save himself and his family, he has moved out. He now spends his nights with friends or in the baggage room of the train station. Fred's monthly income of 320 marks as a telephone operator at the Catholic chancery is barely enough for his family to live on after Käte sets aside eighty marks a month for fixed expenses. She has no money for lipstick and Fred no money for treatment of his periodontitis. Käte even borrows a radio for the baby sitter when she goes out to meet Fred. They live with "the frightful breath of poverty" (p. 85), Käte exclaims as she thinks of the armies of the poor to which they belong. Käte understands Fred's decision to leave his family: "I know . . . that you beat the children only because we have no money" (p. 126), and Fred also understands Käte's depression: "You are sad because we are poor . . . [but] there is no escaping it. I can't promise you that we will someday have enough money . . . to live in a clean house without financial worries . . ." (p. 129).

Standing in a rundown hotel room where she is meeting Fred on this Saturday night, Käte looks at the room and recalls: "I recognized that nothing had changed much since our marriage. We started out in a furnished room that was no less ugly than this one" (pp. 116–17). Only for a brief time were their circumstances different. In 1939 they had a four-room apartment with a bath. But early in the war it was destroyed by a bomb, and from then on they "possessed nothing, neither linen nor furniture" (p. 117).

The circumstances of the Bogners' poverty finds expression not only in the story of the novel but also in its structure. The opening sentence suggests the novel's theme of money: "After work I went to the cashier to pick up my pay." After receiving his wages, Fred counts his money, and before sending the envelope to Käte, includes a note that he has taken ten marks and asks her to meet him that evening. The next few hours Fred spends earning extra cash by giving arithmetic and Latin lessons to children in his son's class and trying to borrow money from his friends.

The second chapter begins as Käte receives Fred's envelope: "Again and again I counted the money Fred sent me" (p. 22). Throughout the novel references to money are used as a means to effect transitions and to provide motivation for the actions of the characters. Money is also for the Bogners a measure of friendship, for Fred values his friends by their ability to lend him small sums, and even Käte is forced to judge which people to buy from on the basis of their willingness to give her credit. Furthermore, the money motif serves as a frame to the story, for it concludes as well as opens the work. In the final chapter the action recurs which begins the novel: "I counted my money" (pp. 179, 186). And in the last lines of the book, as Fred decides to return to his family, he exclaims: "I felt the money in my hand and looked at it. . . . 'Yes,' I said, 'home.'"

Despite the obviousness of poverty as the novel's theme, the work is not without its ambiguity. For example, to what extent can Fred be relied upon as a narrator, or, for that matter, even Käte (although she surely is the more objective of the two); to what extent are Fred's (and his family's) problems related to economics and to what extent do they relate to a moral and spiritual crisis in Fred's and Käte's life? Fred is not simply an innocent victim of society. He drinks, is addicted to playing pinball machines, spends long hours visiting graveyards, and thinks often of death. (To what extent does Fred do these things because he is poor, and to what extent is he poor because he does these things?) Although not an unbeliever or an agnostic, he also begins to question a central dogma of his faith, the resurrection of the dead. Are his feelings of purposelessness, indifference, and boredom economic in origin or merely the malaise of a survivor of the war? The evidence of the novel points to Fred's sickly listlessness as originating in the economic sphere, for Fred is painfully aware of the systematic injustice of society which exploits him and which divides social wealth inequitably. He is totally at odds with society, and his feelings of rancor have not changed during the fifteen years of his marriage from 1936–1951. Although Fred has never been without a job during this period (except when in the army) and at the time of the narration is even tutoring for extra money, he has always been poor.

Still Fred is not a lazy person, he merely lacks ambition and the ability to accept the values of his environment. It is important that Fred has never been integrated into society. He has lived alienated from his milieu during his entire married life, both

under the dictatorial Fascist government and under the democratic capitalist regime. Both systems have inflicted injustices
which he cannot accept and which prevent him from living in
conformity and harmony with society. The novel clearly reveals
Fred's withdrawal both before and after 1945. During the Nazi
period he deserted the war, and during the democratic period
he deserts the peace. Fred is morally and constitutionally incapable of contributing to any society which he despises, and not
being a political activist, he is left with only one alternative—
he drops out. He is the opposite of the aggressive man of business
whom, he suggests, Käte should have married: "Perhaps it would
have been better if you had married an efficient man, a really
industrious fellow who put stock in education. . . . You could
have read good literature together . . . the children could have
slept in stylish beds—you could have had a Nefertiti on the
wall, an Isenheim altar pasted up on wood and van Gogh's
Sunflowers in an excellent reproduction, a Beuron Madonna over
your bed, and a flute in a red, coarse, but very tasteful case . . .
all this shit" (p. 130). Käte is much like Fred. She, too, rejects
the values of society: "I hate efficient men. I can't think of anything more boring than efficient men, their mouths stink from
efficiency" (p. 130), and she realizes that she only fell in love
with Fred after she discovered "how much he really despised the
law" (p. 49).

Fred and Käte are, however, naive in their condemnation of
the values of society. They have never read Marx or studied
socialism, and nowhere in their conversations or narratives is there
the slightest reference to sociology, yet they know instinctively
that they cannot come to terms with their milieu. Although Fred
is an intelligent man and apparently provides his employers with
satisfactory work, he changes his job frequently out of dissatisfac-
tion. He has worked in the pharmaceutical business, in a library,
in a wallpaper factory, as a photographer, and now as a telephone
operator. But neither Fred's protest nor Käte's acceptance of his
discontent leads either of them to social analysis, enlightenment,
or insight; it only produces hostility without compromise. The
protagonists totally reject the injustices in their lives, and they
do not want to work for or be part of any system which exploits
them or others. Suffering has extended Käte's compassion to all

the "generations of the poor who have lived without room to perfect their love" (p. 77).

The injustice in the novel which makes Fred "sick" and which fills Käte with hatred is explicit. While the Bogners live five to a single room, Mrs. Franke, their landlady, who prevents them from obtaining better housing, lives with her husband in four rooms. During confession, Käte reveals her animosity toward priests who live in big houses and have faces like advertisements for skin cream, when she has no money for lipstick. Fred disdains the princely bishop with his chauffeur-driven car and the priests who travel from one conference to another, staying in luxury hotels while he has to meet his wife in a hovel. Fred tells Käte how his friend, a caretaker, sometimes lets him sleep in a closet under the stairs in a thirteen-room villa which has a room for a dog bigger than the Bogners' apartment. Even more irritating to Fred is that the house stands empty most of the year because it is owned by an English "general or gangster" (p. 133) who only occasionally uses the villa.

The social injustice which crushes the Bogners is particularly obvious in the church. Although Fred has a fulltime job with the chancery and his family situation is well known to his superiors, the chancery still does not pay him a "just wage," i.e., does not conform to the guideline for social justice formulated in the nineteenth century by Pope Leo XIII in the encyclical "Rerum Novarum." Furthermore, there is evidence of moral corruption in the church, for the chancery fails to criticize the pharmaceutical industry for advertising contraceptives[1] because the bishop's cousin is the chairman of the association of druggists. The novel also charges that corruption in the drug industry was responsible for defective medicine which during the war caused the death of the Bogners' twins. Käte recalls: "I know and I won't forget it! I know that my children were brought to their death by lice, that we were sold a completely useless medicine by a company which was run by the cousin of the minister of health while the good medicine, the effective medicine, was held back" (p. 50).

Fred's inimical attitude to society has also made him an enemy of bourgeois culture and education. While he is explicit in his condemnation, the reasons for his condemnation need to be deduced. In the novel the representatives of culture are the bishop and the English "gangster," both lovers of Dante. The Englishman has in his villa an outstanding Dante library, and the only person with access to the villa is the bishop, who uses the library for his Dante research. Within the context of the novel, culture is the amusement of the rich, generally unavailable to the poor and the less educated. In such a society education does not serve the creation of better men but provides the wealthy with the means to broaden the gap between rich and poor and to enjoy culture as a pastime. Fred recognizes that life for his children is determined by ironclad class distinctions. He visualizes the future for his son: "I saw my children tied to the deadly cycle which begins with the packing of a school bag and ends somewhere on an office chair" (p. 14).

Despite the negative figure of the bishop and several prelates in the chancery, Böll does not present religion itself as a negative force. The social awareness which the Bogners have comes from their religious understanding. The novel, while it breaks with the mysticism of the war novels, still shows religion as a positive element in man's life with prayer and the sacraments being helpful ingredients for a loving marriage. In the earlier war novels, love always ended in separation and death. In this first novel about the postwar years, despite all the misery and suffering of the protagonists, love ends in union. As in the war novels only love sustained one through the moral abyss of war, so too, now only love brings one through the moral nadir of the *Wirtschaftswunder*. Here, however, the "happy ending" is unconvincing and appears as a false hope. Fred's returning home offers little chance of marital success. Love, the sacraments, and prayer probably will not conquer, as they did not in the past, the poverty that awaits him in the bosom of his family. Nothing has changed for Fred and Käte except for the worse. Fred's income is still the same but their debts are greater; their chances of procuring better housing have been thwarted; they still are five to a room, and now Käte is expecting another child.

Fred's reasons for returning home are complicated. His decision results from a combination of events and feelings: Käte's ultimatum not to visit him again like "a whore" in a cheap hotel, his desire not to lose her and the children, and his conviction that he "cannot leave [her] alone if [she] is pregnant" (p. 147). But, most of all, Fred returns because of an inexplicable change in his perception after seeing Käte "anew" as if "for the first time" while she is shopping: "I saw a woman whose appearance touched my heart and at the same time excited me. The woman was no longer young, but beautiful. I saw her legs, her green skirt, the shabbiness of her brown jacket, and I saw her green hat, but above all I saw her gentle, sad profile . . . my heart went out to her . . . I looked at the profile of this woman and suddenly knew that it was Käte" (p. 187). Whether such an experience will save Fred's marriage each reader will have to decide for himself.

In *Acquainted with the Night* Böll reveals the other side of poverty, the one he did not present in the idyll "Unexpected Guests." In *Acquainted with the Night* he does not proffer poverty with humor and spirituality. Here poverty does not bring the family closer together but drives loved ones apart. It negatively affects all aspects of life: faith, health, and disposition. It causes Fred to beat his children and fills Käte with hatred. The strength of this novel is its realism in showing poverty as a social disease.

II   The Bread of Those Early Years

In *Das Brot der frühen Jahre* [The Bread of Those Early Years, 1955] Böll continues the treatment of man's alienation from the values of the *Wirtschaftswunder*. Here, because the first-person narrator is not a Fred Bogner, a middle-aged, down-and-out castoff of the system about to lose all his teeth, but a prosperous, thriving, automobile-driving, money-in-the-bank, handsome young man with a bright future, Böll's presentation of the estrangement of the hero from capitalist ethics is even more condemning than in *Acquainted with the Night*. The opening metaphor reveals the separation of the protagonist from his own nature which has come about by his adapting his life to a system of injustice: "It was as if I had stepped into the wrong life as a person by mistake boards the wrong train" (p. 8). Until the moment the narrator meets a young girl and falls in love with her, this "wrong life" seemed to him "quite acceptable" (p. 8). After this magic meeting with Hedwig, the narrator—like Fred Bogner seeing his wife through the store window—has his life changed in a sudden manner. He puts all the pieces of his past existence together like a jigsaw puzzle. He sees the picture of his life in perspective. He rejects the compromised person he has become as well as the society he represents, the economic order which puts too high a price on bread and too low a price on human labor; he turns his back on the exploitative society which sees people only in their relationship to the formula for profit.

Despite the social criticism in the work, the central incident which binds together all the events of the story is the meeting of, and ensuing love between, twenty-year-old Hedwig Muller and twenty-three-year-old Walter Fendrich, the narrator. Hence the structure of the story is that of a novella which focuses on a single event. The story is typical of many of Böll's works, depicting a short time span, in this case from about eight o'clock in the morning to about eight o'clock in the evening of a single day in the narrator's life. At 11:47 on Monday, 14 or 15 March 1954 or 1955, Walter goes to the train station to meet a young girl who is the daughter of a friend of his father. She is coming to the city to become a teacher. Walter has previously found her a room and is to take her there and go back to work. Walter feels put upon to have to perform all these services for someone he scarcely remembers from his childhood. He is accustomed to working twelve hours a day and earning good money as an expert washing-machine repairman. But when he sees Hedwig his life changes: "I saw only her dazzling green coat,[2] her face, and I suddenly became fearful with that fear which explorers have when they enter upon a new land. . . . Her face went deep into me. . . . It was as if I had been pierced without bleeding" (p. 44). From this moment on Walter is a new person. He never returns to his job, tears up his old life like a scrap of paper, withdraws all his savings from the bank, repays his old debts, breaks his engagement to the boss's daughter, and marries Hedwig that evening without benefit of clergy.

What happens to Walter can only be compared to St. Paul's experience on the road to Damascus. Walter is struck by divine lightning; Hedwig's "dazzling white face" (p. 44) and her "dazzling green coat" lead him from the path he was taking in life. Hedwig's bright light gives Walter a new vision; he becomes a new man. Walter's new light permits him to recognize that his "acceptable existence" has, in fact, alienated him from his personality, his occupation, and his own body: "I hated myself, my work, and my hands" (p. 10) . . . "I knew now what I had always known, but had for six years not admitted to myself: that I hated this occupation . . . what I liked about it was only the money" (p. 59). His enlightenment permits him to see the fragmented scenes of his past in a new pattern which presents a whole instead of isolated parts. "Today, for the first time all these things occurred to me" (p. 121), he says. The pieces of his past which he rearranges are his postwar experiences of hunger, privation, and injustice.

Walter recognizes that he forced his father to beg bread so he could satisfy his own hunger. He recalls the humiliation of stealing to buy food and the shame of having eaten more because his father ate less. He recognizes that the wolf that was in him has not departed and may never leave. From a visit to the hospital to see his mother he recalls what this wolf can do to a person. In the next bed was a dying woman who fought and argued with her husband over food and money. On the day the woman died, Walter's memory becomes branded with the ugliness of the husband screaming for a can of corned beef which the wife had consumed immediately before she died. Walter remembers also the girl in the factory who shared her sandwich with him and later died of malnutrition. Walter realizes that even drowning can be the result of poverty. Because his school friend's swimming trunks were made of old petticoats, his friend swam apart from his comrades in dangerous waters. Walter recollects the fear of food going bad and kitchens where others ate their fill and never shared what they had. Hence Peter Leiser's observation about the novella is accurate: "Böll's *The Bread of Those Early Years* is a literary contribution that refutes the legend of the 'common sharing of privation' of those bitter years of the great hunger. The dividing line between rich and poor separated the full from the hungry."[3]

As Walter destroys the certainty of his material future by breaking his engagement to the boss's daughter, he asserts his kinship with the poor: with Jürgen Brolaski, the drowned swimmer, and Helene Frenkel, the rickety girl who shared her food, and especially with Alois Fruklahr, the young apprentice with whom he worked salvaging materials from bombed-out buildings. After Alois fell to his death, Walter recalls: "His mouth was as bitter as it ever was: the mouth of a hungry person who did not believe in the justice of this world" (p. 101).[4] When asked by a spectator to the accident: "Was he your brother?" Walter replied: "Yes, he was my brother" (p. 101).[5]

When Walter returned to work and related the death of the apprentice to his fiancée, Ulla Wickweber, Walter watched how she took a pen and drew a neat red line through Alois's name on the list of employees. The experience taught Walter the compassionless manner in which his employers regarded people as a means to profit. In 1953, after Walter established himself with the company and became its most important representative in the field, he bought a boiler from Wickweber at a discount price. When he picked it up he recognized his stencil on the boiler from 1947, the year the boiler was produced at the price of three loaves of bread. He was paying now the discount price of 130 loaves of bread while the regular price was 200. Walter remarks on the enormous profit the company made on the boiler: "I was surprised that unknown factors represented such value, and I thought of all the irons, boilers, immersion heaters, and stoves I stencilled with my F in those years" (p. 61). But Wickweber was not a typical example of the profit-making businessman in the early years of the *Wirtschaftswunder*; Wickweber actually paid his employees above the average wage, gave the customary allowance in kind, and provided free soup at lunch. Thus Walter concludes that one "could be pious and still be a scoundrel" (p. 63). Despite Wickweber's "generosity," Walter's hunger was never stilled. He stole cooking plates from the company to exchange for bread. Now he recalls: "Not for a second did I have qualms of conscience; I had already begun to think about the prices of things" (p. 82). His condemnation of bourgeois morality continues: "I never stole anything again, but it was not because I thought stealing was unjustified" (p. 83). And in reference to the present, he claims: "I would do it again . . . [but] today I would do it better" (pp. 87–88). To Walter the implication of his experience and knowledge leads to a revolutionary ethic. The enormous profits of Wickweber's concern have no justification, and the failure to share the profits with his workers and/or the public is reason enough in Walter's mind to vindicate transgression of the law.

In breaking his engagement to Ulla he says: "You really want me to believe that with a bowl of soup and a little extra pay everything was made all right. . . . You really want me to believe in all seriousness that all of your employees were not entitled to a few extra pieces of bread" (pp. 118–19). And he suggests further to Ulla that she "read each name on the list of employees like a litany and say after each: Forgive us" (p. 118). In contrast to Ulla, Hedwig possesses a social conscience. She tells Walter how he imagined herself married to an accountant for a chocolate factory: "One evening he told me how much the company earned from a piece of candy and forbade me to tell anyone. But I would not keep silent" (p. 129).

Besides depicting the effects of love and revealing the injustices of the economic system, the novella also contains a parable on the responsible use of power. Power, the book reveals, must be used carefully, and when necessary, with compassion. Nowhere is this message more obvious than in Walter's conversation with Ulla. Power is the ability to embarrass, belittle, humiliate, to make people suffer. Walter hates power, although he recognizes that sometimes it has its proper place. In his exchange with Ulla, he is relentless in his accusations against her, her father, and the Wickweber concern. He has the power of righteousness on his side and wields this power vehemently because he expects Ulla to be defensive, but he is filled with a certain remorse when he senses her weakness; he feels he may have been too hard in laying the guilt of an entire enterprise and of an economic system on her head. Ulla responds more positively to his charges then he expected: "The Ulla who sat there altered under my words, under my glances . . . she was no longer the person for whom my words were intended . . . a crying Ulla was an Ulla I never knew . . . I sensed the sour taste of triumph on my tongue" (p. 120). She offers to right past wrongs, but instinctively expresses herself in commercial terms: "I would gladly give you a blank check to remove the curses from our account" (p. 120) and adds, "I know today for the first time that money is unimportant to me" (p. 121). As she releases Walter's hand, it strikes the edge of the table; she says symbolically: "I am sorry, I didn't want to do that," and Walter acknowledges her contriteness: "I believed her—that she did not intend to do what she had done" (p. 122). Because she can cry, can admit wrong, can ask forgiveness, she is no longer one of the strong, the callous, the unfeeling. A little remorse in Böll's world goes a long way towards redemption; whether in Ulla's case it will lead to permanent change is an open matter.

Every writer, even the best, has but a few themes, motifs, and symbols which run through his work. *The Bread of Those Early Years* contains most of Böll's: love, religion, social concern, hands, smiles, and above all bread. Any reader wishing to find out what Böll's work is like could well start with this little book. The hospital scene wherein the husband demands his deceased wife's can of corned beef is as powerful as anything Böll has written. The entire work is rich in detail and exact in its presentation of human situations. Yet a reader may want more from a work, an ending different from *Acquainted with the Night*, an ending which offers more than withdrawal from society as a personal solution to the problems of society. Unlike Fred and Käte Bogner, Walter and Hedwig may be able to renounce the acquisitive values of postwar German society and remain at a level above the poverty line, but because their hatred of the profit system has demonstrated no alternative but *ohne mich* ("without me"), there is no reason to expect that they are capable of working for social change. To point out this failing on Böll's part is certainly not to suggest a weakness in his artistry. A writer is not responsible for presenting social theory in literary form, only for creating life in his work of art. In *The Bread of Those Early Years* Böll does this remarkably well.

CHAPTER 7

Novels of Conquering the Past

I The Unguarded House

"I know and I won't forget," Käte Bogner says in *Acquainted with the Night* (p. 50). This recollection of the Hitler years became a more pressing theme in Böll's work in the mid-fifties as Germans grew reluctant to acknowledge a continuity from past to present and were eager to enjoy the "new life" which began in 1945 for a few, and in 1948 for many. *Haus ohne Hüter* (1954) is the first of two novels to treat thoroughly the theme of conquering the past. The titles of two English translations of the novel, *The Unguarded House* and *Tomorrow and Yesterday*, indicate the subject matter and the manner in which Böll chooses to reveal its theme: the individual suffering of widows and half-orphans in families without husbands and fathers and the attendant phenomenon of wives and mothers living in the past or in future worlds that could have been.

Böll roots his theme in the very structure of the novel. Throughout the work little action occurs in the present; most of the novel consists of recollections of the past or daydreams of an imagined future. Although the exact time of the action cannot be determined, the narrative present encompasses about one week in the late summer of 1953, with most of the slight action occurring on the Friday of that week. Each chapter serves a specific function. As in a drama, chapter 1 introduces the characters and the problematic of the novel. An omniscient narrator relates the random thoughts of eleven-year-old Martin Bach as he lies in bed before falling asleep. Martin ponders his mother's strange habits, the unusual life-styles of the several persons living with him in his grandmother's large house; he thinks of his father, the celebrated poet whom he never knew, of Gäseler, the man responsible for his father's death, of his Uncle Albert, who substitutes as a father for him, and of his school friend Heinrich Brielach, who also lost his father in the war and now lives with a succession of uncles who are his mother's lovers; Martin tries also to distinguish how life in his Grandmother Holstege's household and in the Brielach household reflects what he has learned in school about morality and immorality; however, his young mind is too inexperienced to make the necessary ethical distinctions, and finally he dwells on the pleasant, carefree life at Albert's mother's place in Bietenhahn outside the city. Thus not only does Böll quickly present the main characters but also three important loci of the novel: the rich Holstege, the poor Brielach, and the idyllic Bietenhahn worlds.

Chapter 2 centers on the biography of the Brielach family, their working-class background, their hunger after the war, and their current dire poverty. Chapter 3 shifts to the perspective of Martin's mother as she attends a literary conference. Here she meets Gäseler (the first real action of the novel), the man who, she has been told for eleven years, is the "murderer" of her husband, the man who, as a young lieutenant, deliberately sent her husband to his death. She agrees to go with him on the coming weekend to another literary conference. But as is typical of the structure of the novel, while the lectures drone on, she merely dreams of her past life. At this point, and elsewhere in the novel, as the characters retreat deeper into revery, the narration slips into interior monologue.

Chapter 3 also introduces the fourth locus of the novel, the world of Schurbigels, the Father Willibrords, and the Gäselers, i.e., the intellectual snobs, the opportunists, and the old Nazis, those who during the war prayed for the Führer, Folk, and Fatherland, the people whom the narrators refers to as "buffaloes, men with finely cut features who use words like 'economy' with full seriousness and speak of folk, reconstruction, and the future without irony" (p. 45). These are the men sensitive only to their own ambition, well-adjusted conformists with all their latent emotional links to Nazism still intact, now, however, with their fascistic sympathies disguised by modish dress, speech, and a popular adherence to democracy. These are the people who in Böll's next novel, *Billard um halbzehn* (Billiards at Half-past Nine, 1959), become the powerful buffaloes who persecute the meek lambs.

This chapter and many of those to follow rely heavily on film technique; dissolving scenes and flashbacks, to relate the story. Mrs. Brielach in Chapter 4, Nella in Chapter 11, Albert in Chapter 13, for example, typically gaze out of a window as the present fades away and their dreams come to life to provide the reader background for understanding their personalities and their situations. Film terminology prevails throughout the novel, and references to the similarity of behavior of the characters in the novel to the gestures of actors in movies abound. Furthermore, the characters themselves often go to the movies and tell one another in detail what they saw. This last phenomenon suggests an influence of J. D. Salinger, especially his *The Catcher in the Rye* (1951),[1] on Böll's work at this time.

As Chapter 3 draws attention to a typical day in the life of Nella Bach, a day without financial cares, spent with ambitious hounds of culture who prey on her as the widow of the poet Raimund Bach. Its sequel presents Wilma Brielach, Heinrich's mother, in a typical day fighting the privation and embarrassment of poverty. She visits a dentist's office to discover that she, like Fred Bogner, is soon to lose her teeth if she does not immediately receive expensive dental treatment, costing twelve hundred marks. Through extreme frugality, eleven-year-old Heinrich, who handles the familiy finances, is able to save ten marks a month, only one-third of her minimum monthly payment to the dentist. Overwhelmed by her impossible situation, she too retreats into dreams of the past, but not as totally as her counterpart Nella Bach. Wilma Brielach's poverty does not give her the luxury of using dreams as morphium. She must live in the present, assess her life with her fourth lover, and weigh the advantages of improving her material existence by moving in with her employer, the baker.

One of the concerns of the book is to contrast the lives of people with and without money. Böll does this in several ways: in health care—Mrs. Brielach cannot pay the dentist, while Grandmother Holstege has physicians come immediately to her house when she is known to feign illness; in housing—the Brielachs live in a single room, while the Holsteges have a large house with unused rooms; in food—the Brielachs live on twenty-eight marks a week, while Grandmother Holstege pays eighteen marks for a single meal. But Böll shows poverty to be more than going without food and not being able to pay bills. Poverty is also a source of shame. The Brielachs become paralyzed with the fear of embarrassment at having to move their possessions before the watchful eyes of the neighbors. Heinrich's bed made from a door and the old kitchen utensils from the army become for them public stigmata of suffering. Poverty even affects Heinrich's education. He is never spared by his teachers when his work is poor or his behavior inadequate, as is Martin, who has wealth and his father's name in the newspapers; and although Heinrich is intelligent (capable of doing practical arithmetic before entering school), he is destined to become an apprentice in a trade while Martin is destined to attend the *Gymnasium*.

It is extremely important to recognize that even the idyllic utopian setting in Bietenhahn at the conclusion of the novel rests on the prerequisite of property. Although here the Holstege and the Brielach worlds temporarily come together without social distinction, the amity is based on generosity and not on a shared wealth. Heinrich senses this inequity in the midst of his happiness at Albert's mother's. Three times the narrator varies the sentence: "Everything was good and beautiful, but still something was wrong, it was not for him" (pp. 314, 315, 316.)[2] Heinrich is too closely bound to the present to overlook reality. In the novel he is the shepherd of actuality, not of dreams. He looks after his mother, meets her after work, manipulates every penny for her dental treatment, and cares for his two-year-old sister, even advises Martin and chastises him for unthoughtfulness to his family. Although Uncle Albert too is a shepherd of reality (preempting another motif from *Billiards at Half-past Nine*), no one is more exemplary in this regard than young Heinrich. The two chapters given to Heinrich patently set him apart by their uniqueness. In Chapter 2 the narrator is noticeably more Olympian than subjective as he is when dealing with the other protagonists. In chapter 6, long before the other characters begin to show signs of awareness and change, Heinrich recognizes the truth of his situation: "Slowly it became clear to Heinrich how it was" (p. 86). These opening words of the chapter verify his close attachment to reality. Furthermore, Heinrich is the only main character in the book who does not at some time retreat from the present. Even Uncle Albert has his dream of how life could have been had he gone to Ireland to live on the farm with his deceased wife's parents; and Martin, too, Heinrich's contemporary, shows signs of being infected with his mother's malady. The visits to Bietenhahn, although positive experiences for Heinrich, are clearly seen by him as false idylls.

In chapter 5 the perspective shifts back again to Martin and the Holstege world. On this particular day Nella is having one of her frequent parties with the vapid people who follow Schurbigel, those who speak in clichés of noncommitment: "how sweet," "how charming," "how nice." Although Nella's parties are painful to everyone in the Holstege household, including herself, she is unable to break the habit of this diversion. In chapter 6 the narrator shifts back again to Heinrich and reveals his attempt to understand his world by weighing the experiences which have made him wise beyond his years and more mature than his counterpart Martin. He recognizes what Martin does not yet realize, that the difference between morality and immorality is often a matter of sufficient wealth. People are what they are because they have or have not. He concludes: "Martin's mother was different from his mother only by money" (p. 89).

Up to chapter 7 Böll structures the novel, as he did *Acquainted with the Night*, by alternating the perspective with each chapter, in this case, between the Holstege world and the Brielach world. But beginning with that Chapter 7 and continuing through chapter 10, the novel concentrates exclusively on the Holstege household, revealing the past life of each resident in the old house, including the life of Raimund Bach who died in Russia in 1942. Chapter 8 is important in this sequence because in it Böll develops the house itself into a symbol for the decline of its inhabitants. It needs restoration as do the lives of those who live in it. The roof leaks, windows are broken, water and rats are in the basement. The Holsteges themselves—Nella and the grandmother—are psychologically unable to do anything about the decay. Nella's solution to the problems of the house (her life) is to avoid the basement, i.e., to avoid coming to grips with the past.

For the leaking roof she merely buys pails to catch the rain. The burden of repair falls on Albert. His role as shepherd calls for him to care for others. When his entreaties for change go repeatedly unheeded, he calls the repairmen and exterminators himself. Although he cannot restore order by himself, cannot force a responsible relationship among past, present, and future, he can and does fight the moral malaise around him.

Albert's descent into the basement to retrieve his, Rai's, and Nella's letters of the Hitler years is symbolic of a necessary descent into the past and a return to the present. It is a journey the novel insists every German must make. Albert's discovery in the basement of the "Sunlight-carton" containing his drawings from his years in London is also symbolic of the light that the past can shed on the present, while the current commercial value of these drawings symbolizes in monetary terms the rich reward an honest return to the past can bring.

In chapter 8 Böll contrasts Albert's encouragement to Nella to start anew and his battle against the family's growing *Schlamperei* [disorderliness] with the action of one of Heinrich's recent uncles, "New Life Karl" (p. 21)—so nicknamed because of his frequently stated intention to reform his "sinful" life with Heinrich's mother. For Karl "new life" means the desertion of Heinrich and Mrs. Brielach and the obliteration of them from his memory. The carrying out of his intention results in the dehumanization of himself and the inflicting of pain on others. Böll implies in this comparison that a healthy personal as well as national life is only possible with an honest memory. Böll underlines his meaning by contrasting Albert's and Karl's choice of words. Albert's expression: "Everything will be different" (pp. 284ff.) stresses continuity; Karl's phrase a "new life" emphasizes beginning anew by denying the past.

Chapter 10 contains the memorable scene of Martin's visit to a restaurant with his grandmother. Böll's talent as a writer lies clearly in his ability to present detail. Few authors can write of foods as he can, of their smells, tastes, and appearances. In this regard the novel is a treasure of culinary descriptions. The numerous accounts of foods, however, appear not for their own sake but because each member of the Holstege household cooks his own provisions and eats separately in the large kitchen. The several details of individual meals serve the function of characterizing the members of the household and illustrating the deterioration of family life. At no time among the Holsteges is there a communal meal, the symbol *par excellence* of unity in family affairs. In contrast to the Holsteges, the Brielachs, with their meager means and "immoral" household, live and eat as a family even though Mrs. Brielach works and Leo, Heinrich's current uncle, is a source of discord.

In chapter 10 Martin recalls his first excursion with his grandmother to Vohwinkel's Restaurant. "Now I'll show you what eating really is," the grandmother promises Martin (p. 158). Martin was only five at the time. His age is important, for it dates the event in 1947, during the hunger years before the currency reform. This event, not unlike certain scenes in *The Bread of Those Early Years*, shows clearly that the postwar hunger was not shared by all. In the case of the Holsteges, their wealth is largely profit from the war. Although the family jam factory is not normally what one considers a war industry, Grandmother Holstege explains to Martin the inevitable relationship between the military and the production of foodstuffs: "Whenever Germans wage war, it is accompanied by increased productivity in the jam industry" (p. 122). This remarkable symbiosis accounts for the stability of the Holstege company which was founded by Martin's grandfather in 1913.

In 1947, however, when Martin first visits Vohwinkel's Restaurant, he imagines that the steaming dishes of pink meat are slaughtered children and that this delicate food is being consumed by impatient murderers. Afterward he concludes that "what was done there had to be immoral" (p. 158).[3] Martin's identification of the clients in the restaurant with "children murderers" and hence "immoralists" makes the intention clear: those who eat their fill while the masses starve are, in Martin's terminology, "cannibals."

The restaurant scene in chapter 10 is divided into two parts, the recollection of the first trip to Vohwinkel's in 1947 and the relating of the current visit in 1953. The journeys to Vohwinkel's have become semiannual tortures for Martin for the last six years. On this occasion Martin responds in his usual manner: he sees the customers as "bone crushers" and "hates them all" (p.

159). He is nauseated by all the fat, blood, and flesh around him. He satisfies his sense of justice by vomiting in the middle of the restaurant: "He felt neither shame nor sorrow, only cold triumph" (p. 157). Martin accomplishes this feat without soiling his clothes or leaving a single trace of food on his face. From his point of view "he departed from the battle as victor. He never dirtied his hands nor stained his soul" (p. 157). His grandmother, whose pleasure is always in demonstrating her power by the magic of her bankbook, rights everything with a series of checks, with "that mysterious something called money" (p. 159).

Because Uncle Albert's friend Glum reads books about dogmatic and moral theology, which Martin suspects has something to do with morality, Martin asks Glum about Vohwinkel's Restaurant. According to Glum the people who eat there are not cannibals nor is what they do there immoral. Martin remains unconvinced: "Perhaps Glum's books were too old . . . and perhaps there was nothing in them about these murderers" (p. 159). Böll's point is naively blunt as it penetrates Martin's consciousness: to overeat in a society in which people go hungry can only be done at the expense of those who do not get enough to eat. In the terminology of the novel, the sated eat the hungry; those with money devour those with less money; hence, the former are "murderers," "cannibals," and "bone crushers," and the difference between those who are full and those who are not is only the "mysterious something called money."

Beginning with chapter 11, the remaining action of the novel, except for the last few pages describing the final hours in Bietenhahn, occurs on the Friday on which Nella meets Gäseler to attend the literary conference in Brernich. The next eleven chapters present this day concurrently in alternating chapters through the perspective of several characters. As the first six chapters varied the narrative method of *Acquainted with the Night*, chapters 11 through 21 anticipate the method of Böll's next novel, *Billiards at Half-past Nine*, where the entire action occurs in a few hours on the eightieth birthday of one of the characters.

The appearance of Gäseler is the central event of the novel. The arrival of the "murderer" of Nella's husband forces each of the main characters in the Holstege household to bring the past up to the present, forces each to see the historic continuity between the dictatorship and the democracy. The eleven years of hatred which Nella felt for Gäseler fades in his presence. He is an insignificant, vain, opportunistic, ambitious, adjusted conformist, nothing like the *diabolus* of her fantasy, not even worthy of her hatred. In Gäseler's presence Nella can only feel "cold, uncanny boredom" (p. 239). But his appearance begins, nonetheless, to have its effect. Nella no longer finds her way back to the dream world in which she has lived since 1942. When she asks Gäseler to tell her of the war he reveals his hollowness most completely: "I don't think about it any more. I try to forget it, and I'm successful. It's over . . . I've forgotten everything . . . systematically slaughtered my memory. People have to forget the war" (pp. 247–48). Although Gäseler has "systematically slaughtered his memory," he still sentimentally recalls the first names of generals, his service under Rommel, and his time on the eastern front. He has purged the death, dirt, and suffering from his mind, forgotten the widows and orphans in his rush to build a "beautiful, clean future," putting his "confidence in the Bank" (p. 248). Nella's response to Gäseler is the same as Böll's to the German people: "A slap in the face for all the people who have forgotten the war" (p. 249). As Nella arrives with Gäseler at the resort in Brernich, where the conference is being held, she does not attend the lectures, but goes immediately to the swimming pool. Although the water temperature is a cool sixty-nine degrees, she chooses to go bathing, i.e., she purifies herself in the cold water of reality. She leaves Brernich to return to her family and to a more responsible life.

The appearance of Gäseler also affects Albert's life. It forces him to assess his situation in the Holstege constellation. After his discovery that Nella has gone to Brernich with her husband's murderer, he recites the refrain: "Everything will be different now" (pp. 284ff.) and immediately becomes more active in his concern for Martin by planning to move with him to the protective environment of Bietenhahn.

The day is equally decisive for Martin, who recognizes through conversations with Heinrich that the conditions in the Brielach family are not immoral as he has heard in school. He realizes the prejudices of his teachers and the insufficency of the answers in his catechism. He becomes aware that Mrs. Brielach's living with "uncles" has something to do with lack of money and that there is a silence in the religion class about what this connection is. Maturity comes to Martin on this day. He senses that "something was past, but what it was, he did not know" (p. 324).

Associated with Martin's new awareness and Albert's intention to make things different is Albert's taking Martin to the old fortress, now a mushroom cellar, where he and Martin's father were tortured by the Nazis and where their friend Absalom Billig was murdered. Here Martin becomes aware of the political aspects of the word "immoral." Martin is surprised to discover that Uncle Albert uses the word "terrible" to describe the Nazis, a word his teachers use to talk about immorality. He knows now that his teachers are wrong when they speak of the fascists as "not so bad" (p. 288), and he also becomes suspicious of the school's attempt to play off Nazi "terrors" (p. 288) against Russian brutality. For Albert "making things different" includes educating Martin, showing him the relationship between past and present, illustrating for him the continuity of time. In this fortress scene Albert consciously assumes his role as guide and shepherd. His final advice to Martin, "Don't forget it" (p. 289), stands in direct contradiction to Gäseler's maxim for successful postwar living.

For Heinrich and his mother this Friday is also a day of change and hope. Mrs. Brielach decides to move away from the small room shared with Uncle Leo to the more spacious quarters above the bakery where she works. Her children will have more room to play and with lower rent she will have more money to pay the dentist: grounds for optimism, although diminished in Heinrich's mind because he senses his mother must pay for these material advantages with "immorality" with the baker. Heinrich's fear, however, turns out to be unwarranted. Mrs. Brielach refuses the baker sexual favors because on this decisive day she, like Walter Fendrich discovering Hedwig, meets Albert. There is an immediate love between the two which changes her life: "A gleam of hope was in his mother's and Albert's eyes, and there appeared to be an agreement between them" (p. 306). Heinrich's recollection of his mother's meeting with Albert ends the novel for the Brielachs on a positive note: "He thought of the hope which for a moment had been in his mother's face, *only for a moment*, but he knew *a moment* can mean a lot" (p. 324).

Much in the novel relates it to other works by Böll. Schurbigel, the leader of the Brernich circle of old Nazis, with his dissertation on "The Führer in the Modern Lyric," is the man without a memory who turns to religion after the war without changing his prewar views and without acknowledging any guilt. He is the forerunner of Bur-Malottke in the satire "Murke's Collected Silences." Schurbigel's priestly associate, Father Willibrord, prefigures the popular cultural sermonizer Father Sommerwild in *The Clown.* Grandmother Holstege with her desire to kill Gäseler becomes in *Billiards at Half-past Nine* Grandmother Fähmel, who actually shoots a political leader of Germany's new democratic society because she sees him as a "buffalo," a future murderer of her grandchildren. Glum's detailed wall-size painting of the world, which has become his life's work, preempts the motif of Leni's wall-size human eye which she paints in *Group Portrait with Lady,* and Nella with her beauty and magnificent German blond hair anticipates the physical appearance of Leni, "das deutscheste Mädel der Stadt."

II   Billiards at Half-past Nine

In 1959, as Böll's *Billiards at Half-past Nine* appeared, critics generally praised the work as one of Böll's most important efforts. Today this opinion still prevails. Although the book was more difficult to read than Böll's previous works and was even criticized for its complex structure,[4] it represented no new formal, stylistic, technical, or thematic beginning for the author. Through the perspective of a single family, the novel presents a fifty-year panorama of German history from the turn of the century to the present, from 1907 to 1958, the period of two world wars and two economic recoveries. Böll makes this epic sweep through five decades by concentrating the present time of the novel to a few hours, from about ten o'clock in the morning to about eight o'clock in the evening, on a single day, Saturday, 6 September 1958, the eightieth birthday of Heinrich Fähmel. This method of foreshortening time had been steadily developing in Böll's work. In his interview with Horst Bienek, he explained this tendency as a natural result of his authorial intention: "In my first novel, if I remember correctly, the real action, which is actually very slight, transpires over a few months. In the next two novels, the action is reduced to one or two days, and in this last work [*Billiards*] to eight or ten hours. . . . Ideally, I would say, a novel ought to be able to transpire in one minute. With this exaggeration I can only hint at what I am trying to do with the element of time."[5]

To illustrate Böll's point, a look at the structure of a few works is helpful. In *The Train* the time span was from Thursday till Sunday; in *Acquainted with the Night*, from Saturday morning till Monday morning; in *The Bread of Those Early Years*, from morning till evening; and in *The Unguarded House*, while the present time of the novel was one week, most of the action took place on a single day in a brief time span presented simultaneously through the perspective of various characters. In *Billiards* (1959) Böll simply intensifies the methods of chronological concentration and simultaneity which he used in *House*. The most obvious implementation of this last method is the presentation of the shot fired by Johanna Fähmel. Böll presents the few minutes before seven, the time of the shot, first from the perspective of Johanna and Heinrich, present at the shooting, then from the perspective of Robert and Schrella, playing billiards at the time, then from the perspective of Leonore, telephoning Robert at the moment of the shot, and finally from that of the young Joseph and Ruth Fähmel, returning to the hotel at seven o'clock for their grandfather's birthday celebration. Still, Böll takes more from the technique of *House* than the use of simultaneity. In *Billiards* he assigns individual chapters to each character in order to present events from several points of view, and as in *House*, he shifts the narrative within each chapter between third person and interior monologue.

The main theme of the novel, as the title suggests, is time. Three events, each affecting a different generation, fosters the Fähmels' reconciliation with the past on this day. Heinrich Fähmel's eightieth birthday is for him and his wife Johanna a natural impetus to review their past lives. The unexpected visit after twenty-three years by Schrella, Robert Fähmel's school friend and fellow exile of the Hitler years, becomes the impetus for Robert to come to terms with his wasting life. Schrella's return is, as one critic has said, the arrival of time.[6] In this sense Schrella's sudden appearance functions in *Billiards* as does Gäseler's in *The Unguarded House*. And Robert's son Joseph discovers on this same day that during the war his father had intentionally destroyed the famous monastery which Heinrich Fähmel had built fifty years ago, and which Joseph is now helping to restore. Hence Joseph is forced on this day to make decisions about his own life by contemplating his father's wartime motivation.

In the early chapters, the book deals overwhelmingly with the past, as Heinrich, Robert, and Johanna measure time less by years than by the deaths of relatives, friends, and loved ones, less by narrating the past than by recollecting it. Thus time not only affects the structure of the novel but becomes its theme. The first five of the thirteen chapters cover about six of the ten hours in the novel and bring the time on this day from morning to about four o'clock in the afternoon. The remaining eight chapters cover only the time from about four to eight. Hence there is a converse principle at work between the time of the narration and the time narrated: five chapters for about six hours of real time in which the emphasis is on the past, and eight chapters for about four hours of real time in which the emphasis is increasingly on the present. This unique structure, while complicated, is perfectly suited to the theme of conquering the past. As the present becomes more and more important for each character, each lives less and less a prisoner of convention, routine, and memory; as the structure of the novel itself reflects this change, form and content are closely aligned.

The billiard playing of the novel serves as a paradigm for its structure. As Robert ignores all rules and simply rolls the balls across the table, having one ball strike the other, creating constantly new geometric patterns, the playing reproduces the random chronology of the story and provides a visual image which corresponds to the memories of the characters coming together, reverberating off each other, stimulating new recollections. It is "white over green, red over green, red and white over green" (p. 56); "music without melody, painting without pictures, scarcely color only formula" (p. 40). Not only does the billiard playing symbolize the technique of the novel, but appropriately, modern art itself: formalistic, nonmelodic twelve-tone music and pictureless, nonobjective painting, often of few colors or merely shades of a single color.

Hence it is interesting to see how Böll has constructed this complicated novel. He has commented on his procedure in an interview with Horst Bienek: "When I have the first version of the novel written down, then the work really begins. To help me I use a simple aid: a colored chart divided into three levels: the real, that is, the present, the second, the reflective or the memory level, and the third for the motifs. To the motifs and the characters I assign colors which only appear, however, on the first and second levels. It is very difficult to explain. I can only say that these color charts, which I started using on my first novel, are becoming more and more complicated."[7] In the Böll archive in the Boston University Library the aid which Böll mentions can be found. For *Billiards*, besides this chart (which has been made on a piece of thin cardboard and preserved in Box 6, Folder 3), there are other illustrations by Böll outlining the novel in different ways. One labeled "Stations" (Box 5, Folder 1, on the outside front cover of a *Billiards* manuscript) divides the novel into four parts, listing part I as chapters 1 to 3; part II, chapter 4; part III, chapter 5; and part IV, chapters 6 to the end. To see if the novel has "balance," Böll has tabulated the manuscript pages in each chapter and part, since the length of chapters and episodes in a book is important to him. In several of his critical writings he counts the number of pages it takes an author to relate an incident and defines such divisions in a novel as the breathing rhythm of the work. From this rhythm he characterizes authors as *langatmig* [long-winded] or *kurzatmig* [short-winded], a terminology which has nothing to do with the length of the book.[8]

Böll's divisions are of interest to the critic because he assigns to part I the express purpose of introducing the characters[9] and of presenting Robert Fähmel, the novel's leading character, from four perspectives, from that of his secretary and his father (chapter 1), from that of Jochen, the factotum at the Prince Heinrich Hotel (chapter 2), and from Robert's own perspective by means of his narration and recollection (chapter 3).

In parts II (chapter 4) and III (chapter 5) he allows Heinrich and Johanna, Robert's parents, to reveal themselves in the same manner as did Robert in chapter three. In chapter 6, the beginning of the fourth part, set in the train station at Denklingen, father and son meet for the first time in the novel. Their conversation starts the slow process of lifting the weight off the past which has lain over their lives up to this point. From now on each chapter brings an increasing number of the Fähmels together and transfers each gradually from the past to the present.

To keep his novel under control and to minimize the chance of inconsistencies, Böll has still another chart (Box 5, Folder 1) on which, next to each chapter, he has listed the present time taken up in, and the setting of, each chapter. A final chart (Box 6, Folder 3) lists each chapter with the leitmotifs used in it. These charts are extremely valuable because they illuminate Böll's method of composition and illustrate the structure of the book as the author himself sees it.[10]

Perhaps even more interesting, however, because it reveals the precision and exactness for historical detail that is characteristic of all of Böll's works, is a list of eighteen questions (Box 6, Folder 3) which the author researched or had researched in preparation for writing the novel. Some of this material has found its way into it, and some has not, but the procedure reveals the reliability of the minutiae in Böll's stories. Böll checked the price ranges in the best hotels in Cologne, both for a traditional and a modern hotel, the price for a single and a double room, the price of a breakfast and the cost of service, the exact size of a billiard table, a technical definition of statics, the length of service for an Uhlan around 1880, the style of his headgear and his official insignia around 1907. He also checked out the number assigned to a Rhenish corps of engineers which served in Cologne at the turn of the century, inquired whether officers in the corps wore swords or daggers, and researched the style of their insignia. In addition, he investigated the statute of limitations for attempted murder, as well as the official terminology for the infirmary in a monastery, the exact time of sunset on 6 September 1958, the Latin text and German translation of inscriptions on the graves of Roman children, the text of patriotic songs of 1942, the normal commission fee for an architect around 1909, and the date for a Saturday in the middle of July 1935. These are some of the inquiries Böll made for giving authenticity to *Billiards*. Some of the answers to these questions run over two typed pages and several are found in paragraphs written in a factual telegram style.

Just as *Acquainted with the Night, The Bread of Those Early Years*, and *The Unguarded House* received their creative impulse from specific social problems—the problem of poverty and marriage, the permanent effects of hunger, the plight of half-orphans and widows—so too it is with *Billiards*. Although the theme of that work is conquering the past as in *The Unguarded House*, the creative impulse derives from a different social reality. For West Germany the period 1954–1958 was the era of military restoration, the period when Germany rearmed as an integral part of the West's military defenses. Böll viewed this rearmament as a continuation of the Prussian tradition which, since the turn of the century, had led to two world wars. Hence it is not surprising that in the novel Böll makes no distinction among the militarism of the Kaiser, Hitler, and the federal chancellor. Whether his unwillingness to make these distinctions is thought of as naive historicism or as penetrating moral insight into the development of modern Germany each reader must decide for himself. Surprisingly, the figures whom Böll chooses to represent the continuity of Germany's military tradition from the nineteenth to the twentieth century are not Bismarck and Hitler, but Hindenburg (who was a transitional figure from empire to Republic to dictatorship) and unknown Nazis, people with whom the public does not immediately associate blood, iron, and atrocities. Böll symbolizes this martial spirit in the image of the buffalo which emblemizes these people as unregenerate representatives of power. Germany's militarism, the novel implies, is part and parcel of the capitalist system, one common denominator of Germany's history during this period. Böll presents, then, twentieth-century German history not as three separate eras under an emperor, a dictator, and a federal chancellor, but as a single manifestation of a persistent combination of economics and militarism.

Hans Joachim Bernhard writes of *Billiards*: "The social criticism here is criticism of capitalism in the national form in which it appeared in Germany since the turn of the century."[11] This statement needs some modification. It is valid only insofar as *Billiards* identifies militarism as an essential aspect of capitalism and in-sofar as the work demonstrates that, politically, capitalism can be very flexible, being at one time linked to an intolerent fas-cistic dictatorship and at another to a tolerant liberal democracy, without altering the basic means by which people relate to one another economically. Schrella exposes this aspect of capitalism best when he explains that the reason he was driven out of the country in 1935 is the same as the reason why he is welcomed back in 1958: "Then to make me harmless was to lock me up, now to make me harmless is to set me free" (p. 192).

Still the novel's criticism of capitalism is one-sided—because the work neglects the realm of economics. At no time does the book offer criticism of the economic nature of capitalism, but of only its militaristic and political aspects. In fact, considered from the economic point of view, the novel can be read as an advertise-ment for capitalistic economics. All the representatives of the working class are happy in their jobs as waiters and rivermen and content with their working conditions. Jochen, the hotel fac-totum, even brags: "I have an agreement in my pocket, sealed by a notary, that I have my little attic room for the rest of my life and can even keep my pigeons. I can choose what I want to eat for breakfast and lunch and even receive a hundred and fifty marks cash every month, three times what I need for my tobacco" (p. 32). Nowhere in the novel, which covers the tumultuous years 1907–1958, can the reader find examples of depression, inflation, unemployment, or economic exploitation.[12]

Instead Böll creates two powerful symbols to treat the novel's view of history: the Sacrament of the Buffalo and the Sacrament of the Lamb. With their help he imbues history with a powerful moral correlative. Although the origin of the buffalo is obscure, it is, in part, religious. Most critics cite the Book of Revelations (chapter 13) as a source of the symbolism. This source, however, is far from convincing, for Revelations speaks of two animals which are the enemy of the lamb, the first a nameless beast with seven heads and ten horns, like unto a leopard with the feet of a bear and the mouth of a lion, and the other, also a marvelous beast, with the shape of a lamb but with two horns and the voice of the dragon (Satan). The appearance in the novel of a second villain, the sheep priestess, who masquerades as a lamb and

speaks with the tongue of a dragon, increases the possibility of
the Book of Revelations as a source, but it is more reasonable to
assume that the buffalo symbol derives from Böll's desire to avoid
the stereotype of the wolf as the opposite of the lamb and at the
same time to offer an animal symbol which implies power, cruelty,
hardness, and a lack of sensitivity. Moreover, the symbol was not
new to Böll; he had used it for the same purpose, although only
in passing, in *The Unguarded House*. In any case, the buffalo
in this novel represents the negation of the lamb, i.e., the opposite of Christian values.

On the other hand, the symbol of the lamb requires little explanation, for it is deeply rooted in the biblical tradition as the
sacrificial offering and as the emblem for Christ. Besides calling
Christ the Lamb of God, the New Testament also presents Jesus
as the Good Shepherd who cares for his sheep and exhorts others
to do the same (John 21:15–17). Thus the lamb symbol leads
directly to a third symbolic category, that of the shepherd-pro-
tector. Robert asks Schrella why he is persecuted:

"Are you a Jew?"
"No."
"What are you, then?"
"We are lambs," Schrella said, "and have sworn never to taste of
the *Sacrament of the Buffalo*."
"Lambs." I was afraid of the word. "A sect?" I asked.
"Perhaps."
"A party?"
"No."
"I couldn't become one," I said. "I can't be a Lamb."
"Do you want to taste of the *Sacrament of the Buffalo*?"
"No," I said.
"Shepherd then," he answered, "there are those who will never
abandon the herd." (p. 51)

Throughout the novel it is clear which characters have tasted
of the Sacrament of the Buffalo: Nettlinger, Wakiera, the minister, etc., and which have not: the Fähmels (except Otto, who
died in Russia in 1942, and young Heinrich, who died as a child
in 1917), Ferdi, Schrella, Edith, etc. Furthermore, it is clear
throughout that pacifism and nonviolence are not characteristics

of all the lambs and certainly not of the shepherds. Thus the lamb Ferdi is capable of retaliation and with Robert's help attempts to assassinate the Nazi sadist Wakiera. Also, Robert, to avenge the deaths of Ferdi and the other lambs and to seek retribution from a nation for its capitulation to the spirit of the buffalo, demolishes every building he can in Germany, including the architectural masterpiece the Abbey of St. Anthony, built by his father. Even Johanna, who, during two world wars, would not take a single crumb of food for herself or her family more than the amount allowed the poor and the powerless, contemplates a preemptive murder. Before shooting the minister, whom she had never seen before, she recognizes his "buffalo visage" (p. 270) and identifies him as the future "murderer of her grandchildren" (p. 276). Johanna, then, in her extreme way, is also a shepherd, one who protects the innocent. She and Robert are the scourge of God, claiming the right to vengeance which the Lord maintains is his alone (Deut. 32:35; Rom. 12:19). What justifies the violence of Ferdi, Robert, and Johanna is that they work from a position of weakness, not power, that they strive to right wrong not to do wrong—a distinction some readers will find difficult to accept.

Many critics have found the symbolism of *Billiards* unsatisfactory, have criticized it as too "black and white" to do justice to the complexities of the epoch,[13] as too simplistic to treat the economic roots of the problem of the times,[14] as too allegorical to be effective,[15] or have labeled it a twisting of reality,[16] or simply have found it "unconvincing."[17] All of these criticisms are somehow justified. It is equally unsatisfying that the categorizing of people as lambs and buffaloes is not merely the habit of the circle around Schrella and the Fähmels, where one might expect it and find it fitting, but also the practice of Jochen, the hotel factotum, thus giving the unusual categories a general currency and making the phrases "Sacrament of the Lamb" and "Sacrament of the Buffalo" common figures of speech on the lips of several disparate characters. Finally, the symbolism smacks of unfairness, for it presents all people with power as evil and all people without political power as equal victims in suffering, regardless of whether they are rich like the Fähmels with prestige and social position, capable of extracting privilege, or poor proletarians like the

Trischlers and the Schrellas who can be removed from the face of the earth without a trace.

While the symbolism is not totally successful, the novel succeeds on a different level—probably contrary to the author's intention. The lambs with their shepherds form an association which Schrella acknowledges as a possible sect, but definitely not a political party (p. 51). This circle around Schrella and the Fähmels stands for religion without denomination, politics without party, humaneness without ideology. Such idealism, the novel shows, can foster no social change. The Fähmels' personalism is valid solely on the individual level. Their new activism cannot extend beyond its own circle.

Johanna's shooting of the minister shows the limits of the Fähmel model and points to the new isolation of the Fähmels' position. Her assassination attempt is an attack on the entire West German government[18] because, from Johanna's perspective, all members of the government are corrupt, whether Nettlinger, Wakiera, or the minister; they all have a "buffalo visage" (p. 270). Therefore, to shoot one is as good as shooting the other. They all deserve to be targets. The condemnation of the system extends also to the supporters of the system, to both parties of the opposition. The porter in the Prince Heinrich Hotel observes: "Who belonged to the left and who to the right one couldn't tell" (p. 269). Böll underscores the lack of significant differentiation in the members of the opposition parties by having them eat the same food and listen to the same music at similar conventions on the same day in the same hotel. Singled out for special denunciation is Kretz, the new hope of the left. Robert confesses: "I believe if I would ever kill any one, it would be him" (p. 298). Even Kretz's name subtly condemns him by its similarity to that of the old Nazi Gretz, who, in the novel, betrays his own mother. Furthermore, Schrella concludes after observing Kretz's followers: "These people would really sell their grandmothers for five cigarettes" (p. 298). Johanna, taking her first leave from the sanitarium in sixteen years, offers a scathing blanket condemnation of the representatives of the system, both those who are part of it and those who support it with their loyal opposition: "I'm afraid now even more than then [during the Nazi period]. You [Heinrich] have obviously grown accustomed

to their faces, but I am growing homesick already for my harmless inmates. Are you blind? So easily deceived? Those people
would kill you for less than a gesture of your hand, for less than
a piece of bread and butter" (p. 273).

After this speech Heinrich supports Johanna's decision to shoot
the minister. However, the similarity of her deed to Ferdi's and
Robert's assassination attempt two decades earlier illustrates the
desperation of the act. Johanna, like Ferdi and Robert, is driven
to vengeance not by reason but by a thirst for justice. All three
are cast in the mold of Kleist's Michael Kohlhaas, unable or unwilling to organize or enlighten the public, satisfied with the personal venting of hostility, shunning the arduous task of changing
society. The end result is, as the novel illustrates, a small circle
of people who think alike and feel alike, content with hatred of
injustice and the friendship of their own kind.

The conclusion of the novel thoroughly demonstrates the isolation of this "romantic" position. Johanna is content to hide the
motives of her act from the public behind paragraph fifty-one
(the claim of insanity), is ready to accept again seclusion in the
sanitarium although she is perfectly sane (assuming sanity means
being responsible for one's actions). She accepts the price of in-
carceration for a deed conceived and executed within a few
hours; a high price indeed for a desperate symbolic act of self-
satisfaction. Just as Johanna chooses institutionalized isolation,
the Fähmel circle, by crowding into Heinrich's studio, opts for
the company of themselves, systematically cutting off the outside
world. The novel reveals this isolation in several ways. Hugo
gives up his job at the hotel and joyfully abandons the locus of
the real world with all its vices. Joseph abandons the task of
rebuilding the monastery and decides to study statics and work
in his father's office. Although Robert renounces the seclusion of
his daily billiards at half-past nine to become a father to Hugo,
there is no indication that he will become less formal, less correct, less distant from people not in his circle. Schrella again
leaves Germany, less because he sees no political future for the
Federal Republic than because he is personally incapable of
political activity: "I was always apolitical and still am" (p. 293).
He fears for Germany less because of the buffaloes in power—he
knows what they are like—than because there are so few Chris-

tians, lambs, and shepherds. "I am not afraid because of those down there [marching in the street], but because there are no others" (p. 293), is his final pessimistic conclusion. Heinrich cancels his fifty-one-year-old standing order for breakfast—an act which signifies a repudiation of an empty routine, a snobbish formula, a sign of elitism, a model for role-playing[19]—but, nonetheless, a rejection of the real world. There is undoubtedly great nobility in the Fähmels' decision to choose integrity and loyalty to humane ideals over compromise with a corrupt system, but the inevitable result is isolation, a peculiar form of egoism.

The Fähmels disdain the false world. As Heinrich says on his birthday: "It is the day and the hour to renounce false friendships" (p. 303), but the reader cannot forget that this noble gesture is a rejection not only of a false society but also of the only society there is. Critics have pointed out the positive aspects of the conclusion of the novel. Bernhard characterizes the ending as a *Wandel zur Wirklichkeit*[20] ("turn to reality"). It is precisely this interpretation which needs correction. It is true the Fähmels break out of their prison of time; they step out of the routine that has bound their lives: Johanna temporarily leaves the institution; Heinrich cancels his breakfast at the Cafe Kroner; Robert adopts Hugo. Heinrich comes to understand Robert—father and son now communicate without tension; Heinrich accepts Robert's destruction of the Abbey, and is able to rejoice in Easter fashion: "This day is great; it has returned my wife to me, has given me a son . . . and presented me with a grandchild" (p. 302). Böll even illustrates visually these victories over the past by having the circle of friends sit on stacks of Heinrich's architectural documents piled according to year, showing the family now on top of time, and by having Heinrich himself destroy the birthday-cake model of his Abbey by cutting off the tower and presenting it to Robert.

Despite the positive achievements of this "great day," despite the Fähmels' conquering of time, breaking the dehumanizing barriers of routine and role-playing, indicating a return to life, their actions still rest on a resignation to the status quo, an acceptance of the unchanging political hegemony of the buffaloes. The Fähmels' behavior merely heralds for them a different retreat from reality. Their individual isolation is replaced now by group isolation, the circle of one becomes the circle of a few. Improvement, yes, but far from an adequate solution to the central political problem which the novel poses. The buffaloes still rule the land and are presumably always going to do so. As she shoots the minister, Johanna can only hope that "death will bring a look of surprise to his face" (p. 277). At his party, Heinrich in his pentecostal language exhorts his friends and relatives not be sad: "Do not cry, children, . . . she [Johanna] will come again and stay with us" (p. 302). Her spirit may be among them, but it is not likely the seventy-year-old Johanna will return soon. Heinrich also seems content with the result of Johanna's deed in that he too hopes that "the great surprise on his [the minister's] face will never again disappear" (p. 302).

Hence the book ends positively on one level, but negatively on another. Still, in the aggregate, the work has the power of enlightenment, for it shows very clearly the limits of the effectiveness of an apolitical humanism which tends to deeds of radical moral indignation directed against injustice and which, at the same time, resigns itself to the ineluctability of that injustice. Böll's novel reveals the dead end of solidarity in isolation and implies social change is only possible with a platform, a program, and an ideology for change.

CHAPTER 8

Novels of Intensified Social Criticism and the Abandonment of Social Integration

I The Clown

IN the two novels preceding *Ansichten eines Clowns* [The Clown, 1963] the heroes Albert Muchow and Robert Fähmel seek social integration through the extension of the family; each sees himself as his brother's keeper; each in his way sees to it that innocent youth is protected from moral corruption, instructed about the Nazi past, and given assurance and assistance on the road to maturity. Although both heroes are severe critics of society, Robert even carrying his criticism to the point of attempted assassination, and although both encourage their protégés (Martin and Hugo) to be skeptical of leaders and institutions, still, simply by fulfilling their roles as father figures they convey in a positive manner a message of social responsibility. In *The Clown*, however, Hans Schnier, its protagonist, adds to a wounded psyche like that of Fred Bogner's and the desire for withdrawal from society like that of Walter Fendrich's a new social cynicism and bitterness which reflect Heinrich Böll's own reaction to the sociopolitical events in West Germany during the early sixties.

This sharp sense of rancor in the work does not derive from Hans Schnier's more accurate perception of the shortcomings of German society, nor from the recognition of social injustice that his forerunners did not acknowledge. In fact, much of the criticism in *The Clown* duplicates that found in the earlier novels, all of which, beginning with *Acquainted with the Night*, criticize

Germany's Nazi past, West Germany's postwar development, and the Roman Catholic Church; but in this work the criticism becomes more direct and intense. Hans, the clown, is not, like Albert and Robert, a mature man of middle years, but an emotional young man of twenty-seven with pressing personal problems who views events not objectively but subjectively. His condemnation of the church, his capitalist family, and his opportunistic acquaintances derives from no firmly fixed ideological or philosophical position, but from the position of a sensitive humanist reacting to personal experiences.

The novel's intensified social criticism reflects Böll's developing position in the early 1960s away from optimism toward negativism, away from chastising to pillorying West German society. However, the ailing, jealous, desperate clown cannot be equated with the author. Still Hans's targets—the church, the acquisitive society, the capitalist system, the politics of West Germany, the opportunism of ex-Nazis—are the points of Böll's attack in his essays and sundry writings of the early 1960s. Many critics have recognized this continuity. Klaus Jeziorkowski correctly maintains that throughout Böll's career "the themes of the narrative works are similar to or the same as those of his polemical writings."[1]

In 1963 Böll stated flatly: "My views about Catholic organizations are more bitter and more hardened than those of any of my characters" (*AKR*, p. 458). An analysis of Böll's writings of this period reveals that his views are not only "more bitter and more hardened' than those of the clown on religious topics, but on other topics as well.

In the novellette of 1964, *Absent Without Leave*, the reader recognizes in the title the author's increasing detachment from the sociopolitical course of West German life. The German title of the book, *Entfernung von der Truppe*, makes this interpretation of the story even more obvious. In this tale, the narrator claims his humanity only began with his rejection of society. "Becoming a human being begins when you desert all troops" (p. 116), is his terse assessment of man's social condition. In *Absent Without Leave*, the socially estranged narrator is much like the first-person narrator of *The Clown*. They are brothers under the skin: what can be said of one is valid for the other.

Both lead chaste lives after they lose the women they love; both are indifferent to the wealth of their parents, and both criticize the same things in society.

In the early 1960s, Böll, along with like-minded friends, founded the Christian-Socialist periodical *Labyrinth*, in which he published his first stage play, *Ein Schluck Erde* [A Piece of Earth, 1961]. In this drama, related to his study of St. Francis (entitled "Assisi"), the author presents a wise old man who expresses the harmony Böll finds between Christianity and communism. The old man warns two lovers about the moral danger of worldly possessions: "What you are doing is the worst of all possible things. . . . You are killing love, and you are preventing what should come—the highest love. . . . You are claiming property. Property prevents the highest love and kills both small and great love. Quickly destroy your property" (*Homo viator*, p. 420). In *The Clown*, Hans Schnier not only rejects the wealth of his parents but, after five years as a successful professional entertainer, possesses little more than the clothes on his back, no money at all, and ends his narrative as a beggar rather than compromise his values.

In 1960 Böll completed the essay "Karl Marx," which praises the philosopher and presents him as a secular saint. Because of his sympathy with Marxism, Böll finds it necessary in this work, as does the old Socialist Derkum in *The Clown*, to reprove the German Social Democrats for their falsification of Marxist tradition. This position relates directly to the decision of the SPD at its Party Congress of 1960 to abandon socialism, support rearmament, and endorse atomic weapons for the *Bundeswehr*. In that year even Willy Brandt challenged Adenauer to stop hiding behind NATO and to ask for nuclear weapons. In the 1962 essay "Was heute links sein könnte" [What Could Still Be Leftist Today], in speaking of the "homeless left," Böll further censures the SPD for its tendency to emulate the CDU. He even predicts the development of a type of one-party nation in which the two major parties share the same ideology, as in the United States. Böll's fearful prediction was more than vindicated in 1965 when the two parites formed the temporary "Grand Coalition." Since that time the economic policies of the SPD have become more and more similar to those of the conservative CDU, thus justifying Böll's prognosis even more. These expressions of Böll's feelings of betrayal are reflected in *The Clown* by old Derkum when he tells Hans that he disdains the SPD more than the CDU (p. 237).

In 1963–1964 in the satirical "Brief an einen Freund jenseits der Grenzen" [Letter to a Friend beyond the Border] writing of the SPD, the fictitious author concludes: "I think the body of this party is dead, but its corpse is still alive" (*AKR*, p. 453). In this same satiric manner Böll presents the pointed episode in *The Clown* in which Hans watches a dog standing hesitantly before two election posters, one for the SPD and the other for the CDU. The dog's decision to "piss" on the CDU poster constitutes no vulgar attack on the Christian party, but represents rather a forceful rejection of both the Christian and the Socialist parties, for it makes no difference which poster the dog chooses. Still, in these years Böll reserved his ire for the CDU and its southern affiliate, the CSU. In the satirical correspondence "Briefe aus dem Rheinland" [Letters from the Rhineland, 1963–1964], signed by a sad but witty village schoolteacher named Lohengrin, the writer assures his friend: "You're afraid that in the next election I'll vote for the CDU. Have no fear; it will never come to that; I'll never sink that low" (*AKR*, p. 425). In the same year, 1963, Böll wrote the epilogue to Carl Amery's *Die Kapitulation oder deutscher katholizismus heute* [Capitulation: The Lesson of German Catholicism]. In this essay he continues his criticism of the church begun in his "Brief an einen jungen Katholiken" [Letter to a Young Catholic, 1958]. In the epilogue, he specifically regrets that "German Catholicism is bound in an unholy way to the party which identifies itself with the letter 'C' for Christian" (*AKR*, p. 135).

Still other themes which are found in the polemical writings of these years occur in *The Clown*. The essays "Zeichen an der Wand" [Sign on the Wall, 1960] and "Befehl und Verantwortung" [Obedience and Responsibility, 1961] treat Germany's recent anti-Semitic past as evoked by incidents of swastikas appearing in public places, the publicity of the Eichmann and other war-crime trials, the 1962 scandal of ex-Nazi judge Wolfgang Fraenkel's appointment to chief federal prosecutor, the advancement of Hans Globke, the interpreter of the Nuremberg racial laws, to Chancellor Adenauer's personal aide, and the tactics of Franz Josef Strauss, the minister of defense, in his handling of the 1962 *Spiegel* affair. In *The Clown* the parallel passages are Hans's recollection of his family's *Judenhass* maintained up till the last days of the war and expressed in the exhortations of his mother to her children to drive the "Jewish yankee" (p. 29) from the "holy German soil" (p. 29). In the opening lines of the essay "Hierzulande" [In This Country, 1960], Böll gives an explication of the émigré passage in *The Clown* in which Hans regrets the eager gullibility of returning emigrants duped by the tearful remorse and tactical democratization of old Nazis (pp. 227–28). The following sentences in "Hierzulande": "What is the difference between the people of today and those in 1933?—Nothing. Are there still Nazis in this country?—Naturally; did you expect the mere date of May 8, 1945, to change people?" (*EHA*, p. 429), reflect very accurately the manner, attitude, and tone of the corresponding passages of Hans Schnier's narrative.

In *The Clown* the postwar transformations of Hans's mother, the teacher Brühl, the writer Schnitzler, and the youth leader Herbert Kalick illustrate Böll's criticism. The racist Mrs. Schnier becomes the respected advocate of brotherhood as the president of the Central Committee for the Reconciliation of Racial Differences. The Fascist teacher Brühl, who argued for the execution of all who refused to fight for Germany, becomes a professor of pedagogy and, because he never joined the Nazi party, enjoys the reputation of a man "with a brave political past" (p. 29). The accidentally censured writer Schnitzler capitalizes on his status as a "forbidden author" and develops into an indispensable person in the Foreign Office" (p. 42). The fanatic Hitler Youth leader Kalick, who was responsible for the death of the orphan Georg and the persecution of Götz Buchel, receives a federal Cross of Merit for his work in spreading democratic ideas among German youth. The criticism in *The Clown* is not aimed at questioning the sincerity of these conversions; what is questioned is the opportunism of the ex-Fascists. Such people, Böll implies, believe in nothing except the prevailing ideology. Were it to their advantage, they would adopt any political stance regardless of moral considerations. In other words, these Germans have learned nothing from their political mistakes of the Hitler years.

Finally, in this review of the book *Wie hast du es mit der Bundeswehr?* (1963), Böll concludes: "There exists in this land a fear known previously only in times of great epidemics: a fear of spontaneity, or naiveté" (*AKR*, p. 312). This sentence explains well the discomfort the characters in *The Clown* experience in the presence of Hans Schnier. No two words characterize Hans better than "spontaneous" and "naive." Several characters in the novel recognize his dangerous uniqueness. Thus Kinkel complains that Hans has not the slightest understanding of "the metaphysical" (p. 114) and exhorts him to "be a man" (p. 112), i.e., to be like others. Prelate Sommerwild expresses the idea more positively when he calls Hans "an innocent . . . pure person" (p. 160), but the implication is the same: Hans is an unnerving outsider. Hans reveals his disconcerting naiveté in many ways. He does not like to wash or to wear shoes, he shuns things intellectual, reads only nonserious newspapers and magazines, enjoys the mindless game "Sorry" (*"Mensch-ärgere-dich-nicht"*), and prefers the simplicity of children's movies and the company of young people. He reveals his antisocial spontaneity in his sudden decision to seduce Marie, in his guileless telephone conversations with "friends," in his impulsive honesty with his mother, and in his impromptu miming of a blind man during the conversation with his father. At all times Hans does the unexpected. His first-person narrative, with its angry candor, reveals this aspect of his personality. He cannot conceal emotion, feign friendship, or betray his true nature; he cannot say one thing and think or do another. His innocence is his very weakness and the basis of the near tragic elements of the book. In fact, only the strong strain of satire in the narration undermines the work's tragic dimension. Indeed, Hans's inability to dissemble makes him the "dangerously subjective" (p. 259) and "radical person" ("radikaler Vogel," p. 38) his adversaries think him to be. In each episode his behavior goes to the heart of a relationship or to the root of a problem. His consistent unwillingness to conform to marriage, Christianity, the capitalism of West Germany, or the anticapitalism of East Germany, and his refusal to accept superficial denazification or the social role of money makes him a controversial figure. This radicalism in Hans is the reason why people feel uneasy in his presence and explains the furor produced by the book itself.[2]

As the novel opens, Hans, the clown, recounts his limping back to his pension in Bochum after a disastrous performance the previous evening during which he has injured his knee. Since his "wife," Marie, has left him six months earlier, he has been unable to concentrate on his work and has lost his reputation as a skilled performer. For the last three weeks he has been drinking excessively, although he knows the last performance for a drinking clown is in the gutter. Marie's desertion has so upset the rhythm of his existence that the metaphor "He doesn't know whether he is coming or going" has become a reality. Hans mistakes the train station for the hotel and the hotel for the station; in the hotel he searches for his train ticket and at the station he asks the porter for his room number.

Hans's wounded knee is only the outward manifestation of an inner sickness, a melancholia which has destroyed his objectivity and heightened his subjectivity. Since Marie's departure, he relates to all events and recalls all episodes from the narrow perspective of self. This acute vantage point enhances his critical faculty. Not the slightest hypocrisy escapes his sensitive scrutiny. Whether he measures the moral fluctuations of the past or the present, his feelings, like an ethical seismograph, register the slightest deviations from the norm of personal and social morality while recording the subtlest expressions of humanity.

For such a story Böll has wisely chosen first-person narration.[3] In *The Clown* there is no objectivity, no meticulous weighing of both sides of an issue, but merely the straightforward re-actions of a desperate person. Hans's obsession with self isolates him from others. His isolation in the course of the narrative is interrupted by only two persons, his father, who visits him, and his neighbor's wife, who passes him in the hall. The con-versations in chapter 1 with Kostert, the director of a Christian educational organization, who swindles him out of his fee, take place on the phone and through a closed door. This meta-phor of Hans's isolation and voluntary segregation from the world recurs throughout the novel. In fact, the telephone consistently functions as a reminder of Hans's separation from people. As Hans returns to his apartment in Bonn, it is dusk, about six o'clock.[4] For the next three and a half hours, before he hobbles back to the train station, he has had twelve phone conversations with friends, relatives, and acquaintances of Marie, but little communciation. Hans desires two things from these conversations: to find Marie and to raise money. He discovers the worst possible news about Marie, that she is in Rome on a honeymoon, and he is unable to raise a single penny.

The novel is structured around the several phone calls which Hans makes and receives. Before, during, and after each call, in a stream-of-consciousness narration, Hans relates past events involving each person he talks to on the phone. His recollections range from the war, especially its final days, to the present, but most of them reveal the quality of his life with Marie.

The Clown is both a love story and a social critical novel. Both aspects of the work are of equal importance. From the moment Hans decides to go to Marie's room "to do the things man and wife do together" (p. 48), he never doubts that his relationship with her will be a union for life. He immediately asserts: "I was proud that Marie was my wife" (p. 66) and on returning home, he says to his brother: "I was with a girl, with a woman, my wife" (p. 72). Marie, too, appears to make the same commitment, for she refers to Hans as "my husband" (p. 190) and whispers to him after her miscarriage the words of the marriage ceremony: "Till death do us part" (pp. 197, 286). Thus Hans is insisting on a form of marriage common in the Middle Ages[5] when the church was not involved in effecting the legality of the sacrament, when marriage consisted of mutual consent and a public announcement of the union. His intention is clear when he tells Kinkel: "As far as I have been instructed, according to the Catholic concept of marriage the couple bestow the sacrament on themselves . . . and if they are doubly and triply married by the state and church and do not bestow the sacrament there is no marriage" (p. 113).[6]

Hans's initial refusal to participate in a civil or church wedding, as well as his refusal to raise his children as Catholics,[7] indicates that during his marriage he was consistently an outsider. Thus it is not surprising that shortly after his marriage he becomes a professional clown, i.e., one who stands apart from society in order to criticize it. He attacks the church mainly as a clerical institution which is unconcerned with either the spiritual or physical quality of life of the faithful. The representatives of the church show no interest in preserving an existing union between Hans and Marie, but seek to coerce Marie to bow to "abstract principles of order" (p. 91). Hans intuitively understands and does not hesitate to point out that the insistence on "abstract principles of order" at the price of humanity (whether in religion or politics) leads directly to the "torture chamber" (p. 91). Within the confines of the novel, the church offers no salvation, only damnation. It is not the way to eternal or temporal happiness, but the cul-de-sac of misery and the dead end of charity. The episodes which involve the priest Heinrich Behlen reveal the church's failure in this regard more cogently than those relating directly to the dispute over Hans's marriage. When the young cleric attempts to relieve Hans and Marie's poverty by giving them money from the Caritas Fund, Heinrich's pastor refuses to permit the money for the poor to be used for the young couple. And when Heinrich attempts to comfort Marie at the time of her miscarriage, the church's teaching on the fate of unbaptized infants negates his kind words.

The exact reasons for Marie's leaving Hans and the failure of their marriage remain clouded. Hans seems unable to penetrate to the real cause. Their dispute about marriage seems only part of their problem. Hans readily acknowledges: "So much more was involved than I really understand" (p. 256), and in the first chapter he admits: "Perhaps I had never 'understood' Marie" (p. 18). Although Hans blames Marie's Catholic friends who instill in her a "metaphysical fear" of hell for living in sin, this accusation fails to explain completely the collapse of their marriage. Recent feminist criticism rightly suggests that a contributing factor in Hans's myopic view of Marie, his failure to consider her a person in her own right, and his seeking her as "a valuable property, as an appendage to himself, as a sex object and someone who could be counted upon to fill his every need."[8] In Hans's narrative, the reader also senses her growth of self-awareness and recognizes her search for social approval, which it is impossible to find with Hans. But the irony of Marie's choice of a bourgeois Catholic marriage to save her soul and her search for social fulfillment in the Catholic circle is that both of these decisions will lead to a more emotionally restrictive, more spiritually repressive, and less morally reward- ing existence than her unsatisfactory life with the outsider Hans.

Every incident which treats Hans in the novel: whether as student, son, brother, husband, performer, or guest in East Germany, emphasizes his isolated status. He is, in fact, as he himself asserts, capable of living with only one person, Marie, and even at that he fails. But Hans derives from his detached vantage point a clear vision of truth about society—if not about himself.

Because of his nature, Hans sees things differently from everyone else. A good example is his view of the living and the dead. His sister Henriette and the orphan Georg, because they died victims of a senseless nationalism, are alive while their "murderers," his mother and Kalick, because they prosper in high places without experiencing sorrow for their deeds, are dead. In this manner Hans erects for the victims of Fascism a monument in his mind, and the author Böll provides a power- ful metaphor for the deep structural meaning of the New Testament in which sin is declared the death of the soul (Rom. 6:23) and to die in grace is to be born to eternal life (John 3:36; 17:2–3).

Hans gives another example of his status as clown in the exchange with his mother. When he hears her president-of-the central-committee voice over the phone, he spontaneously answers: "Here is a delegate of the Central Committee of Jewish Yankees. May I speak to your daughter?" (p. 39), and thereby evokes his mother's recriminating response: "You can't forget that, can you?" (p. 39). This exchange focuses on one of the aspects of Hans's personality which sets him apart and makes him dangerous to most of the characters in the novel. He will not forget the Nazi past. In this regard, he resembles those surviving Germans with a memory: Albert, Robert, Nella

Bach, and Johanna Fähmel, while Mrs. Schnier resembles those Fascists who force their consciences into oblivion to more eagerly enjoy the good life: the Gäselers and the Nettlingers.

Even when Hans agrees to marry Marie officially and to sign the papers to raise his children as Catholics, when he is ready to accede to all conditions to keep Marie, and when he is willing to accept his father's money, his unique nature prevents him from conforming to society. In the final, fateful moments that determine the successful social accommodation, Hans proves incapable of an action which betrays his nature. His instinct and intuition save the integrity of his status as clown when his will and reason fail him. This natural protective irrationalism explains his self-defeating impulse to mime a blind man during the conversation with his father over money. This defensive mechanism protects him from making conciliatory gestures of obeisance—no matter how slight—such as accepting coffee made by his father; and it determines his manner of agreeing to marry Marie in a way which makes his offer insulting rather than loving and, therefore, unacceptable.

Also, in his choice of friends, Hans reveals his isolated status. Because he is a clown, he gets on with no one who represents established society. His friend old Derkum is feared by the CDU, denied a mayorship by the Communists, and boycotted by Catholic children; his friend the priest Heinrich Behlen is treated as a social pariah for marrying without laicization; his friend Edgar Wieneken is suspect because of his concern for social justice; and the old priest Strüder, with whom Hans establishes the rudiments of a friendship on the telephone, is the person "nobody takes seriously" (p. 293), the person maintained at the seminary "on sufferance only" (p. 293), the one ostracized in his own community. It is not surprising that Böll chooses Strüder to proclaim the novel's biblical motto (Isaiah 52:15; Rom. 15:21)—which, translated freely, serves as a guiding principle for every social dissident: those who think they are right are wrong, and those who are thought wrong are right. In other words, all of Hans's friends live on the fringes of acceptability.

Hans disdains those who have made their peace with society, especially the intellectuals of the Catholic circle, because they have forsaken what he sees as their responsibility as social critics. Kinkel, Sommerwild, and Blothert represent the intellect betrayed because they find no fault with the status quo in the church, because their intelligence offers no critique of the economic order even though they profess concern for "poverty in the society in which we live" (p. 23). Instead, these men defend the existing order, support the ruling powers, ignore the poor and the suffering to side with political and religious institutions. Kinkel, "the gray eminence of German Catholicism" (p. 110), has given up his vision of social justice and now produces watered-down political tracts out of a mixture of "Marx plus Guardini, or Bloy plus Tolstoi" (p. 103). Blothert bleats incessantly, "Ca ca ca" (p. 130) for chancellor and Catholic (intended or not, a scatological abbreviation for the power structure of the Adenauer era: the church and the CDU-state). Prelate Sommerwild brews "honeywater" sermons out of "Rilke, Hofmannsthal, and Newman" (p. 132) for his following of religious aesthetes and defends a juridical concept of marriage taken from the Council of Trent against Hans's informal theological model of marriage taken from the Middle Ages. And Fedebeul uses his intelligence to campaign for the CDU.

In contrast to such opportunists Hans remains faithful to his ethical status as a clown. No episode makes this clearer than his visit to East Germany. There he refuses to perform anticapitalistic skits because to do so would violate his concept of artistic integrity. Hans's defense of his refusal argues for social responsibility: "I have first to study the living conditions in this country because humor [art] lies in presenting people in abstract situations which are taken from their own reality and not from a foreign one" (p. 262).

Disdain for the intellectuals of the Catholic circle is matched by Hans's contempt for his capitalistic parents. "The holy German soil," of which Hans's mother frequently speaks, remains "holy" only in as far as it produces profit for the family. As soft-coal magnates, the Schniers have lived richly from the earth of Germany for seventy years. The German soil has provided them with wealth and has shielded them from the economic vicissitudes of war and peace. They have, as Walter Hinck maintains, "survived political change because in silent collaboration they have profited from each government, from Hitler's economic buildup as well as from postwar reconstruction, from dictatorship and democracy."[9] The exhortation of Hans's mother to defend the holy German soil is an order to her family to protect their class right to continued exploitation of the nation's wealth for their personal benefit. Although her words fall on the deaf ears of Hans and Henriette, Hans's father takes up the call to defense. With his image as a lovable, wise old man of business, he serves as a symbol and an advertisement for his class. With his kind face, his polite manner, his philanthropic air, he goes frequently into public battle to secure his family's right to profit. Hans avers that his father's investments span so many industries it is impossible for him to go through a single day without enriching his family: "Whether I buy cigarettes, soap, stationery, ice cream on a stick, or sausage, my father has shares in the company" (p. 141).

Hans's brother Leo fails Hans, too. His conversion to Catholicism and his desire to become a priest, while being a sign of his turning away from the convictions and values of his parents, is merely a turn to the religion of Sommerwild and the hypocritical Catholic circle, not to the Christianity of Heinrich Behlen and the old priest Strüder. Religion does not awaken Leo's compassionate understanding of others, especially of his brother. When Hans calls the seminary to speak to Leo, Leo will not risk the consequences of breaking a nine o'clock curfew to bring his brother needed money and consolation. Given the picture of the church as depicted in the novel, the incident confirms the reader's belief that Leo, because of his placing institutional rules before the claims of humanity, will become successful as a cleric but will fail as a person.

When at the end of the novel Hans puts on his makeup to become a beggar, he does not relinquish the idea that his act, his presence on the steps of the train station, will have consequences for those who know him, especially Marie, her Catholic friends, and his family. A spark remains alive in Hans's desperate negativism, the hope that out of his total rejection of the West German status quo, some good may come.

II   End of a Mission

The novel *End of a Mission* (1966) begins with one of the most perfect expositions in all of Böll's works:

Before the county court of Birglar in the early fall of last year, a trial took place about which the public heard very little. Surprisingly, the three newspapers in Birglar county . . . published the identical short report: "Father and son Gruhl found a mild judge. County court judge Dr. Stollfuss, one of the most popular personalities in the public life of our county, in his last trial before retirement (upon which he will be honored in these pages in a coming issue) conducted the proceedings against Johann and Georg Gruhl of Huskirchen, whose inexplicable action of last June caused considerable excitement. After a one-day trial the Gruhls were ordered to make complete restitution of property and sentenced to six weeks' imprisonment. After brief counsel with their attorney Dr. Hermes of Birglar, the two men accepted the mild sentence. With their pretrial detention taken into account, the Gruhls were immediately set free.

The opening lines succinctly present the main characters of the novel, their roles in the events to follow, the time of the defendants' crime, the time and place of the action, and even the outcome of the trial, which seems to be surrounded by an aura of secrecy. But while the reader knows the Gruhls were found guilty, he does not know the nature of their crime, only that it was "inexplicable." Hence the story to follow is in part a mystery novel. The narrator's failure to state the Gruhls' crime creates the suspense the genre needs to hold the reader. Böll doubles the reader's curiosity by suggesting an official conspiracy in the vague but identical reports of three local newspapers.

Irony pervades the novel from the first page to the last. In the third paragraph of the work, Dr. Hollweg, the editor of the liberal newspaper, the last of the three editors who agree to ignore the trial, is shown succumbing to the pressure from above. This same editor concludes the novel with an argument for "free and independent" newspapers, an "indispensable" element, he maintains, for "freedom and democracy." Since the entire novel intervenes between these two scenes, the reader is apt to miss the irony. This kind of authorial subtleness permeates the novel, determines its style, structure, and method of narration, making it formally one of Böll's most successful works.

Most obvious at the formal level is the work's indebtedness to Kleist. The nature of suspense of the Gruhls' trial resembles that of Ruprecht's trial in Kleist's *The Broken Jug* and Kleist's treatment of the mystery of the Marquise's pregnancy in the novella *The Marquise of O*. The long, syntactically complex sentences in Böll's novel, the predominance of indirect discourse, and the ensuing preponderance of the subjunctive seem to come from Kleist. The long periods retard the action of the story, give the tale a relaxed, leisurely pace, at times bringing the events to a standstill, while the use of the subjunctive mood by an omniscient narrator puts the very reality of the story and the motives of the characters into question—another aspect of the novel's irony. The long sentences characterized by hypotaxis show a controlled world and a controlled society with everything in its place and everyone knowing his job and fulfilling it. This stylistic device is the opposite of the paratactical style used by Böll in his early war stories to emphasize the ineluctability of fate which claims the lives of his characters.

Only on page twenty-six when the formal charges against the Gruhls are read does the reader discover that their "inexplicable" crime is the burning of a jeep belonging to the *Bundeswehr*. As the reader has his curiosity satisfied in one matter, it is aroused, in the typical fashion of a mystery story, by another. Why would the Gruhls burn a jeep? After the protest character of their deed becomes obvious, the reasons for the official conspiracy of silence becomes known and the Gruhls confess, the reader would like to discover how the Gruhls will merit the light sentence mentioned in the first paragraph, one equivalent to acquittal. What will be their defense? Only on page 212, four-fifths of the way through the novel, does Dr. Hermes, the defense attorney (significantly named after the Greek god of trickery and cleverness), reveal that his clients produced a "happening" and should therefore be seen as artists, not as political troublemakers. It is also at this point, where moral protest hides behind society's acceptance of artistic freedom, that the novel, despite its formal accomplishments, compromises its moral dimension. More will be said on this topic later.

In Böll's essay "Einführung in Dienstfahrt" [Introduction to *End of a Mission*, 1966], which appears in the collection *Aufsätze, Kritiken, Reden*, Böll discusses the genesis of the novel and explains his intention. A friend told him of a young soldier who was ordered to drive a jeep until the speedometer recorded the appropriate number of miles for inspection. The absurdity of the situation seemed good material for a short story. The first version, according to Böll, was fifteen pages long, the second forty, the third seventy. By now none of the original characters remained and the material became less fascinating to him than the form that the story would take. "At this point," Böll continues,

I thought how the complete niceness (*Nettigkeit*) of society to art is nothing more than a kind of padded cell. At the same time I was reading about the provos in Amsterdam and their Happenings. I recognized that all art is taken seriously by this bewildering and incomprehensible society. This recognition brought me to the idea that art, that is, a Happening, is perhaps the last chance to break out of this padded cell; it can become a time bomb or the way to take the director of this madhouse out of action with a poisoned chocolate sweet. I decided on a combination of poisoned chocolates and a time bomb. (*AKR*, pp. 264–265)

Böll's story, then, became in his mind a novelistic attack on society's values. To deliver this package, Böll concludes, "I would . . . need several very nice people, and several chocolate sweets very nicely packaged" (*AKR*, p. 265). By now Böll had reached the fifth version of the novel, which was much too long; after some editing by his wife, a seventh version was ready for the publisher.

In the published version of the novel, Böll's time bomb appears as the burning of the jeep and his poisoned chocolate sweets as the several nicely packaged criticisms of society, delivered in the testimonies of several very nice people who are, for the most part, model citizens, exemplars of social efficiency and humanity. After publication, however, Böll felt that the critics failed to recognize his purpose. In a conversation with Christian Linder, he complained that the main point had been missed: "In *End of a Mission* the burning of an army jeep is violence against things in the form of a work of art; it is naturally pure satire or irony, a challenge to produce art" (*Drei Tage im März*, p. 89). And in an interview with Ludwig Arnold, he was more explicit: "In *End of a Mission* my intention was not recognized. I believe that the demand for action in the work, the connection between the Happening as a recognizable work of art and as a political act was unjustifiably slighted. Very little of that intention was recognized by critics. I find, however, that my intention is presented legitimately and clearly enough in the book. That art can be a vehicle for political or social action was the idea" (*Im Gespräch*, p. 34).

The misunderstanding Böll refers to can be corroborated by a few quotations. The *Rhein-Neckar Zeitung* called the novel "a savory entertainment" (10 October 1966). The *Hannoversche Allgemeine* saw in it "no aggressiveness, just humor" (24 September 1966). The leftist periodical *Konkret*, to which, after December 1975, Böll became a regular contributor, referred to the novel as a "cool, ironical, happy, pleasant mature work" (No. 9, 1966). Other reviewers found it "roguish" and called it a "little comedy."[10] Although Werner Hoffmeister recognized the novel's satirical anger, he concluded that it "is articulated in a form more relaxed and yet more controlled than before; there is more playfulness and more subtlety."[11] But Werner Ross acknowledged most succintly the novel's failure to achieve its goal: "Böll employs his entire shining narrative talent to make a flame out of a fire" (*Der Schriftsteller HB*, p. 86).

Since Böll's intention is so often misinterpreted, Rainer Nägele inquires if the fault is not Böll's own. He wonders "if this misunderstanding is not placed in the novel itself and, therefore, is no misunderstanding" (*H.B. Einführung*, p. 148). Nägele's question is to the point. Several reasons exist for the book's failure to carry out its author's purpose. The intention underlying the novel becomes lost in the very decency of Rhenish village life with all its potential for humanity. The source of the social evil which the book attacks is attributed to the big city which never appears in the novel. The wonderful people of Birglar with their sympathy for the defendants present the society of the novel as positive if not as perfect. In the village, respect for others flourishes, as exemplified by the villagers' attitude toward the prostitute Sani Seiffert; tolerance for the opinions of others prevails, as exemplified by the esteem shown Pastor Kolb; civility is the standard for human intercourse, as exemplified by the representatives of the differing parties, and simple wisdom and openness to art blooms, as exemplified by the villagers' attitude toward the exhibition of the erotic paintings and to the craftsmanship of the Gruhls. Hence what comes from this province, including its system of justice, appears to have a merciful face. This demonstration of provincial goodness dampens the novel's intended criticism of society's corruptness because Birglar does not stand apart from society, but is a part of the order the novel attacks.

Böll intends, no doubt, some irony in the humaneness of the life of the village; for these good people of the village carry out the functions of the corrupt system. Judge Stollfuss, bailiff Hall, the officer of the court Schroer, the police chief Kirfel, the court stenographer Aussen, and the editors of the newspapers with all their humor, compassion, and respect for people are, nonetheless, willing administrators of the corruption depicted in the novel. They execute the conspiracy, conceived in the big city to thwart the Gruhl's protest. This state of affairs gives rise to several questions. Are the Stollfusses, etc., really such good people after all? If so, then the society that is run by them cannot be such a corrupt place because good people administer the laws as humanely as possible. Or are the Stollfusses really not such good people because they knowingly function as cogs in a corrupt system? Stollfuss himself refers to the economic process and to the society he serves as "merciless' and "pitiless" (p. 239). Nonetheless, the reader, even the one familiar with Böll's work and his comments on the novel, still inclines to see the county of Birglar as that positive model of *Heimat* Böll speaks of in his *Frankfurter Vorlesungen*, that corner of the earth for which one can feel homesickness, as in fact Frau Kugl-Egger, does, as that place where people have names and faces and are not anonymous numbers, where there is community and not just society, where art is appreciated as natural human expression and not as a commercial product.

The positive picture of the village, indeed, overwhelms the reader, and this in spite of the general opportunism on the part of some of its inhabitants. The judge is a humanist, but his expression of humanity in the Gruhl case is just as much prescribed from on high as it is the inclination of his personality. His desire to help the Gruhls in an orderly, unobtrusive manner serves his own career as much as it benefits the Gruhls. His clever leniency permits him to retire from the bench with distinction and the hope of a Federal Service Cross. Opportunism is obvious elsewhere also. Hollweg and the other editors agree to go along with the conspiracy of silence concerning the trial because it is in their own interests to serve the powers of society. The attorney Hermes pursues a course of defense worked out in advance with the judge and the authorities in the big city (but not with the prosecutor) to save his clients, a defense designed not to assist the Gruhls' desire to protest against absurdity in the system, but rather to acquit his clients and to aid the authorities in thwarting the protest. Hermes thus furthers his own career by proving he is a capable lawyer with whom the state can work and on whom it can depend. The prosecutor Kugl-Eggers, when he discovers Hermes's intention and realizes that the judge and his superiors have already agreed to this defense, exclaims: "At this moment I knew that I had been betrayed and sold out. . . . Higherups and high places have forced me into a position which compels me to irresponsibility and to act against my nature" (pp. 212, 217). However, he quickly recognizes his best interests and goes along with the intended direction of the trial. The opportunism in the Gruhl case embraces all parties and all participants.

The net result is a picture of kindly justice leading to a happy ending. The Gruhls are effectively freed; damages for the jeep are paid by the wealthy Agnes Hall, who plans also to pay Johann Gruhl's outstanding tax debt. Georg Gruhl will marry the prettiest girl in the village and take over his father's shop. A jeep, provided by Agnes Hall, will be burned annually, an event destined to become an occasion rather than a social protest, and Agnes Hall even makes Johann Gruhl the heir of her estate. In the midst of this victorious happy ending for the Gruhls, the triumph of the corrupt system goes by almost unnoticed. The system has kept the potentially dangerous political character of the Gruhls' act out of the public eye and has managed to present itself, in the process, as a nice, pleasant, friendly, institutionalized but fair social order, clever in its own interests, perhaps, but not vicious, even mild and humane.

Böll's failure to get across his idea also lies in the presentation of the novel's central event, the happening, and in the attitude which the Gruhls display toward it. The Gruhls are no less opportunists than the others involved in the trial. They retreat from their intention of social protest, permit higher authorities to play down their case by agreeing quietly to mild treatment. They refuse to demand a jury trial and do not force the trial to a higher court in order to effect a public hearing of their cause. The narrator has a point when he claims this obligingness "betokened a tacit but palable concession and at the same time a request for concession" (pp. 17–18). The Gruhls accommodate society in spite of their claim of "having not the slightest regard for justice and the law" (p. 20) and their insistence that their cooperation with the court is out of "respect for the judge" and "respect for the witnesses, especially Police Chief Kirffel, whom [they do] not want to leave in the lurch or cause diffculty for" (p. 20). This kind of participation, although partly a manifestation of friendship, retreats from principle, destroys the cutting edge of Böll's novel, defuses his time bomb, and neutralizes the poison in his chocolate creams. The effectiveness of the novel's moral criticism is diminished, however, not because the actions of desertion and arson are done by less than perfect heroes, but because these less than perfect heroes do not recognize that they have sold out their cause. For the Gruhls' compromise still to have been an effective protest against the military establishment, they would have had to acknowledge that they have in them a degree of the soldier Kuttke's moral ambivalence. They would have had to recognize that they are in collision with the state to avoid punishment for their protest just as the state is in collusion with them to keep the protest meaningless. In contrast to the Gruhls, Private Kuttke effects better Böll's critical intention by crassly flaunting his profitable symbiotic relationship with the military.

The system (state, military) indicates its own weakness and shows it fears the effects this trial could have on the public by charging the Gruhls with the lesser crimes of gross misdemeanor and destruction of property instead of desertion and arson. The Gruhls compromise their position also in that they do not press their advantage. In accepting their lawyer's line of defense (they may just as well have pleaded temporary insanity or extenuating circumstances due to extreme emotional and financial pressure), they weaken their moral and ethical position. Their presumed intention of using art as a vehicle for political-social action becomes merely the use of art as an apology for political-social action. Thus, they severely diminish the moral persuasiveness of the novel. In the story, art becomes less a means of protest than a way to avoid confrontation, less a challenge to society than a way to avoid responsibility. For the generation of Americans who grew up with the civil disobedience and nonviolent protest of Martin Luther King and the movement against the war in Vietnam, the Gruhls offer a very ambiguous moral model. From the standpoint of strategy for social change, the novel shows art more as an avoidance of personal consequences than as a raising of collective consciousness.

In comparing the Gruhls to the hero of the short story "Du fährst zu oft nach Heidelberg" [You Go to Heidelberg Too Often, 1977],[12] although here the protagonist intends no social protest, believes, in fact, that the system will treat him fairly, the reader discovers that there the protagonist is not intimidated by the corruptness of the state. He maintains his friendship with Chilean Communist exiles against pressure from his family, sweetheart, future in-laws, and even the representatives of the state, who all suggest his frequent trips to Heidelberg will affect his future career. This story offers a more successful protest against the social evil of job discrimination (Berufsverbot) than the novel does against the military and the tax structure. This occurs because the rhetorical means of persuasion in these two works is not primarily logos but ethos, and the young would-be teacher communicates his ethics without adulteration; the Gruhls do not.

Commenting on End of a Mission, Manfred Durzak argues that in the course of Böll's writing the novel the original theme (demasking the absurdity of the military, its waste of time, money, and human resources) became coupled with the new theme of the social role of art. The element that successfully binds the two themes, he claims, is lacking. The moral protest gets lost in the manner in which the Gruhls assert their protest is art.[13] This observation penetrates the heart of the novel's problem.

In the Gruhls' compromise, in the demonstrated ability of the system to control the press, judges, lawyers, the course of justice, society has shown that it has the power, at least on the level of the model presented in the novel, to contain the social effects of art. This is the exact opposite result of Böll's intention. Still the novel shows by omission that without rational political action, preferably with a broad base of support, nothing changes in society—certainly not the tax structure or the wastefulness of the military.

CHAPTER 9

Novels of the 1970s: The Search for a Social Alternative

I   Group Portrait with Lady

FIVE years after *End of a Mission* Böll published his next major prose work, the novel *Group Portrait with Lady* (1971). When the Swedish Academy awarded him the Nobel Prize for literature in 1972, it singled out *Group Portrait* for special praise. Although Böll had often been a nominee for the Nobel award, it is safe to say that had *Group Portrait* not appeared in 1971, he would not have received the award in 1972. Kiepenheuer & Witsch's publicity for the novel proclaimed the book as Bölls "most comprehensive, encompassing work," labeling it a "summation" of his previous oeuvre. The claims of the publisher Böll found "a little too pretentious" but accepted the use of the word "summation" "as far as such expressions apply."[1]

In *Group Portrait* the first paragraph introduces the main character Leni, giving her age (forty-eight), her height and weight, her maiden name (Gruyten), reporting that she was married for three days in 1941 to a career soldier named Pfeiffer, that she has been a working woman for thirty-two years (five years in her father's office and twenty-seven in a garden nursery), suggesting that the cause of her current poverty began with the selling of her valuable house for a pittance during the inflation at war's end, stating without explanation that she no longer works although she is relatively young, in good health, and in need of money, and concluding with the comment that her son is serving a prison sentence.

Böll states his intention with the story in an interview with Dieter Wellershoff: "I tried to describe or to write the story of a

German woman in her late forties who had taken upon herself the burden of history from 1922–1970."[2] In the novel, the third-person narrator states the same intention with only slightly different emphasis: "He has one and only one thing in mind: to put a quiet and silent, proud, unrepentent person like Leni Gruyten-Pfeiffer in the proper light" (p. 237).

After the opening paragraph, the narrator or, as he calls himself, the *"Verfasser"* (*Verf.*), rendered in the English version as the "Author" (Au.), proceeds to introduce the characters who will be his informants in his search for the real Leni, the naive woman who was a candidate in the Nazi years for the title "most German girl" in her city (Cologne, but unnamed in the novel), who was called at various stages of her life a "stupid goose" (p. 33), a "proletarian materialist" (p. 35), a "mystic" (p. 37), and an "innocent" (p. 134), but who is now denigrated by the world as a "Russian sweetheart" (p. 376), a "Communist whore" (p. 9), a "tramp" (p. 9), a "used mattress" (p. 9), and as someone who could best serve the world by letting herself be gassed (pp. 10, 20).

After introducing Leni and the informants who will provide the facts for Leni's early life in chapter 1, the narrator opens chapter 2 with a reference to Leni as a school girl in 1938. Chapter 2 presents Leni's prewar and early war years, showing the failure of her formal education and her rejection of organized religion because it neglected the sensual side of her existence. Chapter 2 carries Leni's life to the year 1940, the time of the death of her brother Heinrich and her cousin Erhard in Denmark. Chapter 3 gives the background of Leni's youth by presenting the lives of her father, mother, and brother, dwells on Leni's abortive love affair with her cousin Erhard and explains that her cousin and brother did not die as war heroes in Denmark, but were executed there for the absurd crime of trying to sell an antitank gun to the Danes. Thus Heinrich's farewell statement to his family before leaving for Denmark: "Garbage, garbage—garbage is all I want to be, nothing but garbage" (p. 58), besides introducing the key motif of "refuse," betrays his self-condemnation for serving in Hitler's army, prophesies his act of protest against Nazi Germany, and prepares the way for the suicidal despair in his last words before the firing squad: "Shit on Germany" (p. 78). Cousin Erhard, the poet and Leni's shy lover, manages before his death a more humorous, ironic statement of disdain: "We are dying for a noble profession, for the weapons trade" (p. 79).

Chapter 4 continues the Gruyten story in June 1941 with Hubert Gruyten's reaction to the death of his son. Gruyten loses interest in his prosperous construction company and turns it over to his employees, while at the same time founding a new fictitious company with make-believe Russian workers. With this new firm he becomes even wealthier and more generous, hoping, by swindling the government and by distributing his wealth, to take revenge on the regime and to justify his existence. At a company party given for the Gruyten employees, Leni meets Alois Pfeiffer. She mistakes his sensual dancing for an indication of a loving sensuality; she is seduced, only to discover in Alois a crude, egocentric lover. On 24 June 1941, three days after their wedding, Alois is killed in battle. Leni's laconic comment sums up the marriage and the relationship: "He died for me before he was dead" (p. 125).[3] After Alois's death, Leni renews her visits to the convent where she was educated in order to see her old friend and mentor in materialistic sensuality, the mystical Jewish nun, Sister Rahel. Because of the miserable way her order conceals and feeds her, Sister Rahel dies of malnutrition near the end of 1942. At this time a Slavist named Scholsdorff, working for the revenue office, discovers Hubert Gruyten's fraudulent company of "dead souls," Schelmm and Son.[4] He becomes suspicious of the names of Gruyten's Russian workers, all of whom are characters from Russian literature. As a result of the crime, Leni's father goes to prison and all the family wealth and property except the house in which Leni lives are confiscated. The series of family disasters— the business scandal, the imprisonment of Hubert Gruyten, the execution of Heinrich—combine to cause the death of Leni's mother also at the end of 1942.

Chapter 5 begins in 1943 with Leni at the age of twenty-one, bereft of father, mother, brother, lover, friend, husband, and a comfortable existence, forced to start a new life as a worker. She makes the transition from bourgeois to proletarian existence without knowing the transition has been made. She is naively unaware of social classes as she is innocently unaware of what a Jew is in Nazi Germany. She finds employment in a wreath factory attached to a nursery adjacent to the city cemetery. Here she works with Nazis, neutrals, and two anti-Nazis (a Communist, Frau Ilse Kremer, and a Jewish woman with false papers, the erstwhile Rhenish separatist Frau Liane Hölthohne, born Elli Marx).

The owner of the nursery and factory is Walter Pelzer, one of Böll's most successful literary creations. Pelzer's unscrupulous acquisition of wealth is less a manifestation of greed than a reaction to his boyhood fear of poverty and repossessors who frequently came to his father's door. He decided early in life to avoid financial misery. By collecting gold teeth during World War I from dead American soldiers (an occupation he justifies with the pragmatic rationale that the Americans were dead and he was alive). Pelzer returns from World War I with a nest egg that keeps the bailiff from his door for the rest of his life. Always adjusting to the times, he joins after the war in turn the *Freikorps* and the Communist party, by 1929 becomes a Storm Trooper and a Nazi party member, reverts to anti-fascism in the 1940s with the rationale: "Ich bin doch kein Unmensch" [After all, I'm not a monster] (p. 208), and a few days before the end of the war officially resigns from the party and becomes a democrat. Pelzer possesses the existential agility to have his conscience and his pocketbook survive unscathed the vicissitudes of history. He helps the right people at the right times for both noble and selfish motives, risks as little as possible to invest in good deeds when they promise to pay dividends. He is an arch-opportunist, a Rhenish mixture of "criminality and humanity" (p. 195), a man who can persuade his friends, associates, and even his enemies that he is not a thorough scoundrel.

Chapter 6 picks up Leni's story in December 1943 after she has been working for Pelzer for about one year. In that month Boris Lvovich Kolotovski, a Russian POW, comes to work in Pelzer's wreath factory. Chapters 6 and 7 present the central episodes of the novel, the secret love affair between Leni and Boris. These chapters introduce Bogakov, Boris's fellow POW and confidant, and the "exalted personage" (Herr Hochgestellt), an anonymous German industrialist and behind-

the-scenes politician who during the war protects Boris because of a prewar business friendship with Boris's father. These
chapters are also structurally the center of the novel.

On Boris's first day at work, Leni offers him a cup of her
precious coffee. To the Fascists who work in the nursery this
simple and natural act of humanity to a Russian prisoner attacks
the foundations of the Third Reich and insults those who have
fought and died in the war. Kremp, a war amputee, dashes the
cup (of kindness) from Leni's hand. Leni picks it up in
silence (estimated meticulously by the "Au." to have lasted
approximately forty-eight seconds), washes it "like a holy
chalice" (p. 185), and immediately offers Boris a second cup
of her priceless coffee. This gesture, both knowing and naive,
is typical of her character—knowing, in that she will not tolerate, much less perpetrate, an act of inhumanity even as slight
as the failure to offer a cup of hospitality; naive, in that she
is not fully aware of all the ramifications and implications of
her act: "Leni only knew what she did when she did it; she
had to materialize everything" (p. 190). Yet, with her gesture
she transforms the subhuman Russian into a human being.
On the second day, when Leni again brings Boris his coffee,
"she laid her left hand on his right and it went through him . . .
like an electric shock" (p. 191). Both immediately "dissolved
in flames" (p. 191). Boris sat upright "like a resurrection,"
(p. 191), and Leni experienced something "more beautiful"
(p. 191) than her spontaneous orgasm on the heath when she
was sixteen years old. In this scene of the "laying on of hands"
(p. 190), Böll obviously expands further the love-at-first-sight
motif of his earlier works. Here there is fulfillment of love
prior to a word being exchanged between the lovers.

Chapter 7 continues the story of Leni's love affair with Boris
from their whispered "I love you" (p. 214) before the door to
the toilet, their first kiss behind the bales of peatmoss (February 1944), to their first sexual union in the nursery on 18 March
during a daylight air raid when everyone else in the factory
flees for shelter. Leni calls this day her "engagement" (p. 226).
At this time they do not yet know each other's full name
because they rarely had more than a few fleeting seconds together. During the frequent air raids after February 1944

Boris and Leni meet in a crypt in the adjacent cemetery. One of these meetings, 28 May, she calls her "wedding day" (p. 226). In October, nine daylight raids take place, causing Leni to call October "the month of the glorious mysteries" (p. 226). By the end of 1944 in consequence of her providing coffee, cigarettes, and extra food for herself and Boris, Leni has accrued a huge debt. To satisfy it she sells her house to an old friend and bookkeeper of her father's, Otto Hoyser.

Beginning with chapter 8 the structure of the novel changes. Up to this time there have been no long narrative passages, only the reporting of phrases and sentences uttered by the informants, accompanied by long pedantic commentary by the "Au." evaluating his information. It seems as if Böll himself had tired of his method at this point. The method, in fact, curtailed one of his greatest talents—his narrative power. Up to this point, the story moved lengthwise, chronologically forward from 1938 to 1945. With chapter 8, it begins to move crosswise. The "Au.," instead of assembling and commenting on his collected quotations and documents, lets each important character tells his own story about the end of the war, especially the circumstances of 2 March 1945, the day of the nine-hour Allied raid on the city of Cologne, the event which marked, for many people, the end of the war. During this raid, Leni's son is born. The birth of Lev and his baptism by Pelzer highlight what is the shortlived "soviet paradise in the tombs." During these separate narrations, in which the personae of the novel bring their lives up to 1970, Böll demonstrates his remarkable skill, not alone in narrative, but also in his mastery of various levels of everyday language. Each informant speaks in his own voice. The reader is able to identify the informants individually by the tone of their sentences and their diction.[5] Thus with chapter 8 the investigation of Leni's life shifts from a diachronic to a synchronic presentation. The various accounts of the war's end fill in the background of Leni's life from January 1945 to June 1945, the month Boris, in a German uniform, carrying false papers, is captured by the Americans, transferred to the custody of the French, and dies laboring in a mine in Lorraine.

Chapter 9 begins with an account of Leni's postwar asso-

ciation with the Communist party. This section of the book is
Böll's strongest attack against institutionalized communism. The
party has no understanding of Leni's natural proletarianism and
no comprehension of her instinctive communism. She is a
Communist as Böll once said he was a Catholic: the way a
black man is black. Leni simply lives communism every day
of her life. "She obstinately, inarticulately, but consistently
avoids every form of profit-thinking, doesn't reject it, that pre-
supposes some form of articulation, but simply shrinks from it"
(p. 348). Leni wants to be a Communist for the simple reason
that Russia produced a man like Boris. This section of the book
also pillories the Communist party for the Soviet non-aggression
pact with Hitler in 1939, the persecution of dissident party
members, and the invasion of Czechoslovakia in 1968.

Nothing is reported on Leni's life between 1945 and 1970.
The story in chapter 9 quickly shifts to the present, as the role
of the "Au." changes from a reporter and commentator to a
character in the story he is telling. In effect, he takes over as
protagonist. He travels to Rome to follow up the investigation
of Sister Rahel and the church's second betrayal of her, now
by concealing her sanctity. As it was awkward for the church
to have a Jew in a religious order in the Nazi era, it is em-
barrassing in the post-Vatican II era to have roses grow from
the grave and even from the cremated ashes of a nun denied
by the church. In Rome the "Au." meets Sister Klementina, the
investigator of the Sister Rahel affair, and falls in love with
her. On his return from Rome, the "Au." is invited to a meeting
of Leni's friends to save her from an eviction instigated by
Otto Hoyser, her father's old friend and present owner of her
house.

Chapter 10 recounts this meeting and the successful tactic
of blocking Leni's street with garbage trucks to delay her eviction until her friends can pay her debts. To round out the story,
the "Au." in chapter 11 quotes a psychologist's report on Leni's
son Lev, explaining his practice of "deliberate underachievement" in the realm of business, accompanied at times in the
realm of human relations by a policy of "deliberate over-
achievement." The report also explains the reason for Lev's imprisonment: crude forgeries designed to regain for his mother

the ownership of her house. Chapter 12 relates, in a letter to Leni from an attending male nurse, the death of Leni's friend Margret, who, in a clinic for treatment of venereal disease, dies blushing because of her "damned innocence" (p. 390). Although the compassionate Margret is considered a prostitute, she claims the only thing she ever did for money was to marry. According to the nurse, "She could not say no when she thought she could spread a little joy" (p. 387).

The final chapters grow increasingly short, consisting of only a few pages. Chapter 13 relates the death of the old Communist Ilse Kremer, and the final chapter provides a thorough "happy ending" for all of Leni's friends. Lev will soon be out of prison to provide for his mother. Leni's way of life seems secure for herself and her lodgers, and Sister Klementina has left the order to be by the narrator's side.

The structure of the novel is indeed complex, combining a diachronic and synchronic treatment of time and the integration of over one hundred and twenty-five characters into the story. Böll's own color diagram of the novel[6] with its outline of the characters, time levels, motifs, and incidents resembles more a modern nonobjective painting than a design of a novel. But even with a basic overview of the structure of the plot, the reader is far from having come to terms with this distinctive work. The style at times intentionally approaches philistinism in the "Au.'s" fanatic desire for objectivity. He constructs periods, some over a page in length (designed to exaggerate the style of the fiercest bureaucrat), with all the punctuation marks the language offers to make such a style possible: commas, colons, semicolons, dashes, parentheses, and ellipses. When the narrator enters the story as a character he even objectifies himself by writing of his activities in the third person. Even though the "Au." quotes his material, provides his sources, and verifies his informants' statements, he still struggles for a more pronounced cachet of objectivity. At one point he maintains he is not an "idealist," a "materialist," or a "realist," denies that he "has been to college," that he is a "Catholic, Protestant, Rhinelander, socialist, Marxist, liberal, for or against the sex wave, the pill, the pope . . . , for or against a free or planned economy" (p. 337). However, his objectivity must be taken lightly. He is not neutral

and not at all disinterestedly objective. He loves Leni, everything about her and all that she stands for. His whole report
glorifies that unique woman and calls nothing about her into
question. It claims objectivity only insofar as its intention is
to show that a woman who opposes society's values can be a
positive figure. Böll's *Group Portrait*, like several other works
of modern German literature—take any work by Günter Grass:
*The Tin Drum, The Dog Years, Cat and Mouse, Local Anaes-
thesia, The Flounder*, as an example—is informed with the most
intricate structural and symbolic patterning, but motivated by
the challenge to gain aesthetic control over the experience of
Nazi Germany, postwar guilt, and the inadequacies of West
German democracy. Any attempt at interpretation which concentrates on the patterning and ignores the purpose—or vice
versa—is wanting. In the case of *Group Portrait*, any criticism
which concentrates on the religious myth, the symbolism, the
structure, etc., without acknowledging the novel's intent of
offering an alternate model to Western capitalist society is similarly deficient.

Some of the complexity of the novel can now be dealt
with. Who is this "Au." for whom is he writing? That he is
writing for an audience, and not for himself, is clear in the
text. He apostrophizes a future audience and gives part of his
manuscript to the wife of the "exalted personage" to read. But
more puzzling than the intended audience of the report is the
identity of its author. Is he a journalist, a police, insurance, or
tax investigator, a free-lance writer? That he is working in a
professional capacity is proved by his frequent references to
legitimate tax deductions for the expenses of his research. This
method of reportage and montage which Böll has chosen has
several predecessors: Uwe Johnson's *Das dritte Buch über Achim*
[The Third Book about Achim, 1961], Hans Erich Nossack's
Der Fall d'Arthez [The Case of D'Arthez, 1968], Christa Wolf's
Nachdenken über Christa T. [The Quest for Christa T., 1968],
Siegfried Lenz's *Das Vorbild* [The Exemplary Model, 1973]; but
in each of these works the reader knows the narrator: a journalist trying to write a book about a famous sports figure, a security
agent preparing a dossier on a political suspect, a writer hoping
to understand her deceased friend, and a group of pedagogues

searching for a model for young people. In each of these works the reader knows why the narrator is writing and for whom. Böll's failure to provide these answers detracts from the book's wholeness. The format, as Böll admits in his interview with Heinz Ludwig Arnold, emulates that of a detective story.[7] Thus the reader has the right to expect the necessary information as a means of answering his legitimate questions, especially since the "Au." is not a postulated narrator but one of the major characters in the book. Böll's refusal to provide answers to the questions about the narrator is surely part of the work's intended irony, its sense of aesthetic play; but in this case it results in mere titillation and coquetry, diverting the reader's attention from the story itself.

Theodore Ziolkowski does much to throw light on the artistic function of the narrator[8] but cannot definitively answer the question who the narrator really is. His analysis focuses on the form and the strategy of the novel. He concludes that the "Au." functions as an *advocatus dei* in a beatification process. Important, however, to keep in mind is that the "Au." is a secularist working against the church's and society's accepted models of sanctity. He does not argue for the sainthood of Leni according to institutional or clerical conventions but according to religious, humanist standards. The body which renders the decision on the beatification of Leni is not the Congregation of Sacred Rites, but the reader himself. Leni is presented as a model of wholeness and innocence, of love and loyalty, of humanity and humaneness, of generosity, compassion, sexuality, and naturalness, all in contrast to the prevailing values of church, state, and economy. To destroy the old "iconography" is certainly Böll's intention, but to formulate a new one in the process, he recognizes, is inevitable.

The iconography of which Böll speaks in his interview with Manfred Durzak[9] has received general treatment, most notably from Ralph Ley, Ingeborg Carlson, Margareta Deschner, and Theodore Ziolokowski.[10] In chapter 1 the "Au." states: "She [Leni] has an intimate relationship with the Virgin Mary. She receives her almost daily on the T.V. screen. Each time she is surprised that the Virgin Mary is blond and no longer young as she expected. This meeting takes place in silence, usually

late at night when the neighbors are asleep and the usual T.V.
stations—even the one from Holland—have signed off" (p. 18).
This motif, introduced early in the novel, suggesting an identification between Leni and the Virgin Mary, justifies itself on
the last page: "It is she herself. It is she who appears to herself,
in some way still to be explained, as a reflection" (p. 400).
Hence Leni's association with Mary is a frame for the entire
novel. However, this identification is not merely stated at the
beginning and end of the work, but is reinforced throughout
by a network of motifs.

Leni is born on 17 August 1922 during the time the church
celebrates the feast of the Assumption of Mary into heaven.
Probably because she is born near this Marian holy day (15
August) she is christened Helene Maria (p. 135). At the age
of sixteen, in the summer of 1938, while lying on her back in
the heather on the heath, staring at the sky, she experiences a
spontaneous orgasm, a "Seinserfüllung." She felt "opened," having been "taken," and having "given." Leni confesses she would
not have been surprised if she had become pregnant. From this
moment on she claims the virgin birth is no longer incomprehensible to her (p. 29). Although she soon afterwards stops
practicing her Catholic religion, she continues to pray the *Ave
Maria*.

Because of Leni's inclination to spiritualism, her tendency to
experience things sensually rather than comprehending them
intellectually, she inclines to silence. Leni's silence also recalls
the Mary of the Gospels, to whom the evangelists attribute very
few words. Furthermore, the approximately thirty-year gap in
Mary's life from the time of the birth of Jesus until he is an
adult is reproduced in Leni's story. From the time of Lev's
birth in 1945 till he is an adult of twenty-five in 1970 little is
known of either Leni or Lev. At the time of Lev's birth, Leni,
Lev, and Boris are specifically referred to as the "holy family"
(p. 257). Boris, in the manner of Old Testament orthodox Jewish
practice, refrains from sexual intercourse with Leni from the
sixth month of her pregnancy to the third month after her
delivery.

The "Au." emphasizes in his account the miraculous quality
of Lev's birth on 2 March 1945. He reports Pelzer checked his

records and discovered that nine months prior, on 2 June 1944, no daylight raids occurred and that the factory had no night shift (p. 274). (However, the reader should not forget that two daylight raids occurred on 28 May 1944 and that Leni called the twenty-eighth her "wedding day," p. 226.) Even Lev's delivery on peat moss and straw mats in Pelzer's nursery recalls Christ's birth on straw in a stable.

These several references in the novel associating Leni with the Virgin Mary are, indeed, striking, but most important in the identification of Leni with Mary is her innocence. After her seduction by Alois Pfeiffer, the "Au." concludes: "In Leni's case it was not a question of a moral mistake, but of an existential one" (p. 120). What the "Au." is emphasizing is Leni's innocence, or in theological terms, her inability to sin—or one might even say the "Au." implies her immaculate conception. In his interview with Dieter Wellershoff, Böll stresses the importance of Leni's innocence if the reader is to understand her character: "The woman [Leni] is naive, but, I believe, also innocent, not in a judicial or moral sense, but in a metaphysical sense. That is the problem that excited me—to present an 'innocent' person."[11] The "Au." in his attempt to explain Leni, because, as he says, "'everything that Leni does, she does in all innocence'" (p. 135), tries to look up the word "innocence" in his seven-volume lexicon but is surprised to find no such entry, only a long one on guilt. After pondering a society that knows guilt but not innocence, he wonders how to proceed with his report because "without this word Leni cannot be understood" (p. 135).

Leni is not only Mary, but also Magdalen and Eve. Her name is not only short for Helene but for Magdalene as well. As a young girl, according to her friend Margret, she "could have appeared in a mystery play as a saint or as Mary Magdalen" (p. 51); and, of course, in the eyes of the world she is thought of as a sinner because of her affairs with the Russian Boris and the Turk Mehmet. In his *Frankfurter Vorlesungen* Böll speaks of Eve, Mary, and Magdalen as the trinity of womanliness which is "never pure and never separate in the female character" (*FV*, p. 101). In making Leni into a new model for humanity, Böll has created in her a new Eve—as the mother of Christ is often called. When asked if Leni were a Rhenish

Madonna, Böll replied: "That could be. I never actually thought about it, but naturally I have all that in me. I know the Madonna cults in the Rhineland. I know the Rhenish Madonnas, the Madonna as protectress, the strange figure of St. Ursula with her virgins. All of that may be in the book."[12]

Since Leni is identified with the Virgin Mary, Boris is naturally her Joseph. The references to the "holy family" (p. 257) are unavoidable. Pelzer actually calls Boris Leni's "St. Joseph" (p. 273). Lotte Hoyser says specifically: "They lived together for six months [referring to Boris's six months of abstinence from sexual intercourse] as Mary and Joseph" (p. 257). Boris's familiarity with Jewish practice and belief stems from his childhood. During the Russian civil war he was sent to the country and reared by an old Jewish woman, who even had him circumcised. With his capture in June 1945, he is removed from the life of Leni and Lev as Joseph suddenly disappears from the Gospel accounts of the holy family. Thus, if Leni is Mary and Boris is Joseph, Lev should emerge as a Christ figure. And he, indeed, assumes this role. He associates with the underprivileged of society, the garbage collectors and street cleaners. He has even learned Russian and Arabic in order to mediate between peoples. For the poor he is a leader who serves their interests and understands their problems. He is also the prophet of the Gospel of secular salvation: "deliberate underachievement." The German word *Leistungsverweigerung* is a direct attack on the dehumanization which attaches to the Western concept of production for profit and the ever increasing pressure to produce more whether it is needed or not if only profit can thereby be derived. Lev's theory is to reduce the constant pressure on the worker and the nation for an ever larger gross national product.

It represents Böll's ideal: "People shouldn't work for more than they really need in order to live. That may be a lot—but spend a lifetime working for things that are superfluous?"[13] The fisherman in "Anekdote zur Senkung der Arbeitsmoral" [Anecdote on the Decline of the Work Ethic] serves as the model for *Leistungsverweigerung*. But the principle can also be seen at work in the behavior of Hans Schnier, the clown, and in the Gruhls of *End of a Mission*.

In part because of their *Leistungsverweigerung,* Lev and his mother have become the center of a counterculture, of which Böll says:

I believe it is necessary, absolutely necessary, and probably the only possibility man has to protect himself from fascism, automation, and the computer world. I see in the mechanization of the world the appearance of fascism, the development of fascism. . . . The priority of economic considerations in the planning of cities, factories, of existence, is growing more pronounced. Profit is the controlling factor.[14]

Böll believes this model of society which Leni and Lev represent "is realizable when there is solidarity,"[15] i.e., when there is cooperation between the working people in a society. When asked what this new ideal is, Böll replied simply: "a profitless and classless society, therefore, a socialist society."[16] Hence Lev with his Gospel of *Leistungsverweigerung* is a Messianic figure with a message of salvation to the industrialized world.

The character most strongly contrasted with Leni, the Madonna, is her friend Margret, a pronounced Magdalen. While Leni is pure, Margaret is a "sinful," "loose" woman dying of syphilis. Margret is, however, best described not as a prostitute, but as a *Freudenmädchen* in the literal sense of the word, in the meaning Böll gives the expression in the play *Aussatz*:[17] a woman who gives pleasure. As a young girl Margret exclaims: "It is wonderful how the boys enjoy it; some scream with pleasure (*Freude*)" (p. 49). The "Au." comments: "It simply gave Margret joy (*Freude*) to give them pleasure (*Freude*)" (p. 49). Like Mary Magdalen, Margret too reforms in the eyes of the world. Her last two years she has lived in seclusion on a farm inherited from her parents (p. 387), and in the clinic she is well on the way to recovery from venereal disease.

What interests Böll in the combination of Leni and Margret is the concept of holiness. *Group Portrait* is, in part, an attempt by Böll to put into question the traditional idea of sanctity—a person remaining pure from the beginning to the end of life. Such people, Böll argues, often have behind them a series of sinful people without whom they could not have become saints. Behind the saintly Leni there is Margret.[18] In this sense, Böll claims, "Margret is the second most important character" in the novel.[19] Still in her way she is sinless like Leni. Her numerous contacts with men were not "commercial." She simply allowed herself to be used to help others. In some way she too is innocent. Actually the manner of her death verifies this innocence. Shortly before she is to be released, the hospital personnel as well as other patients discover she blushes at the jargon of prostitutes. The constant teasing she then receives affects her nervous system and causes her death. The nurse writing to Leni claims she died of "blushing" due to her "damned innocence" (pp. 390–91). Thus, in her way, Margret is also an example of the trinity of womanliness, Mary, Magdalen, Eve— saint, sinner (in the eyes of the world), female.

The most saintly of characters in the novel, however, is Sister Rahel. She too is associated with the Madonna through her real name, Maria Ginzberg (a Jewish woman named Mary), and through Leni, who entitles one of her large wall paintings *Part of the Tissue of the Left Eye of the Virgin Mary Called Rahel.* Furthermore, Rahel has visions of Christ as she is kept in an attic chamber by her order. "The Lord is nigh, the Lord is nigh, He is here" (p. 99) was her constant refrain. Later when the order assigns Sister Rahel to the cellar because of her smoking in the attic, she refuses to take her crucifix with her, maintaining: "That is not he, that is not he" (p. 132) as if she knew what Christ really looked like. After her death she is associated with one of the most stereotypical forms of all miracles in the Cahtolic church; from her grave and ashes bloom roses in winter. The church tries to suppress the information concerning the miracles, not least because it had oppressed Sister Rahel, but also because a beatification process would destroy the church's progressive image. Although Sister Rahel is associated with many traditions of saintliness—she is a virgin, a martyr, has worked with the poor, and has had visions of Christ—her life is far from one that the church would like to make public and offer as a model. She was imprisoned as a Socialist and pacifist during World War I (pp. 325); she was suspended from teaching because of her emphasis on philosophical biologism and reduced to a menial by her order despite her training as a physician, scientist, philosopher, and theologian (pp. 39, 325). Her oppression by the church was not only caused by her beliefs, but also because in the Nazi era her Jewishness produced fear in her order. The church simply does not know how to deal with the phenomenon of Sister Rahel.

Sister Rahel, besides being Leni's mentor in sensualism, i.e., enjoyment, acceptance, and pleasure in the senses, is the first to acknowledge her as an "unrecognized genius of sensuality" (p. 33). Later the "Au." reinforces this observation by referring to her "materialistic sensual concretism" (p. 52), maintaining it is impossible to think of Leni in "unreal terms" (p. 128). Böll expresses his intention with this aspect of Leni's personality as "the attempt to bring to materialism or the materiality of human life a new dimension, to explain the sacredness of materia."[20]

David Myers has done much to explain how the apparently incongruent combination of urgent moral protest and self-conscious aesthetic play dominates the structure of the novel.[21] Many critics have failed to recognize this playfulness in the work and have come to misunderstand the figure of Leni by failing to grasp her double function. One of the central statements of the book points to this difficulty of interpretation: "Yes, she exists and then, she doesn't. She doesn't exist, and then, she does" (p. 373). The meaning of this sentence lies in the recognition that Leni lives on two levels, the real and the symbolic. At times her real life dominates and her symbolic qualities fade, and at other times her symbolic qualities dominate and her real life fades. As Leni is a combination of her real and symbolic function she exists sometimes more at one level and sometimes less at the other. Therefore, she is and she is not; she is not and she is.

The word "garbage" is a key motif in the novel. Böll's use of it recalls his *Frankfurter Vorlesungen*: "To me there is only one humane possibility of humor: to show in all its majesty that which society has declared as garbage and considers refuse" (*FV*, p. 107).[22] Leni is not only the "Soviet whore," but "the tramp" who ought to be "gassed" (p. 10), hence the garbage of society that ought to be disposed of. Her son Lev epitomizes Böll's concept of humor in regard to garbage. As a garbage collector, he has united "vocation and avocation" in a job that "serves cleanliness but is thought to be dirty" (p. 385).

What concerns Böll in *Group Portrait* is the presentation of a model of humanist community which can serve as an alternative to the prevailing form of competitive existence in a capitalist, profit-oriented society. Three examples, all with Leni at their center, are offered. The "Soviet paradise in the tombs" at war's end, the circle around Leni in her house, and the "Help Leni Committee" initiated by Leni's admirer Schirtenstein may serve as evidence. Each of these models is based on the Communist ideal: from each according to his ability, to each according to his needs. In the community in the cemetery each person contributes what he can by supplying food, necessities, and electric power; each brings something different and essential to the community. In Leni's house the rooms are given to families, couples, and friends according to their needs, and each pays rent in proportion to his income rather than the market value or the space occupied. Also the "Help Leni Committee" saves Leni's house by each person helping in the way he is best able: by work, money, the arrangement of legal details. What characterizes these three groups is solidarity and community.

Hans Joachim Bernhard correctly maintains that a significant development occurs in Böll's work when the Turkish, Portuguese, and German garbage collectors unite in solidarity behind Leni to prevent her eviction.[23] Even at this relatively nonpolitical level their action is a social step forward. The exploited class unites to help itself—an improvement over being helped by a "shepherd" figure, a Fähmel or an Albert, who acts for them. Still, Bernhard misinterprets the "Help Leni Committee" as proletarians united. The group has, in fact, a much broader social base. It is called into existence by Leni's nonproletarian neighbor Schirtenstein, the music critic. Its members are, besides the Turkish and Portuguese workers, the rich opportunist Pelzer; the "Au." and his friend the ex-nun Klementina; Leni's old friends Lotte Hoyser and Marja van Doorn; Boris's old friend and fellow POW Bogakov; the civil servants Scholsdorff and Hans Helzen and his wife, Grete; Leni's friend, previous employer, and owner of a flower shop, Liane Hölthohne; and the old gardener Grundtsch. In other words, the "Help Leni Committee" is a cross-section of society, a microcosm of the real world, a symbol of solidarity that transcends the proletariat and simply comprises people of goodwill, a model of a classless society.[24] At least temporarily all class, religious, and national differences are leveled. Catholics, Moslems, Protestants, Jews, Germans, Turks, Portuguese, and Russians work together, each person contributing what he can with his own expertise and his own resources.

Although *Group Portrait* is a fictional argument for a Socialist alternative, and although in the novel communism is idealized by the circle around Leni, the Communist party fares no better in the book than the capitalist system. In the 1920s the party attracted fine people: Ilse Kremer and her husband Willi, also "Fritz" (the 68er), and after the war, Leni. But it betrayed each in a different way: Willi Kremer by turning him over to the Fascists after the Hitler-Stalin pact of 1939 as a way of purging dissidents from the party, "Fritz" by supporting the 1968 suppression of the Czech experiment in liberalization, and Leni by showing no understanding for her natural proletarianism and no sympathy for her religious convictions. Russian communism is further rejected in the novel in that several Russian POW's prefer to stay in Germany after the war.

Still the criticism of communism in the novel is essentially different from that of capitalism. The criticism of communism is of its practice, of a betrayal of noble principles. In this sense it duplicates that leveled at the Catholic church. The failing of the church and communism lies not in their message or their teachings, but in their failure as institutions to live by their tenets, in their willingness to compromise their ideals for power. The criticism of capitalism, on the other hand, is of its fundamental principles of profit, private ownership, and self-interest, of the very nature of the system which considers people as objects to be exploited. The rejection of capitalism lies in the inhumanity of its foundations—that of party communism and the institutionalized church in their deviation from principle.

Böll's *Group Portrait* follows an existing and expanding pattern of anticapitalist literature produced in Western countries. When a figure in Western literature represents humanist ideals, that character demonstrates a disharmony with the vital principles of capitalist society. Whether he appears in a novel of critical realism or of romantic inwardness, is a character of the *renouveau catholique* or of the Socialist school, he inevitably opposes the values surrounding him. In Böll's oeuvre the incompatability of capitalism with humanism is universal. Whether the protagonist is Leni or Lev, Hans Schnier or Uncle Albert, Walter Fendrich or Fred Bogner, he is invariably at odds with his society. Of necessity such characters suffer the fate of outsiders—disdain, rejection, mistreatment, and frequently poverty. When Böll's heroes are rich, their wealth results from birth or circumstances, never from their ambition. In *Group Portrait* the fate of Leni and Lev crystallizes the radical message of Böll's novel, which, reduced to a single sentence, proclaims: It is impossible to be a Christian (a humanist) and support a society based on exploitation.

II   The Lost Honor of Katharina Blum

In 1974 Böll published *The Lost Honor of Katharina Blum*, the most political of all his works. Because the novel polemicizes against false practices of journalism and serves, in the author's own words, as a "political pamphlet" in narrative form, an examination of the work for its sociological content seems an appropriate starting point. Moreover, from this standpoint Böll considers the work very successful: "I am astonished at the effect of *Katharina Blum*. That justifies its weakness. I am indifferent to what people find wrong with the book. They may be correct. But it does not matter when I see the direct political effect of the work. . . . Naturally I am interested in criticism, especially that which is justified. But in this case—and that is an exception in my whole career and in my reaction to criticism— I am satisfied. That is a stupid word—let's say: content with the effect this book has had."[25] This statement by Böll recalls a similar one he made in 1962 in his interview with Horst Bienek: "For me commitment is a prerequisite; it is a foundation, and what I build on this foundation is what I understand as art."[26]

When he refers to the positive effect of *Katharina Blum*, Böll has in mind the echo of his criticism within that novel, of the

Bild-Zeitung which has resounded in the responsible German press. Despite its biased sensationalism or because of it, the *Bild-Zeitung* enjoys the widest circulation of Germany's dailies. In every way it illustrates the worst characteristics of yellow journalism, for it goes beyond mere melodrama in reporting. Besides emphasizing sensationalism in headlines and photos, specializing in shocking stories of crime, sex, and scandal, employing colloquial language and vulgar expressions, besides appealing to and stimulating the reader's hunger for sensation, the *Bild-Zeitung* prints assumptions as fact, promotes an hysterical political climate, and encourages lynch-justice. Of the reporting in the *Bild-Zeitung* Böll has said: "It is no longer cryptofascistic, no longer fascistoid, it is naked fascism: incitement, lies, garbage."[27]

The film version of *Katharina Blum* makes clear that Böll's indictment of the Fascist practices of the *News* (as the *Zeitung* is called in the American version) extends as well to the representatives of the law for their toleration of the newspaper's methods of defamation. In the narrative Böll does not inform the reader of the ages of the police officials and prosecutors, but in the movie version of the book these characters are clearly portrayed as under forty—a point important to Böll[28] because it emphasizes his criticism that none of these characters is an old Nazi. Hence the problems of Fascism which the story treats—intimidation, fear of communism, distortion of truth, wire tapping, failure of society to protect the dignity of man in accordance with the constitution—are those of the Federal Republic, not of the Hitler past.[29]

In the story of a young woman deprived of her good name and driven to murder, Böll reveals the gap between society's promise and its performance; in this case it is the gap between the claim of the West German constitution that "the dignity of man is inviolable" and the reality: West Germany's toleration of yellow journalism which assaults the dignity of the individual and, therefore, the dignity of man. Böll writes: "The constitution of the Federal Republic is probably the best possible constitution a state could give itself in the twentieth century" (*NPLS*, p. 260). To substantiate this claim he quotes paragraph 1 of its first article: "The dignity of man is inviolable. To

preserve it and protect it is the responsibility of all state power."
The betrayal of the promise of the constitution is, then, the
theme of Böll's narrative. He emphasizes this point in an exchange between Katharina Blum and a federal prosecutor
during her interrogation by the police. Katharina takes the
News out of her purse and asks if "the state—thus she expressed
it—[here Böll stresses the word *Staat* because that is the word
used in the constitution] couldn't do something to protect her
from this dirt and restore her lost honor" (p. 81). The prosecutor replies that she is free to file a private complaint. The
lack of encouragement in the prosecutor's answer is one of the
motivating factors in Katharina's murder of the reporter who
assasinates her character. She assumes that there is no practical
recourse to justice within the system, that the state has no interest in procuring justice for her as a powerless, insignificant
individual.

After his article attacking the *Bild-Zeitung* for its reporting
on the Baader-Meinhof group appeared in *Der Spiegel* (10 January 1972), Böll was subjected for several months to numerous
personal attacks in the press.[30] Many readers of *Katharina Blum*
naturally assumed his book was a reaction to his public mistreatment. Böll denies this motivation for his book. In an interview with Christian Linder he confesses that his intention to
write against the practices of yellow journalism in the Federal
Republic existed long before 1972: "The whole Baader-Meinhof
affair has little to do with *Katharina Blum*. A long time ago
I asked one of my occasional collaborators to keep an eye on
the *Bild-Zeitung* and other boulevard newspapers for striking
examples of defamation of known and unknown persons."[31] Böll
maintains the story of Katharina Blum has its basis much more
in the Brückner-affair[32] than it does in his personal experience
with defamation: "What I actually wanted to present [with
Katharina Blum] was the frightening role of Prof. Brückner
in his connection with the Baader-Meinhof case. He was simply
a man who came in touch with members of the Baader-Meinhof
group; he gave them a place to stay, something entirely natural,
and was destroyed psychologically because of it. . . . That is the
starting point of the problem: not the [Baader-Meinhof] group
itself, but the people who are treated as lepers."[33]

The psychological destruction of the individual by the press which Böll tries to recreate in *Katharina Blum* is accurately described by Brückner himself in an interview of 1973:

I saw myself in a situation in which I became a victim, subjected to general disdain. . . . A new reality developed around me. Whenever an article about me appeared in the newspapers, I was deluged day and night by anonymous telephone calls. There were threatening letters. Many people turned away from me on the street. I suddenly saw myself assailed, oppressed, and defamed, and I asked myself: is this me or someone else?

The problem of isolation became immediate. There was publicity about me which was not a result of any service or crime. In the fall of 1972, I discovered my likeness in a Sunday newspaper under an article with the title: "Ulrike Makes Her Men Happy in Bed." A new Brückner was being produced whose image no longer corresponded to the image the victim had of himself. Through this negative publicity I was made into a nonperson and at the same time made the object of personal defamation. The distance between the official nonperson and society grew. Every meeting—even with friends and people of my own political persuasion—became an event. The possibility of natural intercourse with people disappeared. . . . [Brückner ends this statement with a sentence that applies directly to the reporter Tötges in Böll's story.] I met some [journalists] who were capable of anything.[34]

To strengthen the polemical intention of his story, Böll uses three obvious devices: the structure of his narrative, the manner in which it is related, and the perspective from which it is told. By the choice of an anonymous, objective narrator who writes exclusively from the viewpoint of Katharina, and by his method of handling the chronology of events, he emphasizes the background of the murder rather than the murder itself. In this sense, he creates a model of reporting in direct contrast to that of the *Bild-Zeitung*.

The narrative technique of *Katharina Blum* is not new with Böll. It is a variation of the method he originated in *End of a Mission* and developed in *Group Portrait*. In *End of a Mission* the objective reporter develops into an omniscient narrator because he relates information impossible to know through investigation, but in doing so still maintains the impression of reporting facts rather than telling a story. In *Group Portrait*, although the narrator eliminates this ambivalence, insisting always that he is writing a report, he, nonetheless, never reveals why he is writing about his heroine. The narrator of *Katharina Blum* avoids these incongruities; he gives his reason for writing in the subtitle of his work and identifies his sources of information on the first page: "For the following report there are a few minor and three major sources which are to be named at the beginning and not mentioned again. The major sources are the records of the police department, the lawyer Dr. Hubert Blorna, and his school and college friend, the prosecutor Peter Hach.... The minor sources, a few of greater, the others of lesser importance need not be mentioned here because they... reveal themselves in the course of the report" (pp. 9–10). The reporter-narrator of *Katharina Blum*, like his counterparts in *End of a Mission* and *Group Portrait*, tells his tale by means of montage, reportage, and flashbacks. He pieces together the story of a young woman in an attempt to explain the facts behind a murder, maintaining, like his predecessors, an objective distance by sustaining a tone of irony and persiflage.

The narrator's presentation of the crime at the beginning of the report is dry, cool, and factual: "On Wednesday the twentieth of February 1974 on the evening before *Weiberfastnacht*, a young woman of twenty-seven leaves her apartment in the city at 6:43 in the evening to attend a private party. Four days later . . . on Sunday evening, at approximately the same time— more exactly 7:04—she rings the bell to the apartment of police commissioner Walter Moeding, and informs the shocked Moeding that this afternoon in her apartment, at 12:15, she has shot the journalist Werner Tötges. . . . She feels no sorrow and asks to be arrested because she would like to be where her 'Dear Ludwig' is" (pp. 11–12).

In the second chapter of the story, the narrator constructs a metaphor for the method he uses to organize his report. He compares the amount of available information about the murder to puddles of water that have accumulated after a rain. Like a child who builds dams and channels in order to drain the standing water into a single stream, he releases his facts and controls the flow of details into the main stream of his narration, occasionally damming up one source to go back to another.

Another structural element Böll uses to keep the polemical content of his work in the foreground is to present the main event of the story (Katharina's shooting of the reporter) in a few sentences at the beginning of the narrative and to have Katharina retell the incident in her own words at the end, thus leaving the entire middle ground of the tale free to expose the reasons for the murder, and leaving the murder itself as a frame for the narration. With this structure Böll keeps the violent death of Tötges looming in the background while placing the causes for that violence in the foreground. Böll's structure allows, then, the motives for the murder to become his polemical argument and justifies the subtitle of the book: "How violence can originate and where it can lead."

In the center of the story Böll places the worlds of money, business, the press, the police, and the law. The murder by Katharina is caused by the interaction of these five social forces. In the course of the report, Böll shows, through the example of Katharina Blum, how these five elements operate in social alliance. Where the limits of one world begin and those of the other end remains vague in the report as in reality. These forces represent the superstructure of society, which primarily seeks to maintain, increase, and secure wealth and power for those in position to exploit those who lack the social means to defend themselves. Seen in this light, the mistake of Katharina Blum is having gotten into a situation which appears to place her against the forces which represent society.

Read from this perspective Böll's story reveals the divisions of class society. Although Katharina Blum is a legitimate subject of police investigation and criminal reporting because of her contact with a suspected criminal, so too is the wealthy, influential politician Alois Sträubleder. But the different treatment each receives relates to his or her position in society. Sträubleder's name is kept out of the newspaper, and he is never held or interrogated by the police even though, on the surface, his connection with the same criminal is as suspicious as Katharina's. Thus, the rich and the powerful are exempt from the treatment accorded the little man. Through Sträubleder, Böll also brings institutionalized religion into the conglomerate of power. When the first report on Katharina appears in the *News*, Sträubleder is attending a conference for Christian businessmen at which he is the main speaker and discussion leader. As a single individual Sträubleder represents the alliance of power in society. He is a prominent Christian, a rich businessman, a leader in politics and science (p. 148) with close connections to the police, the courts, and the press—illustrated by his friend Lüding who "has the *News* in the palm of his hand" (p. 123).

What Böll shows in *Katharina Blum* is the vulnerability of anyone suspected of being against the system. Whether he in fact is, is unimportant; mere suspicion of disloyalty to the ruling forces in society makes one an enemy of the state and liable to assassination of character and the destruction of one's existence. The boulevard press becomes the spokesman, judge, and jury for the ruling interests in society. It pronounces sentence and metes out punishment. Because it fulfills this function for the ruling class, the *News* is in turn protected and permitted to make profit with its lies and distortions. That the *News* clearly violates a citizen's constitutional right to dignity is no concern to the representatives of the law. Böll remains fair, however, to the press, for while Katharina is waiting in a jail cell, an officer brings her fifteen clippings from responsible newspapers which have treated her case in a few lines on inside pages without photos. There is, however, little comfort for Katharina in this knowledge, for she says: "Who reads that. Everybody I know reads the *News!*" (pp. 83–84).

Böll strengthens the argument of the book that mere suspicion of disloyalty to the system is basis enough for condemnation by making Katharina's life before her accidental involvement with the police, the law, and the press an advertisement for the capitalistic system and its claimed advantages for the hardworking proletarian. Böll complains that many readers have missed this point. In an interview in the Munich *Abendzeitung* he responds to the charge of having idealized Katharina Blum: "Glorified? What is she then? A domestic who behaves in an absolutely conformist manner, a person who to me is not very likeable. She has accommodated society all the way to owning her own condominium. Unglorified. No one can be more average than she."[35] And in an interview with Manfred Durzak, Böll argues: "She is a pure career woman in a conventional pattern of the economic miracle. She intelligently recognizes her chances in her profession and takes advantage of them. She is interested in material success."[36]

Thus, in the story of Katharina Blum Böll intends no positive presentation of the main character. Still, despite Katharina's unquestioned acceptance of the ideology of achievement against which Lev struggles in *Group Portrait*, there is much that recommends Katharina's character. She is generous, humane, and "radically ready to help" (p. 56). Although prudish, she is secure in her sexuality. In short, she is a woman who knows who she is and has a positive realistic image of herself. But, most of all, she is capable of love and does not hesitate to risk her whole painstakingly acquired existence for her "Dear Ludwig." Also Katharina's desire to get ahead can be judged positively. Her success is at no one's expense, and others beside herself benefit from it. Her several jobs are not an example of greed, but her effort to avoid loneliness and her desire to find security from the poverty of her youth. Her possessions represent less her materialism than they do her success in jobs she likes to do and does well. In this regard she is much like an author or professor who prospers moderately from good writing or teaching. Still she epitomizes one serious failing: she is totally noncritical of society. Her lack of formal education, however, does not excuse her in this matter. One does not need an education to be socially alert; one needs simply to observe the world. She does not reconsider her social assumptions even after her suffering at the hands of the police, law, press, and the business world. From her experience she learns nothing. While in prison she calculates, in her methodical manner, the time of her and her lover's release (in about eight to ten years); she estimates the amount of interest her savings will have accumulated in that time and plans with her Ludwig to open a "restaurant with a catering service" (p. 113). Hence Katharina is a person who goes through life never gaining insight into the fundamental structure of society.

But in this regard she is like the other positive figures in the story, especially the Blornas. Although they sacrifice a com-

fortable existence to help Katharina, Hubert and Trude Blorna
never see anything behind the mistreatment of Katharina except injustice. Neither Blorna, although he is a lawyer, nor his
wife, although she is called "red Trudy," is capable of ideological
thinking or even of being critical of the social organization of
power; neither sees behind the injustice in the Blum affair to a
pattern of social abuse; neither recognizes that the system simply
views everyone as a source of profit, as a resource ready to be
exploited because it places the right to make profit before the
right of the person. Blorna and his wife fail to see the manipulation of the powerless by the powerful, the systematic elimination
of all who even appear to think differently or appear to challenge the organization of society. The Blornas react only out
of emotion, a sense of outrage. They, along with Katharina,
do not attempt the slightest induction, never move from the
particulars of their situation to a general conclusion about society. Their failure to generalize is the failure to learn from
their experience. The Blornas disdain their old friend Sträubleder because, out of cowardice and expediency, he does not
aid Katharina. They are angry at the total injustice of the Blum
affair, but they do not try to penetrate to the ideology of dehumanization behind it. Blorna, according to Böll, is the model
for a social liberal,[37] "totally unintellectual and unideological."[38]

Böll's criticism of yellow journalism, however, comes through
more effectively in his narrative than does his criticism of the
structure of society because his narrator relates his story from
the perspective of Katharina Blum. Therefore, most readers see
her as a positive figure and react, like the Blornas, merely to the
injustice accorded her. Böll's other message, the book's deeper
criticism of society, fails to make a similar impact because the
narrow perspective of Katharina Blum inhibits the reader's objectivity. While the narrative point of view brings out one social
problem, it forces related social problems into the background.[39]

In his interview with Manfred Durzak, Böll compares Katharina to Walter Fendrich in The Bread of Those Early Years.
He claims of the scene in which Katharina smashes her apartment: "She destroys her bourgeois existence which she has acquired with such effort. I cannot see that that is less reflective
and less psychologically founded than in The Bread of Those

Early Years."[40] In fact, Fendrich's destruction of the remnants of his past life after meeting Hedwig, symbolized in his breaking his engagement with the boss's daughter, quitting his job, and withdrawing all his money from the bank, arises from quite different motivations than does Katharina's destruction of her apartment. Fendrich destroys his chances of success because he turns his back on the values of society. Katharina, as has been explained, never does this; she remains to the end a child of the economic miracle. She destroys her apartment not out of love or knowledge, but out of desperation. She realizes at this moment that the life which she has established with such effort lies in ruins, that she has lost her honor; thus, in a moment of despair she destroys the symbolic remnants of what is left. She does not reject society's values, as her later planning for a new existence with Ludwig proves. The reader assumes that, after her release from prison, her life will be as successful and as bourgeois as it was before. Only the lives of the Blornas, in comparison to their past, will be ruined ones. The catastrophe is greater for them than for Katharina because they struggle against injustice, whereas Katharina does not struggle at all; she simply reacts to the loss of her good name.

Although "on Thursday[41] after reading the first article" (p. 172) in the *News* Katharina considers killing the journalist Tötges, Böll argues in his interview with Durzak that the shooting of Tötges, remains "an almost exclusively erotically determined act."[42] There is truth in Böll's statement as Katharina's account of the murder indicates: " 'Why are you staring at me like that, Blumikins, as if scared out of your wits? I suggest we have a little bang for starters.' In the meantime I had my hand in my purse, and he went for my dress, I thought 'O.K., I'll give you a bang,' I pulled out the pistol and shot him on the spot" (p. 185). But if Böll's statement is true, it weakens the book's argument that the mechanism of society elicits its own violence. The more important the sexual motivation in the murder, the less important are the social motives. In fact, the book's argument that society produces its own violence and that this violence is reflected in the press's misuse of language, is more effective than Böll seems to realize. The sexual aspect of the murder demonstrates the way language has dehumanized Katharina.

Tötges is not a sexual pervert, a man with a rapist mentality; he is, like Sträubleder, a healthy product of capitalism, an aggressive opportunist and exploiter. Normally he would not approach a woman in the way he does Katharina, whom he treats as a sexual object only because he believes the image he himself has created of her as the "Robber's Moll" and the receiver of "Male Visitors." He does not recognize his own lies. At this point Tötges is less a reporter for the *News* than he is a member of the public duped by the power of false rhetoric. He is no different from the people who make the anonymous calls and write the anonymous letters to Katharina. Thus his murder is a crime which has its origin in the perversion of language as well as in the mechanism of capitalist society.

Because of Katharina's unwarranted suffering, she appears as a martyr; thus Böll's comment on *Group Portrait* applies even more to *Katharina Blum*: "My attempt in *Group Portrait* to destroy iconographic clichés failed; I created new ones.... To destroy iconography without creating a new one appears impossible."[43] Responsible for the iconography created in *Katharina Blum* is not only the narrative perspective of the work, but also the religious element incorporated into the story. As usual in Böll's work, the religious element relates to love, which for Böll forms a moral category, not the legal one defined by marriage. Love manifests itself as a mysterious composite of psychology, sex, and grace. It brings out man's noblest impulses, as in Katharina's attraction to Ludwig, not merely man's sexual desire, as in Sträubleder's and Tötges's attraction to Katharina. Katharina is, as her name implies and her nickname, "the nun," suggests, "the pure one." The name of her lover, Götten (from *Gott*, God), also indicates his religious role in the story; he is Katharina's Messiah. His coming is an advent in her life. She speaks of him as John the Baptist speaks of Christ: "My God, he was the one who should come" (p. 80). The reader cannot help but notice the similarity of her expression to that in Matthew 11:2–3. And as the heroic aura around Katharina stands in contrast to her real bourgeois life, so does Ludwig's stand in opposition to the reality surrounding him. Ludwig is no principled political activist, but just an ordinary criminal. He is a deserter, a defrauder, a safecracker, and a thief (of a car and weapons); still, he is not, as the *News* proclaims, a murderer and a bankrobber. His accomplices are not political radicals but corrupt members of the military. However, when the mystery of love envelops him, he becomes transformed, if not into a hero, at least into a candidate for the bourgeois life, a possible restaurateur in Katharina's dream of the future— certainly something better than he was before.

As the reader accepts the transformation of Ludwig because of the conviction of Katharina's language, so, he accepts the narrator's image of Katharina because of the sympathetic portrayal of her. This aspect of the work underscores the principal theme of the book: the responsibility of language. The reader of the report assents to the positive image of Katharina and Ludwig although the former becomes a murderer and the latter is a criminal, just as the reader of the *News* consents to the image of Katharina as moll and Ludwig as murderer when each is totally innocent of these crimes. Böll's story recalls his commitment to responsible language made years ago in his speech "Die Sprache als Hort der Freiheit" (1958): "What divided beings words are in our world. Scarcely spoken or written and they transform themselves and burden him who spoke or wrote them with a responsibility whose weight he only seldom can bear. . . . He who uses words, as everyone does who writes a newspaper article or puts a line of poetry on paper, ought to know that he sets worlds in motion" (*EHA*, pp. 439–440).

The story of Katharina Blum demonstrates the wisdom of this commitment. The work indicts the *News* and all yellow journalism for neglect of its greatest responsibility, the proper use of language, the service of truth. Placing the perversion of language into the category of crime does not distort Böll's intention; it does not raise aestheticism above justice, misuse of language above abuse of the individual because often crime against a person cannot be carried out without first perverting language. Whether it is the destruction of Katharina Blum, the murder of millions in concentration camps, the "wasting" of villages in Vietnam, the ground work for such crimes is always first laid by manipulating the perpetrators of such actions as well as their victims with false rhetoric and the distortion of truth. The message of *Katharina Blum* is not only a warning against the obvious excesses of the *News*, but a plea for responsible use of language in print and in speech, in public and in private, by every journalist, politician, and citizen.

The importance of words comes through in the story in several ways. Not only do the names of Katharina and Götten symbolize something about their roles in the story, but so too does the name of the murdered journalist Tötges (from *töten*, to kill). He is the one who kills Katharina with words and the one killed by Katharina because his language leads directly to physical aggression. Böll makes sure the reader does not miss the connection between word and deed. When Tötges suggests that they start the interview with a "bang," Katharina's response is literal: "O.K., I'll give you a bang" (p. 185), and shoots him.

Katharina's sensitivity to language manifests itself early in the narrative: "The interrogation lasted so long because Katharina checked every word in the transcript with astonishing pedantry" (p. 39). She argues against the substitution of the word *zärtlich* ("tender," "delicate") for *zudringlich* ("aggressive," "forceful"). She makes the distinction that in love "tenderness [*Zärtlichkeit*] is a reciprocal activity, whereas aggressiveness [*Zudringlichkeit*] is a one-sided activity" (p. 39). The police find such distinctions superfluous and blame Katharina for the prolonged interrogation. The insensivity of officials to both language and people pervades the story. That order is not accidental. Böll implies that insensivity to the former leads automatically to insensitivity to the latter. The commissioner Beizmenne begins the interrrogation of Katharina with a direct attack on her dignity: "Did he fuck you?" (p. 25), to which, after "blushing," Katharina replies in "proud triumph": I wouldn't call it that" (p. 25).

Throughout the work the perversion of truth, the distortion of reality always precedes physical aggression. Before society can condone its attack on the innocent, the innocent must first be made into objects deserving destruction: into molls, Communists, criminals, nonpersons. Once the labels stick, violence follows as justice. In this way, Böll explains the subtitle of his work: "How violence can originate and where it can lead." Thus the story conveys the meaning that a society which puts profit before people, or which perverts language to achieve its ends unintentionally, sows the seed for an inevitable harvest of bitterness.

Because everything—even, as Böll shows, a punch in the nose— in capitalist society has commercial value, Böll can turn the art which society rewards against society. In this manner art can break out of the padded cell in which it is confined and play a positive social role. In the scene where the celebrated artist Frederick Le Boche fashions an abstract painting from Sträubleder's blood absorbed on a blotter, Böll demonstrates both the marketability of things in Western society and the way art can subvert society's inhuman values. After Le Boche confers monetary worth and cultural status on his "One Minute Work of Art" (p. 179) simply by placing his signature on it, he presents the painting to Blorna with the suggestion that he exploit the market by selling the work to raise funds for Blorna's cause. At this point Böll reaffirms his own social commitment by having his narrator proclaim the practical message of the book: "Art still has a social function" (p. 179).

CHAPTER 10

Conclusion

THIS monograph has traced Heinrich Böll's literary career from his earliest short stories of 1947 to 1978. In following his evolution over thirty years, the book has pointed out some obvious development, such as his change from a Christian existentialist in religious and political matters in the immediate postwar years to a Christian Socialist in his later years. But equally as important as showing the change in Böll's *Weltanschauung* has been to point out the consistent humanism in his life and works.

The final evaluation of Böll cannot yet be written, but the available evidence suggests that Böll will always be seen in the dual role as artist and public figure. As public figure, he will be recognized for his compassionate interest in his fellow human beings, whether they be in Europe or elsewhere, and he will be remembered for his courage in publicizing the plight of dissidents in Russia and that of Palestinian refugees in the Holy Land, in pleading for understanding of Ulrike Meinhof while arguing for changes in the German social conditions that produce terrorists. Comment on Böll's public life has been both kind and harsh, depending upon agreement or disagreement with his positions, but those critics who recognized in Böll a weakness for the suffering of people surely have discovered the strength of his character and his work.

As an artist Böll has never received universal critical acceptance, not even from those who find his stories some of the best written in the middle decades of this century. That sentimentalism and idealism dominate his work and that he cannot always adequately execute his intentions are the charges most often heard. Minor weaknesses in Böll's work, however, seem

196

not to affect his popularity with a discriminating public. Already he stands in the company of two of his favorite writers: Dostoevski and Tolstoi. Like them, he has produced eminently readable work imbued with moral power.

Notes and References

Page references to quotations from Böll's works appear parenthetically in the text whenever appropriate. All translations in this book are by the author of this monograph unless otherwise stated. The books and articles cited are those given in the bibliography; all references to *Die Zeit* are to the North American edition, and the abbreviations used in the text and notes are as follows:

AKR—	*Aufsätze, Kritiken, Reden*
EHA—	*Erzählungen, Hörspiele, Aufsätze*
Ee—	*Einmischung erwünscht*
E 50–70—	*Erzählungen 1950–1970*
FAZ—	*Frankfurter Allgemeine Zeitung*
FV—	*Frankfurter Vorlesungen*
NPLS—	*Neue politische und literarische Schriften*
Querschnitte—	*Querschnitte aus Interviews, Aufsätzen und Reden von Heinrich Böll*
UDR—	*University of Dayton Review*
47–51—	*Heinrich Böll 1947 bis 1951.*

Chapter One

1. In Albrecht Beckel, *Mensch, Gesellschaft, Kirche bei Heinrich Böll* (Osnabrück, 1966), p. 10.

2. "An einen Bischof, einen General und einen Minister des Jahrgangs 1917," *AKR*, p. 258.

3. "Interview mit mir selbst," in Beckel, pp. 10–11. Another example of the parents' liberality was their tolerance of young Heinrich's lax religious practices. In the four years (his fourteenth to eighteenth) in which Böll did not attend mass or receive the sacraments, his parents did not pressure him to conform to church law (see *Querschnitte*, p. 17).

4. See Hermann Stresau, *Heinrich Böll* (Berlin, 1964), p. 6.

5. Günter Wirth, *Heinrich Böll* (Berlin, 1967), p. 38.

6. At this time Böll read the entry in Bloy's diary for Christmas

199

1916: "My satisfaction would be greater if I had the complete certainty that in this moment as we eat our Christmas meal all Germany would die of hunger." Bloy's expression of his wartime hatred of the Germans coincided with the period when, according to Böll, his own family was "not far from starvation." Böll's reaction to this diary was to "give up Bloy" (see "Brief an einen jungen Katholiken," *EHA*, p. 385).

7. Böll's mother was in fact killed in an air raid in November 1944.

8. Pertinent to Böll's position on collective guilt is his statement in an interview with Jean-Louis de Rambures in *Le Monde*, 13 December 1973: "Not to see that Nazism was a terrorist regime, one would have had to be blind. What, on the other hand, I did not know was the systematic and bureaucratic elimination of millions of human beings, as practiced by the Third Reich. Apparently Albert Speer himself was completely unaware of this. It may seem crazy. But this is a fact, and will doubtless always remain inexplicable. Just once, however, I came near the truth. It was during a train journey. I was returning from the East, on leave. In the middle of the night our train stopped in a small German railroad station. Suddenly, I saw an immense flock of shaven creatures invading the platform. A few raised their emaciated arms towards us travelers. We threw them bread and cigarettes out of the carriage windows. It was hallucinating. But I had no idea that this was genocide. It was only later, after the war, that I brought the two facts together; the little railroad station was Buchenwald. . . . I don't believe that an individual can be guilty just because he is born in one place rather than another. But neither is he for that reason innocent. That's the rub. Neither innocent, nor guilty, that's what we all are. The hardest thing for a German is to accept himself as such." Reprinted in *Commonweal*, 10 May 1974, p. 237, trans. Anne Femantle. The *Commonweal* version of the interview is, however, incomplete. For the complete text see *Le Monde* or *FAZ* (13 December 1973).

9. See "Interview mit sir selbst," in Beckel, p. 10.

10. Ralph Ley, *Böll für Zeitgenossen* (New York, 1970), p. 59.

11. For Böll's account of this loss of life see "An einen Bischof, einen General und einen Minister des Jahrgangs 1917," *AKR*, p. 248.

12. Böll maintains: "Between 1945–1947 I published about sixty novellas in ten different newspapers" ("Interview von Jean-Louis Rambures mit Heinrich Böll," *FAZ*, 12 December 1973, p. 24). However, only two other short stories besides "Die Botschaft" and "Kumpel mit dem langen Haar" are known from 1947: "Aus der Vorzeit"

and "Der Angriff." Both appeared originally in the *Rheinischer Merkur*. They are now collected for the first time in Heinrich Böll, *Werke: Romane und Erzählungen*, 5 vols.

13. Horst Beinek, *Werkstattgespräche* (Munich, 1962, 1965), p. 171.

14. "Group 47" was founded in Munich in 1947 (hence the name) by Hans Werner Richter. It was an informal organization with no official members, no dues, no officers; it was in fact no organization, simply a group of writers and critics who came together at the invitation of Richter to read from their latest works and receive criticism. The meetings, however, were frequented from their inception by *ecrivains engagés* dedicated to an honest treatment of Germany's recent past. The most prominent names in postwar German literature and criticism were associated with the group at some time between 1947 and its gradual demise in the late 1960s: Böll, Grass, Johnson, Lenz, Celan, Andersch, Hildesheimer, Enzensberger, Aichinger, Bachmann, Koeppen, Handke, and the critics Marcel Reich-Ranicki, Walter Jens, et al. In the 1950s and 1960s "Group 47" was the single strongest force in West German writing and in large measure responsible for the rebirth of German literature after the war. It awarded one prize each year to the best reading at its annual meeting.

15. Ley, *Böll für Zeitgenossen*, p. xiv.

Chapter Two

1. For Böll's comments on the vocabulary of the Nazis see "Wie das Gesetz es befahl," his review of H. G. Adler's *Der verwaltete Mensch: Studien zur Deportation der Juden aus Deutschland*, in *Ee*, pp. 126–31. Here he writes: "I hesitate to say murdered for *sonderbehandelt* because to call this process, which meant the death of more than six million people, murder, would be a euphemism" (p. 127); and "Himmler, Eichmann, Hitler, Goebels, and Göring cannot be defined with words like murderer and criminal. To call them such seems to me too humane and an insult to murderers and criminals" (p. 128).

2. Bienek, p. 178.

3. Günter Eich, *Gesammelte Werke* (Frankfurt, 1973), I, 35.

4. Theodore Ziolkowski, "Heinrich Böll: Conscience and Craft," *Books Abroad* 34 (1960): 215.

5. See Frank Trommler, "Der 'Nullpunkt 1945' und seine Verbindlichkeit für die Literaturgeschichte," in *Basis: Jahrbuch für deutsche Gegenwartsliteratur*, Band I, ed. Reinhold Grimm and Jost Hermand

(Frankfurt, 1970), pp. 9–25; and Heinrich Vormweg, "Deutsche Literatur 1945–1960: Keine Stunde Null," in *Die deutsche Literatur der Gegenwart*, ed. Manfred Durzak (Stuttgart, 1971), pp. 13–30.

6. See David J. Parent, "Böll's 'Wanderer, kommst du nach Spa . . .': A Reply to Schiller's 'Der Spaziergang,'" *Essays in Literature* 1, no. 1 (Spring 1974):109–17.

7. Although Böll has a profound interest in the drama of moral situations, he has never treated directly the major moral dilemma of individual responsibility in cooperating with the Third Reich even by unwilling participation in its activities. There is no doubt, however, that this major moral problem of recent German history is on his mind as an author. At a writer's conference in 1962 on his first trip to the Soviet Union, Böll was challenged with the question: "What did you do during the war?" He responded: "I could say that I never fired a shot in the war, took no part in any battle. But still I was a soldier in Hitler's army. I was in your country, in the Ukraine, in Odessa. And I am constantly aware of my part of the responsibility for what that army did. Everything that I write comes from the consciousness of this feeling of responsibility. . . ." Quoted from "Heinrich Böll und wir" in Lew Kopelew *Verwandt und verfremdet*, trans. Heddy Pross-Weerth (Frankfurt: Fischer, 1976), p. 70, English trans. by Robert C. Conard in *UDR* 13, no. 1 (Winter 1976): 6.

8. Theodore Ziolkowski, "Albert Camus and Heinrich Böll," *Modern Language Notes* 77 (May 1962): 291. Important also in this comparison between Böll and Camus are Böll's own words: "I believe, the most important book for me after 1945 was Camus's *The Stranger*" (*Querschnitte*, p. 65).

9. Samuel Beckett, *Waiting for Godot* (New York: Grove Press, 1970), pp. 60–61.

10. Albert Camus, "The Myth of Sisyphus," in *The Myth of Sisyphus and Other Essays*, trans. Justin O'Brien (New York: Knopf, 1967).

11. "Wiedersehen in der Allee," in *47–51*, p. 357.

12. In *Children Are Civilians Too*, trans. Leila Vennewitz, p. 127. One change in punctuation has been made to conform more closely to the original.

13. Enid MacPherson, *A Student's Guide to Böll* (London, 1962), p. 46.

Chapter Three

1. Walter Jens claims: "Böll's work reached its peak in the Murke

satires," *Deutsche Literatur der Gegenwart: Themen, Stile, Tendenzen* (Munich: Piper, 1962), p. 148. Jens's reference to the Murke satires is to the book *Dr. Murkes gesammeltes Schweigen und andere Satiren* (Cologne: Kiepenheuer & Witsch, 1958), which contains, besides "Murke's Collected Silences," "Christmas Every Day," "Action Will Be Taken," "Bonn Diary," and "The Thrower-away"—all but "Christmas" can be found in Heinrich Böll, *18 Stories*. Not all critics admire Böll as a satirist. Günter Blöcker feels Böll's humanity prevents him from being too severe in his chastisement: "The blows which he administers are not far removed from absolution. And many who praise his satiric talent are merely expressing their relief at getting off so lightly" ("Der letzte Mensch," in Werner Lengning, ed., *Der Schriftsteller H.B.* [Munich, 1977], p. 87). And elsewhere Blöcker claims: "Whatever he may be, I would scarcely consider him a satirist. For that he lacks not only gall, but above all lightening sharpness and the piercing power of formulation" ("Heinrich Böll als Satiriker," in *Die Bücherkommentare* 7, no. 1 [1958]:2).

2. In a report on the Böll reception in Brazil Erwin Theodor Rosenthal observes: "Böll's works are received in Brazil as contemporary critical observations which do not apply exclusively to Germany, but to the entire Western World (and perhaps not only there!)" ("Böll in Brasilien," in Manfred Jurgensen, ed., *Böll: Untersuchungen zum Werk* [Bern, 1975], p. 150).

3. Klaus Jeziorkowski, *Rhythmus und Figur* (Bad Hamburg 1968), p. 33.

4. "[Böll] is neither Kleist nor Hebel, but he wrote 'Murke's Collected Silences,' and that no other living writing has been able to duplicate" (Cesare Cases, " 'Die Waage der Baleks,' dreimal gelesen," in Marcel Reich-Ranicki, ed., *In Sachen Böll* [Cologne, 1970], p 225).

5. See Chapter 3, note 1.

6. Dieter E. Zimmer, "Dr. Murkes gesammeltes Schweigen," in *In Sachen Böll*, cites critics who claim the "broadcasting industry" and the "culture industry" are the main objects of the satire, but Zimmer himself sees the "pompous wordiness, and oily insincerity" of society as the point of the work (pp. 268–69).

7. Quoted from a summary of the Ahlen Program and the Düsseldorf Principles in "Dokumente zur Zeit," *Die Zeit*, 21 November 1975, p. 7.

8. *Ansichten eines Clowns*, p. 132.

9. Among all of Böll's satires only two others are written in the third person: "Der Bahnhof von Zimpern" (1958) and "Keine Träne um Schmeck" (1961), both in *E 50–70*. "Zimpern" is not available in

English; "No Tears for Schmeck" can be found in *Encounter* (London) 32, no. 5 (May 1969).

10. Jost Hermand, ed., "Vorwort" to *Jugendstil* (Darmstadt, 1971), p. ix.

11. Erhard Friedrichsmeyer, *The Major Works of H.B.* (New York, 1970), p. 68.

12. Wilhelm Johannes Schwarz, *Der Erzähler H.B.* (Bern, 1968), p. 31.

13. Wirth, *Heinrich Böll*, p. 86.

14. Léopold Hoffmann, *Heinrich Böll* (Luxembourg, 1973), p. 29.

15. Friedrichsmeyer, *The Major Works of H.B.*, p. 52.

16. Cesare Cases, " 'Die Waage der Baleks,' dreimal gelesen," in *In Sachen Böll*, p. 227.

17. Ibid., pp. 227–28.

18. John Fetzer, analyzing the story from a legal point of view, asserts there is no evidence that the scales were intentionally false or that they were inaccurate for five generations. He sees the story as Böll's attempt to demonstrate the need for caution before jumping to revolutionary conclusions. See his "The Scales of Injustice: Comments on Heinrich Böll's 'Die Waage der Baleks,' " *German Quarterly* 45, no. 3 (May 1972): 472–79. Although Fetzer makes some valuable observations on the tale, the article seriously violates the spirit of the work, uses false methodology (legal evidence is not the same as literary evidence), and at times contradicts the facts of the story.

19. "On Simple and Sentimental Poetry," *Complete Works of Friedrich Schiller in Eight Volumes* (New York: Collier & Son, 1902), 8 (*Aesthetic and Philosophical Essays*), p. 319.

20. For Böll's comments on the "Seven Corporal Works of Mercy," see "Ich habe die Nase voll!" in *Ee*: "I find them [the Seven Corporal Works of Mercy] very beautiful. Perhaps we ought to make a litany of them: feed the hungry, etc., even when they are Chilean Communists and Soviet dissidents . . . I can imagine a poem made of them; I am ready to collaborate with someone on it" (p. 186).

21. See Curt Hohoff, "Die roten Fliessen im 'Tal der donnernden Hufe,' " in *In Sachen Böll*, pp. 251–58. For more on Böll's color symbolism, see Gertrud Bauer Pickar, "The Symbolic Use of Color in Heinrich Böll's *Billard um halbzehn*," *UDR* 12, no. 2 (Spring 1976): 41–51.

22. Hohoff, p. 255.

23. In the story the word "death" is seldom used in the medical sense, but in the biblical sense of the death of the soul—the state which separates the sinner from God, as expressed in such epigrammatical

phrases as: The wages of sin is death (Rom. 6:23), To be carnally minded is death (Rom. 8:6), and The sting of death is sin (I Cor. 15:56).

24. Mirzova's outsider status is also reflected in her name. Her classmates follow the Russian practice of feminizing the father's last name when referring to her.

25. For information on Böll's relationship to the new morality and situation ethics, see Robert C. Conard, "The Humanity of H.B.: Love and Religion," *Boston University Journal* 21, no. 2 (Spring 1973): 35–43.

26. In this story the female's superior moral strength is even indicated in physical terms: "The girl's hands were larger and firmer than Griff's hands, larger and firmer than his own too: he felt this and was ashamed of it" (*E 50–70*, p. 242).

27. Occasionally Böll demonstrates the power of the female for the negative development of the male, like Bertha in the short story "Wie in schlechten Romanen" [Like a Bad Dream, 1956], in Heinrich Böll, *18 Stories*, and Frau Franke in the novel *Und sagte kein einziges Wort* [Acquainted with the Night, 1953].

28. Bienek, p. 177.

29. Wolfdietrich Rasch, "Zum Stil des 'Irischen Tagebuchs,'" in *In Sachen Böll*, p. 264.

30. Wilhelm J. Schwarz, "Heinrich Böll," in Otto Mann, ed., *Christliche Dichter im 20. Jahrhundert* (Bern, 1968), p. 435.

31. Ibid.

32. Hoffmann, p. 32.

33. Inge Meidinger-Geise, *Perspektiven deutscher Dichtung I* (Nuremberg: Glock und Lutz, 1957), p. 54.

34. Schwarz, *Der Erzähler Heinrich Böll*, p. 33.

35. See Rainer Nägele, *H.B.: Einführung in das Werk und in die Forschung* (Frankfurt am Main, 1976), pp. 133–35.

36. Rasch, in *In Sachen Böll*, p. 266.

37. "One could dare call these creatures 'angels' if one would give the word its original meaning: messengers of hope." See "Mut und Bescheidenheit: Krieg und Nachkrieg im Werk Heinrich Bölls," in *Der Schriftsteller H.B.*, p. 57.

Chapter Four

1. Böll sees the novel *Katharina Blum* also in this light. He calls it a "political pamphlet," "a pamphlet in the form of a report," a "polemic" (*Streitschrift*). Then he adds the sentence which applies to

"The Seventh Trunk": The pamphlet in the form of a story is a form which perhaps is not yet commonly practiced" (*Gespräche über den Roman*, ed. Manfred Durzak [Frankfurt, 1976], p. 150). In general, postmodernist literature often has literary scholarship and literature itself as the subject of literature: for example, Vladimir Nabokov's *Pale Fire* and many works by Jorge Luis Borges.

2. See Böll's comments on the literary influences on him in "Interview mit mir selbst" in Beckel, p. 7; in Bienek, pp. 177–78; and in "Interview von Marcel Reich-Ranicki," in *AKR*, p. 508, where Böll claims that of the many writers who have influenced him Hebel and Heinrich von Kleist are the most important.

3. Bienek, p. 182. Böll expresses the same idea in "A Plea for Meddling," *New York Times*, 19 February 1973, p. 15.

4. From Alan Pryce-Jones's review of *Miss MacIntosh, My Darling* by Marguerite Young, *New York Herald Tribune*, 16 September 1965, quoted from Margret Gump, *Adalbert Stifter* (New York: Twayne, 1974), p. 92.

5. Stifter develops his theory of the "sanftes Gesetz" in his "Vorrede" to *Bunte Steine*.

6. All references to ruling monarchs, the Kaiser, and to historic names and dates are excluded from the work, even the subtitle, "A Narrative for Our Times," was shortened by Stifter simply to "A Narrative" because, he maintained, "The reader himself must find out the time" (quoted from Gump, p. 112).

7. Quoted from Gump, p. 112.

8. Quotations from *Der Nachsommer* are from the edition Goldmanns gelbe Taschenbücher, Band 1378/79/80 (Munich: Wilhelm Goldmann, 1964).

9. Stifter himself, however, was not an apolitical man who disregarded the social realities of his day. He authored several cultural and political essays. He acknowledged the Revolution of 1848 as the most important social event of his time and at first welcomed its newly won political freedom. He was even a delegate from his district to the preparatory meetings for the Frankfurt Parliament. In his position as school superintendent for Upper Austria he was much concerned with the poverty of teachers and their lowly social position, but eventually he sided against the social disruption caused by the revolution and was fearful of political change. Ultimately he showed little understanding of politics and retreated into a utopian world of moral and ethical *Bildungs-* and *Humanitätsidealismus* which supported the reactionary powers in Austria. On one point in *Der Nachsommer*, however, he veers from the prevailing conservative attitudes of Romanticism. He

sees with optimism the coming age of technology as a boon for mankind: "Won't the goods of the earth, then, through the possibility of easy exchange become so common that everything becomes available to all? . . . A time of greatness will come which in history has not yet been." It is this double view of Stifter's work (his progressive vision and his conservatism) that leads the East German critic Günter Wirth to characterize Stifter as a representative of what today would be called "the third way" ("Tradition 'im Futteral,'" in *Böll: Untersuchungen zum Werk*, p. 127).

10. See Böll, "Annäherungsversuch: Nachwort zu Tolstois *Krieg und Frieden*," in *NPLS*, pp. 163–87.

11. Risach also makes this same argument, *Der Nachsommer*, p. 515.

12. Quotations from the foreward to *Bunte Steine* are from the edition, Goldmanns gelbe Taschenbücher, Band 1375 (Munich: Wilhelm Goldmann, n.d.).

13. From this point of view Böll's epilogue continues in the manner of Arno Schmidt's critique of Stifter in "Der sanfte Unmensch: Einhundert Jahre Nachsommer," in *Dya na Sore: Gespräche in einer Bibliothek* (Karlsruhe: Stahlberg, 1958), pp. 194–229, and of Horst Albert Glaser's critique in *Die Restauration des Schönen: Stifters "Nachsommer"* (Stuttgart, 1965).

14. In *FAZ*, 29 January 1976.

15. Published under the title "Ich habe die Nase voll!" in *Ee*, pp. 183–88.

16. *Time*, 5 July 1976, p. 46.

17. Willy Brandt admits the mistake of these decrees: "I erred at the time. . . . There have been gross deviations and grotesque abuses" (*Time*, 5 July 1976, p. 46).

18. *Time* magazine reports that of 496,000 applicants for government jobs 428 have been denied employment under the Radical Decrees (*Time*, 5 July 1976, p. 45). Two years later *Die Zeit* reports that over 2 million persons seeking employment with the government have been investigated and 611 cases of denied employment for political reasons are known (*Zeit*, 28 July 1978, p. 6). *Die Zeit's* charge that job discrimination based on interpretation of the Radical Decrees is much greater than 611 cases is supported by *Neues Deutschland*, which reports that the number of *Berufsverbote* in West Germany is 4,000 (*Neues Deutschland*, 17 July 1978, p. 3).

19. *rb* = rotbrüchig, red sympathetic; *sb* = schwarzbrüchig, black (church) sympathetic; *bb* = braunbrüchig, brown sympathetic; *rf* = rotfaul, red contaminated; *Likaki* = Linkskatholischer Kirchengänger, leftist Catholic churchgoer; *Kaki* = rightest Catholic churchgoer be-

cause the word is pronounced *khaki*. Also combinations such as *sbrf* and *rbrf* appear.

20. In a discussion of *Berichte zur Gesinnungslage der Nation* during an interview with René Wintzen, Böll declares: "[I] reread one of the few classical German satires, *Briefe der Dunkelmänner*. That is a wonderful German work although written in Latin in the period of Humanism against the Dominicans in Cologne who were playing a shady role. I had the form then, and the idea: secret fictitious reports by informers on red radicals in public service, etc. With that the organizational preparation was complete" (*Querschnitte*, p. 136).

Chapter Five

1. The brief section of the book which deals with the family background of the blond soldier, the section which hints at a relationship between war and business by showing the family wealth of the soldier derives from the production of flags and war insignia, prefigures Böll's development as a writer with social concerns.

2. Gert Kalow, "Heinrich Böll," in *Christliche Dichter der Gegenwart*, ed. Hermann Friedmann and Otto Mann (Heidelberg, 1955), p. 428.

3. Theodore Ziolkowski, "H.B.: Conscience and Craft," p. 217.

4. Ibid.

5. Walter Kaufmann, *From Shakespeare to Existentialism* (New York, 1960), p. 36.

6. Böll says of his method of treating time: "Ideally, I would say, a novel ought to take place in one minute. I can only indicate with this exaggeration what I am trying to do in my treatment of time" (Bienek, p. 177).

7. Hannah Arendt, *Eichmann in Jerusalem: A Report on the Banality of Evil* (New York, 1963).

8. Carl Amery, *Die Kapitulation oder deutscher Katholizismus heute* (Hamburg, 1963), p. 23.

Chapter Six

1. Böll's position in this 1953 novel is in full accord with the church's teachings on birth control, as is his position in the 1954 novel *The Unguarded House* in full accord with the church's position on abortion. But with time Böll's attitude to these matters has been influenced more by the existential necessities of life. See his 1968 critique of the encyclical "Humane vitae" in *NPLS*, pp. 32–35.

2. As at the end of *Acquainted with the Night,* when Fred Bogner sees Käte through the store window wearing her green skirt and hat and turning into Green Street, so here, too, Böll uses the color green (in Hedwig's coat, p. 44, and her pullover, p. 125) as the symbol of new life. Color symbolism is not uncommon in Böll, and in *The Bread of Those Early Years,* besides green, he uses red to symbolize the coldbloodedness and the viciousness of the economic order. Notice especially Walter's metaphor about the red coloring in the spring (p. 121), Ulla's red coat and Walter's comment that he used to love to see her in it (p. 107), the pink of the bathing trunks which killed Jürgen Brolaski (p. 71), the red line used to cross out Alois Fruk-lahr's name (p. 102), and the frequent references to the triumvirate of Prussian militarism, classical education, and the profit system in the leitmotif of the blood red of General Scharnhorst's collar, Iphigenia's lips, and the ace of hearts (pp. 12, 13, 102).

3. Peter Leiser, *Heinrich Böll: Das Brot der frühen Jahre/Ansichten eines Clowns* (Hollfeld, 1974), p. 40.

4. Compare this line with the hymn sung by the villagers in "The Balek Scales": "The justice of this earth, Oh Lord, hath killed Thee," *EHA*, pp. 60, 61.

5. Here the reference is to the biblical imperative, derived from the story of Cain and Abel, that each man must be his brother's keeper (Gen. 4:9).

Chapter Seven

1. The first German translation of *The Catcher in the Rye* appeared in 1954. Böll's revised translation of this work appeared in 1962 (Cologne: Kiepenheuer & Witsch).

2. It is precisely this aspect of the conclusion that Hans Joachim Bernhard ignores in his analysis of the novel and in his argument that the ending is idyllic and utopian. See *Die Romane Heinrich Bölls* (Berlin, 1973), pp. 170–81.

3. In the adult world of the novel the word "immorality" is used exclusively for things sexual. Significantly, Martin concludes on his own that immorality also has a relationship to food, money, and politics. These pasages recall Böll's criticism in "Brief an einen jungen Katholiken": "Morality is always identified with sexual morality. . . . What an immense theological mistake lies in this identification. . . . From this one-sided interpretation of morality the whole of European Catholicism has suffered for about a hundred yers" (*EHA*, p. 379).

4. Paul Hünerfeld in a review of *Billard um halbzehn*, in *Die Zeit,* 9 October 1959.

5. Bienek, p. 177.

6. Therese Poser, "Billard um halbzehn," in Möglichkeiten des modernen deutschen Romans, ed. Rolf Geissler (Frankfurt, 1962), p. 249.

7. Bienek, pp. 147–75.

8. See especially Böll's "Annäherungsversuch," his postscripts to Tolstoi's War and Peace, in NPLS, pp. 163–87, where he refers to Tolstoi as langatmig and Dostoevsky as kurzatmig.

9. Böll finds it important that the main characters be introduced early in a novel. See his postscript to War and Peace, NPLS, p. 171. The only novel by Böll in which this does not occur is his first, Adam, Where Were You?

10. Since these charts are made from manuscripts of the novel, not from the printed text, their details vary somewhat from the published edition. For excellent analysis of the structure of Billiards see Poser and Klaus Jeziorkowski, Rhythmus und Figur.

11. Bernhard, p. 210. Böll's own statement on Billiards supports Bernhard's assertion. In an interview with René Wintzen in 1976, Böll clearly lays the blame for Hitler's coming to power on a coalition of capitalist interests: "I believe that the Nazi party would have again been reduced by natural election processes. At the moment when its decline started and the leadership of the Nazi party was rather desperate after a loss at the polls [November 1932] and a loss of money— at that moment the German nationalists together with the industrialists and the bankers took the party and put it in power" (Querschnitte, p. 113).

12. While Böll fails to deal with economic realities in Billiards, he does so successfully in several other works: "The Balek Scales," Acquainted with the Night, The Unguarded House, The Bread of Those Early Years, and Group Portrait with Lady.

13. Paul Konrad Kurz, "Heinrich Böll: Die Denunziation des Krieges und der Katholiken," Stimmen der Zeit 96 (1971): 26.

14. Horst Haase, "Charakter und Funktion der zentralen Symbolik in Heinrich Bölls Roman 'Billard um halbzehn,'" Weimarer Beiträge 10 (1964): 225.

15. Karlheinz Deschner, Talente, Dichter, Dilettanten (Wiesbaden, 1964), p. 19.

16. Marcel Reich-Ranicki, Deutsche Literatur in West und Ost (Munich, 1963), p. 137.

17. Schwarz, Der Erzähler Heinrich Böll, p. 37. Böll's own explanation of his symbolism lies in the historical situation of November 1932 (see Note 11). He labels the coalition that brought Hitler to

power as the Buffaloes: "This alliance of Junkers and bankers and German nationalists was for me the Buffaloes . . . because they simply trampled over everything like a herd of buffaloes. The others, the victims, I called the lambs" (*Querschnitte*, pp. 113–14).

18. Böll's praise, however, in his essays for West Germany's democratic constitution is lavish: "The constitution of the Federal Republic of Germany is probably the best possible constitution that a state can have in the twentieth century" ("Die Würde des Menschen ist unantastbar," in *NPLS*, p. 260). In another essay Böll writes of the constitution as a means of legally introducing socialism to West Germany and as a weapon against the abuse of private property: "It is a great and crucial mistake on the part of the West German Social Democrats that they have never quantitatively defined the magic word 'expropriation' (which is legal according to the Federal German constitution)," "Inflation," in *New York Times Magazine*, 2 May 1976, p. 63.

19. For an analysis of Heinrich as actor, role-player, and manipulator of people and circumstances, see R. Hinton Thomas and Wilfried van der Will, *The German Novel and the Affluent Society* (Toronto: University of Toronto Press, 1968), pp. 45–55.

20. Bernhard, p. 215.

Chapter Eight

1. Klaus Jeziorkowski, "Heinrich Böll. Die Syntax des Humanen," in *Zeitkritische Romane des 20. Jahrhunderts*, ed. Hans Wagener (Stuttgart, 1975), p. 302.

2. Between 10 May and 21 June 1963 eight review articles of *The Clown* appeared in *Die Zeit* alone.

3. From the manuscripts of *The Clown* in the Boston University Library one can see that Böll began the novel in the third person and switched to the first. Interesting also are three large sheets of thin cardboard on which Böll outlined the time structure and the content of each chapter of the novel, which at the time carried the title *Augenblicke* [Moments]. See Box 2, Folder 2. For review of the Böll archive see Robert C. Conard, "Report on the Heinrich Böll Archive at the Boston University Library," *UDR* 10, no. 2 (Fall 1973):11–14.

4. In the outline mentioned in the previous note, Böll indicates the time of Hans's arrival in Bonn at seven o'clock, but judging from the published text, six o'clock seems more accurate.

5. See Edward Schillebeeckx, *Marriage: Human Reality and Saving Mystery*, trans. N. D. Smith (New York: Sheed and Ward, 1965), pp. 378–80.

6. Böll's statement—"As an author really only two themes interest me: love and religion" (*AKR*, p. 510)—is from the political point of view an acute narrowing of the themes in his works, but, nevertheless, an extremely accurate observation for some of his minor works. In the radio play *Hausfriedensbruch* [Disturbing the Domestic Peace] Böll pursues the dramatic conflict of two people separately married who leave their spouses to return to each other, because in their youth they loved one another and lived together, and now believe that that union consisted of marriage and their present marriages are adulterous. In the stage play *Aussatz* [Leprosy], published together with *Hausfriedensbruch* in 1969, Böll explores the idea of divorce by mutual consent. In the third act of this drama, Gerta Buhr has been given her freedom by her husband on the condition she create no scandal. Hence she is in effect divorced and can therefore take a lover who despite her existing marriage is able to claim her as his spouse: "You are my wife and married to someone else." In the short story "Bis dass der Tod euch scheidet" [Until Death Do You Part, 1976], the main character argues that a marriage exists until the "death of the marriage," not until the death of one of the partners separates the spouses. At this point the reader recalls Leni Pfeiffer's words in *Group Portrait* which effect her "divorce" from her husband: "For me he was dead before he had died." Hence throughout Böll's work a consistent source of drama is the idea that it is not marriage that sanctifies love; rather it is love that sanctifies marriage.

7. Hans's refusal to get married by the state or the church and his refusal to sign papers to raise his children Catholic is not, although he is an unbeliever, a signal of disdain for religion. Hans is merely insisting that marriage and child rearing are private matters between spouses. Hans's total openness to religion is seen clearly in the comfort he finds in the church liturgy and in his efforts to have Marie continue to practice her religion when she herself is prepared to abandon it (pp. 266–67).

8. Evelyn T. Beck, "A Feminist Critique of Böll's *Ansichten eines Clowns*," *UDR* 12, no. 2 (Spring 1976):19. See also Gertrud B. Pickar, "The Impact of Narrative Perspective on Character Portrayal in Three Novels of Heinrich Böll," *UDR* 11, no. 2 (Winter 1974): 25–40. Here Pickar alludes to Hans's "bad faith" in his relationship with Marie.

9. Walter Hinck, "Ansichten eines Clowns—heute," in *Böll: Untersuchungen zum Werk*, p. 20.

10. See Bernd Balzer, "Vorwort" to *Heinrich Böll Werke: Romane und Erzählungen* (Cologne, 1977), I, 93.

11. Werner Hoffmeister, "Heinrich Böll: *Ende einer Dienstfahrt*," *Novel* 1 (1968): 291–92.

12. In *Heinrich Böll Werke: Romane und Erzählungen*, 5, 521–29.

13. Manfred Durzak, *Der deutsche Roman der Gegenwart* (Stuttgart, 1971), p. 96.

Chapter Nine

1. Dieter E. Zimmer, "Das Gespräch mit dem Autor Heinrich Böll. Für Sachkunde und für Phantasie," *Die Zeit*, 10 August 1971, p. 9.

2. Böll/Wellershoff, *Akzente* 18 (August 1971):331.

3. See Chapter 8, note 6.

4. Böll obviously intends a pun. The word *Schelm* means knave, rogue, villain.

5. Marcel Reich-Ranicki is mistaken in his criticism that all the characters "speak the same idiom, a Böllian colloquial German" ("Nachdenken über Leni: Heinrich Bölls neuer Roman *Gruppenbild mit Dame*," *Die Zeit*, 10 August 1971). While it is obvious that the language of each character has an informal quality, Reich-Ranicki seems to forget that the characters are being interviewed. Anything but a colloquial language would be out of place. Still, within this single level of speech, each character has his own voice; his own level of linguistic crassness, decorum, and sophistication.

6. Böll reproduced this diagram as a thank-you card to send to well-wishers on the reception of his Nobel Prize.

7. Böll/Arnold, *Im Gespräch* (Munich, 1971), p. 55.

8. See Theodore Ziolkowski, "The Author as *Advocatus Dei* in Heinrich Böll's *Group Portrait with Lady*," *UDR* 12, no. 2 (Spring 1976), and "Typologie und 'Einfache Form' in *Gruppenbild mit Dame*" in *Die subversive Madonna*, ed. Renate Matthaei (Cologne, 1975).

9. Manfred Durzak, *Gespräch über den Roman*, p. 139.

10. Ralph Ley, "Compassion, Catholicism, and Communism: Reflections on Böll's *Gruppenbild mit Dame*," *UDR* 10, no. 2 (Fall 1973); Ingeborg L. Carlson, "Heinrich Bölls *Gruppenbild mit Dame* als frohe Botschaft der Weltverbrüderung," *UDR* 11, no. 2 (Winter 1974); Margareta Deschner, "Böll's 'Lady': A New Eve," *UDR* 11, no. 2 (Winter 1974); Theodore Ziolkowski, "The Author as *Advocatus Dei*."

11. Böll/Wellershoff, pp. 332–33.

12. Ibid., p. 345.

13. Böll/Linder, *Drei Tage im März* (Cologne, 1975), p. 91. See also the interview with D. Zimmer: "I believe we are probably killing

ourselves with work [Leistung]," *Die Zeit*, 10 August 1971, p. 10. It would be unfair to absolutize the position of *Leistungsverweigerung* into an atavistic model of personal agriculture and craft guilds and then criticize the model for its inherent romanticism, and infeasibility in meeting the needs of a nation or the world. In *Group Portrait* Böll's critique is of a system of production that drives the worker, creates anxieties by stimulating unnecessary consumption, and exploits natural resources for the profit of those who do not work, but who manipulate the resources, buy the advertising, and control the means of production.

14. Böll/Arnold, pp. 56–57.

15. Ibid., p. 57.

16. Ibid., p. 58.

17. Heinrich Böll, *Hausfriedensbruch: Ein Hörspiel/Aussatz: Ein Schauspiel* (Cologne, 1969), p. 85.

18. See Böll/Wellershoff, p. 343, and Böll/Linder.

19. Böll/Wellershoff, p. 343.

20. Böll/Arnold, p. 59.

21. See David Myers, "Heinrich Böll's *Gruppenbild mit Dame*: Aesthetic Play and Ethical Seriousness," *Seminar* 13, no. 3 (September 1977).

22. Also on the subject of Böll's humor see Wilhelm H. Grothmann, "Zur Struktur des Humors in Heinrich Bölls *Gruppenbild mit Dame*," *German Quarterly* 50, no. 2 (March 1977):150–60.

23. Bernhard, p. 372.

24. See Bernd Balzer, "Einigkeit der Einzelgänger," in *Die subversive Madonna*, ed. Renate Matthaei (Cologne, 1975), pp. 11–33.

25. See the Böll interview in Durzak, *Gespräch über den Roman*, p. 151.

26. Horst Bienek, p. 182.

27. "Will Ulrike Gnade oder freies Geleit," *Der Spiegel*, 10 January 1972, p. 55.

28. See the interview with the directors of the film, "Sieben Fragen an Volker Schlöndorff und Margarethe von Trotta," *Die Zeit*, 17 October 1975, p. 15.

29. For an even sharper attack on conditions in Germany, see Böll's poem "sieben Jahre und zwanzig später" in *Gedichte, Klaus Staeck: Collagen*, Querheft 1 (Cologne, 1975), pp. 37–40. In this poem Böll speaks ironically of "the free / democratic / system / of *Bild* / by *Bild* and / for *Bild*." And the poem contains one of Böll's bitterest lines: "In this German house / murderers make the laws."

30. See Frank Grützbach, ed., *Heinrich Böll: Freies Geleit für Ulrike Meinhof. Ein Artikel und seine Folgen* (Cologne, 1972).

31. Böll/Linder, p. 68.

32. Peter Brückner was chairman of the psychology department at the Technical University in Hannover. Because of his rumored association with the Baader-Meinhof group, he was suspended in 1972 from his university duties while being subjected to considerable calumny in the press. In December 1973 he was reinstated in his position. In 1977 he was again suspended, this time for the publication of a political pamphlet, "Die Mescalero-Affäre—ein Lehrstück für Aufklärung und politische Kultur." As of this writing his case for reinstatement is pending in the courts. See *Die Zeit*, 5 May 1978, p. 16.

33. Dieter Zilligen, "Interview Heinrich Böll," in *Bücherjournal*, NDR television, 19 October 1974, quoted from Hanno Beth, "Rufmord und Mord: Die Publizistische Dimension der Gewalt," in *Eine Einführung in das Gesamtwerk in Einzelinterpretationen*, ed. Hanno Beth (Kronberg, 1975), pp. 57–58.

34. Quoted from a letter to *Der Spiegel*, "Betroffen, belastet, diffamiert," 19 August 1974, p. 7.

35. Quoted from *Die Zeit*, 28 May 1976, p. 19.

36. Durzak, *Gespräch über den Roman*, p. 136.

37. Ibid., p. 149.

38. Ibid., p. 148.

39. See Durzak, *Gespräch über den Roman*, p. 140.

40. Ibid., p. 143.

41. Actually Böll means Friday, not Thursday, because Katharina's first interrogation was on Thursday and the first article could only have appeared the next day. The story contains several similar mistakes. On Friday during Katharina's second interrogation the text reads: she took "both issues of the *News*" (p. 81) out of her handbag. Two issues could not have appeared by this time (see Beth, p. 77, note 66.) Also Moeding is referred to as the "chief commissioner" (p. 12) when, in fact, he is the assistant to the commissioner Beizmenne (see Beth, p. 76, note 35). Furthermore, the suspicion of the police that Katharina was also the murderer of the *News*-photographer Adolf Schönner, killed on Tuesday (26 February), seems an inconsistency in the text, for Katharina was in custody from Sunday evening (24 February) on, the time she gave herself up to Moeding (pp. 13–15) (see Rainer Nägele, *Heinrich Böll: Einführung in das Werk und in die Forschung*, p. 76). Such mistakes lead Joachim Kaiser in his review in *Süddeutsche Zeitung* (10–11 August 1974, p. 76) to conclude that no reader scrutinizes Böll's manuscripts anymore before publication. Such errors, however, have been common in Böll's work throughout the years, notably in *Adam* and "Collected

Silences." Many of these errors are corrected in the American translations.

    42. Durzak, *Gespräch über den Roman*, p. 36.

    43. Ibid., pp. 138–39.

Selected Bibliography

Note: Several bibliographies of Böll's work and work on Böll exist. One of the most useful because of its intelligent organization, making it easy to find isolated translations in anthologies and periodicals, is Werner Martin's *Heinrich Böll: Eine Bibliographie seiner Werke*. Hildesheim: Georg Olms Verlag, 1975. More comprehensive, however, containing information not elsewhere available on performances and recordings of Böll's work and a thorough list of secondary literature, all periodically brought up to date, is Werner Lengning's *Der Schriftsteller Heinrich Böll: Ein biographisch-bibliographischer Abriss*, 5th ed. Munich: Deutscher Taschenbuch Verlag, 1977.

PRIMARY SOURCES

1. Böll's Works
Ansichten eines Clowns. Cologne: Kiepenheuer & Witsch, 1963.
Aufsätze, Kritiken, Reden. Cologne: Kiepenheuer & Witsch, 1967.
Berichte zur Gesinnungslage der Nation. Cologne: Kiepenheuer & Witsch, 1975.
Billard um halbzehn. Cologne: Kiepenheuer & Witsch, 1959; 6th ed., 1963.
Das Brot der frühen Jahre. Cologne: Kiepenheuer & Witsch, 1955.
Einmischung erwünscht: Schriften zur Zeit. Cologne: Kiepenheuer & Witsch, 1977.
Ende einer Dienstfahrt. Cologne: Kiepenheuer & Witsch, 1966.
Entfernung von der Truppe. Cologne: Kiepenheuer & Witsch, 1964.
Erzählungen, Hörspiele, Aufsätze. Cologne: Kiepenheuer & Witsch, 1961.
Erzählungen 1950–1970. Cologne: Kiepenheuer & Witsch, 1972.
Frankfurter Vorlesungen. Cologne: Kiepenheuer & Witsch, 1966.
Gedichte, Klaus Staeck: Collagen. Querheft 1. Cologne: Verlag Lamuv, 1975.
Gruppenbild mit Dame. Cologne: Kiepenheuer & Witsch, 1971.
Hausfriedensbruch: Ein Hörspiel/Aussatz: Ein Schauspiel. Cologne: Kiepenheuer & Witsch, 1969.

Haus ohne Hüter. Cologne: Kiepenheuer & Witsch, 1954; 4th ed.,
   1965.
Heinrich Böll 1947 bis 1951. Cologne: Friedrich Middelhauve Verlag,
   1963. Contains *Der Zug war pünktlich, Wo warst du, Adam?,* the
   twenty-five stories in *Wanderer, kommst du nach spa . . .,* and
   the story "Die schwarzen Schafe."
Heinrich Böll Werke. Ed. Bernd Balzer. 10 vols. Cologne: Gertraud
   Middelhauve Verlag and Kiepenheuer & Witsch, 1977 and 1978.
   The first five volumes, which appeared in 1977, comprise the most
   complete collection of Böll's novels and stories. The second five
   volumes, which appeared in 1978, contain the most complete
   collection of Böll's radio plays, dramas, film texts, poems, essays,
   reviews, speeches, commentaries, interviews, and sundry writ-
   ings.
Irisches Tagebuch. Cologne: Kiepenheuer & Witsch, 1957.
Neue politische und literarische Schriften. Cologne: Kiepenheuer &
   Witsch, 1973.
Querschnitte aus Interviews, Aufsätze und Reden von Heinrich Böll.
   Ed. Viktor Böll and Renate Matthaei. Cologne: Kiepenheuer &
   Witsch, 1977.
"Ein Schluck Erde." In *Homo viator: Modernes christliches Theater.*
   Cologne: Verlag Jakob Hegner, 1962, pp. 381–432.
*Die verlorene Ehre der Katharine Blum oder: Wie Gewalt entstehen
   und wohin sie führen kann.* Cologne: Kiepenheuer & Witsch,
   1974.
Und sagte kein einziges Wort. Cologne: Kiepenheuer & Witsch, 1953.

2.   Böll's Interviews
Conversation with Heinz Ludwig Arnold. In *Im Gespräch: Heinrich
   Böll mit Heinz Ludwig Arnold.* Edition Text + Kritik. Munich:
   Richard Boorberg, 1971.
Conversation with Horst Bienek. In Horst Bienek, *Werkstattgespräche
   mit Schriftsstellern.* Munich: Hanser, 1962; Deutscher Taschen-
   buch Verlag, 1965, pp. 168–84.
Conversation with Christian Linder. In Heinrich Böll/Christian Lin-
   der: *Drei Tage im März: Ein Gespräch.* Cologne: Kiepenheuer &
   Witsch, 1975.
"Das Gespräch mit dem Autor Heinrich Böll. Für Sachkunde und
   Phantasie." An interview by Dieter E. Zimmer. *Die Zeit,* 10 Aug-
   ust 1971, p. 9.
"Ich habe nichts über den Krieg aufgeschrieben." Ein Gespräch mit
   Heinrich Böll, Hermann Lenz, Nicolas Born und Jürgen Manthey.
   In *Literaturmagazin 7: Nachkriegsliteratur.* Ed. Nicolas Born and

Jürgen Manthey. Reinbeck bei Hamburg: Rowohlt, 1977, pp. 30–74.

"Ich tendiere nur zu dem scheinbar Unpolitischen: Gespräche mit Heinrich Böll." In Manfred Durzak, *Gespräche über den Roman.* Frankfurt: Surkamp, 1976, pp. 128–53.

"Interview mit Heinrich Böll." An interview by Dieter Zilligen. In *Bücherjournal,* NDR television, 19 October 1974.

"Interview mit mir selbst." Böll interviews himself. In *Albrecht Beckel, Mensch, Gesellschaft, Kirche bei Heinrich Böll.* Osnabrück: Fromm, 1966, pp. 7–12.

"Interview von Marcel Reich-Ranicki." In Heinrich Böll, *Aufsätze, Kritiken, Reden.* Cologne: Kiepenheuer & Witsch, 1967, pp. 502–10.

"Heinrich Böll/Dieter Wellershoff: *Gruppenbild mit Dame.* Ein Tonband-Interview." *Akzente* 18 (August 1971): 331–46; rpt. in *Die subversive Madonna: Ein Schlüssel zum Werk Heinrich Bölls.* Ed. Renate Matthaei. Cologne: Kiepenheuer & Witsch, 1975, pp. 141–56.

"Weil dieses Volk so verachtet wurde, wollte ich dazugehören." An interview by Jean-Louis de Rambures. *Frankfurter Allgemeine Zeitung,* 13 December 1973, p. 24; also *Le Monde* on the same day and abridged in *Commonweal* under the title "Heinrich Böll on Work, Faith, Germany," translated by Anne Femantle, 10 May 1974, pp. 236–38.

3.   English Translations

Absent without Leave and Other Stories. Translated by Leila Vennewitz. New York: McGraw-Hill, 1965.

Acquainted with the Night. Translated by Richard Graves. New York: Holt, 1954.

Adam and *The Train:* two novels. Translated by Leila Vennewitz. New York: McGraw-Hill, 1970.

Adam, Where Art Thou. Translated by Mervyn Savill. New York: Criterion Books, 1955.

And Never Said a Word. Translated by Leila Vennewitz. New York: McGraw-Hill, 1978.

Billiards at Half-past Nine. No translator. New York: McGraw-Hill, 1973.

The Bread of Those Early Years. Translated by Leila Vennewitz. New York: McGraw-Hill, 1976.

Children Are Civilians Too. Translated by Leila Vennewitz. New York: McGraw-Hill, 1970.

The Clown. Translated by Leila Vennewitz. New York: McGraw-Hill, 1965.

Eighteen Stories. Translated by Leila Vennewitz. New York: McGraw-Hill, 1966.

End of a Mission. Translated by Leila Vennewitz. New York: McGraw-Hill, 1968.

Group Portrait with Lady. Translated by Leila Vennewitz. New York: McGraw-Hill, 1973.

"Inflation." In *New York Times Magazine*, 2 May 1976, p. 63.

Irish Journal. Translated by Leila Vennewitz. New York: McGraw-Hill, 1967.

The Lost Honor of Katharine Blum. Translated by Leila Vennewitz. New York: McGraw-Hill, 1975.

Missing Persons and Other Essays. Translated by Leila Vennewitz. New York: McGraw-Hill, 1977.

Tomorrow and Yesterday. Translated by Mervyn Savill. New York: Criterion Books, 1957.

The Train Was on Time. Translated by Richard Graves. New York: Criterion Books, 1956.

The Unguarded House. Translated by Mervyn Savill. London: Arco, 1957.

SECONDARY SOURCES

AMERY, CARL. *Die Kapitulation oder deutscher Katholizismus heute.* Hamburg: Rowohlt, 1963.

ARENDT, HANNAH. *Eichmann in Jerusalem: A Report on the Banality of Evil.* New York: Viking, 1963.

BALZER, BERND. "Einigkeit der Einzelgänger." In *Die subversive Madonna: Ein Schlüssel zum Werk Heinrich Bölls.* Edited by Renate Matthaei. Cologne: Kiepenheuer & Witsch. 1975, pp. 11–33.

————. "Vorwort." In *Heinrich Böll Werke: Romane und Erzählungen I, 1947–1951.* Edited by Bernd Balzer. Cologne: Gertraud Middelhauve Verlag and Kiepenheuer & Witsch, 1977.

BECK, EVELYN T. "A Feminist Critique of Böll's *Ansichten eines Clowns.*" *UDR* 12, no. 2 (1976): 19–24.

BECKEL, ALBRECHT. *Mensch, Gesellschaft, Kirche bei Heinrich Böll,* mit einem Beitrag von Heinrich Böll: "Interview mit mir selbst." Osnabrück: Verlag A. Fromm, 1966.

BERNHARD, HANS JOACHIM. *Die Romane Heinrich Bölls: Gesellschaftskritik und Gemeinschaftsutopie.* 2nd ed. Berlin. Rütten & Loening, 1973.

BERRIGAN, PHILIP. "Report on a Talk by Philip Berrigan." *Flyer News* [University of Dayton Student Newspaper], 18 November 1975, p. 5.

BETH, HANNO, ed. *Heinrich Böll: Eine Einführung in das Gesamtwerk in Einzelinterpretationen.* Kronberg: Scriptor Verlag, 1975.

—————. "Rufmord und Mord: Die publizistische Dimension der Gewalt. Zu Heinrich Bölls Erzählung 'Die verlorene Ehre der Katharina Blum." *In Heinrich Böll: Eine Einführung in das Gesamtwerk in Einzelinterpretationen.* Edited by Hanno Beth. Kronberg: Scriptor Verlag, 1975, pp. 55–82.

BIENEK, HORST. *Werkstattgespräche mit Schriftstellern.* Munich: Hanser, 1962; Deutscher Taschenbuch, 1965.

BLÖCKER, GÜNTER. "Der letzte Mensch." In *Der Schriftsteller Heinrich Böll: Ein biographisch-bibliographischer Abriss.* Edited by Werner Lengning. 5th ed. Munich: Deutscher Taschenbuch Verlag, 1977, pp. 87–90.

—————. "Heinrich Böll als Satiriker." In *Die Bücherkommentare* 7 (1958): 2.

BORKIN, JOSEPH. *The Crime and Punishment of I. G. Farben.* New York: The Free Press, 1978.

BRÜCKNER, PETER. "Betroffen, belastet, diffamiert." *Der Spiegel,* 19 August 1974, p. 7.

BRUMMACK, JÜRGEN. "Zu Begriff und Theorie der Satire." *Deutsche Vierteljahrsschrift für Literaturwissenschaft und Geistesgeschichte* 45, Sonderheft (1971): 275–377.

CARLSON, INGEBORG L. "Heinrich Bölls *Gruppenbild mit Dame* als frohe Botschaft der Weltverbrüderung." *UDR* 11, no. 2 (1974): 51–64.

CASES, CESARE. " 'Der Waage der Baleks,' dreimal gelesen." In *In Sachen Böll.* 3rd ed. Edited by Marcel Reich-Ranicki. Cologne: Kiepenheuer & Witsch, 1970, pp. 224–32.

CONARD, ROBERT C. "Report on the Heinrich Böll Archive at the Boston University Library." *UDR* 10, no. 2 (1973): 11–14.

—————. "The Humanity of Heinrich Böll: Love and Religion." *Boston University Journal* 21, no. 2 (1973): 35–43.

DESCHNER, KARLHEINZ. *Talente, Dichter, Dilettanten: Überschätzte und unterschätzte Werke in der deutschen Literatur der Gegenwart.* Wiesbaden: Limes, 1964.

DESCHNER, MARGARETA. "Böll's 'Lady': A New Eve." *UDR* 11, no. 2 (1974): 11–24.

DURZAK, MANFRED, ed. *Die deutsche Literatur der Gegenwart.* Stuttgart: Reclam, 1971.

————, ed. *Gespräche über den Roman*. Frankfurt: Suhrkamp, 1976.

————. *Der deutsche Roman der Gegenwart*. Stuttgart: Kohlhammer, 1971.

————. "Heinrich Bölls epische Summe? Zur Analyse und Wirkung seines Romans 'Gruppenbild mit Dame.'" In *Basis: Jahrbuch für deutsche Gegenwartsliteratur*. Band 3. Edited by Reinhold Grimm and Jost Hermand. Frankfurt: Athenäum Verlag, 1972, pp. 174–97.

EICH, GÜNTER. *Gesammelte Werke*. Frankfurt: Suhrkamp, 1973.

FETZER, JOHN. "The Scales of Injustice: Comments on Heinrich Böll's 'Die Waage der Baleks.'" *German Quarterly* 45 (1972): 472–79.

FRIEDRICHSMEYER, ERHARD. "Böll's Satire." *UDR* 10, no. 2 (1973): 5–10.

————. *The Major Works of Heinrich Böll: A Critical Commentary*. New York: Monarch Press, 1974.

————, et al. "Workshop in Translating Literature." *Unterrichtspraxis* 7, no. 2 (1975): 81–85.

GLASER, HORST ALBERT. *Die Restoration des Schönen: Stifters "Nachsommer."* Stuttgart: Metzler, 1965.

GROTHMANN, WILHELM H. "Zur Struktur des Humors in Heinrich Bölls *Gruppenbild mit Dame*." *German Quarterly* 50 (1977): 150–60.

GRÜTZBACH, FRANK, ed. *Heinrich Böll: Freies Geleit für Ulrike Meinhof. Ein Artikel und seine Folgen*. Cologne: Kiepenheuer & Witsch, 1972.

HAASE, HORST. "Charakter und Funktion der zentralen Symbolik in Heinrich Bölls Roman 'Billard um halbzehn.'" *Weimarer Beiträge* 10 (1964): 219–26.

HERMAND, JOST. "Verwort." In *Jugendstil*. Edited by Jost Hermand. Darmstadt: Wissenschaftliche Buchhandlung, 1971, pp. i-xvi.

HINCK, WALTER. "'Ansichten eines Clowns'—heute." In *Böll: Untersuchungen zum Werk*. Edited by Manfred Jurgensen. Bern: Francke, 1975, pp. 11–30.

HOFFMANN, LÉOPOLD. *Heinrich Böll: Einführung in Leben und Werk*. 2nd ed. Luxembourg: Verlag Edi-Centre, 1973.

HOFFMEISTER, WERNER. "Heinrich Böll: *Ende einer Dienstfahrt*." *Novel* 1 (1968): 291–92.

HOHOFF, CURT. "Die roten Fliessen im 'Tal der donnernden Hufe.'" In *In Sachen Böll*. 3rd ed. Edited by Marcel Reich-Ranicki. Cologne: Kiepenheuer & Witsch, 1970, pp. 251–58.

HÜHNERFELD, PAUL. Review of *Billard um halbzehn. Die Zeit*, 9 October 1959.

JEZIORKOWSKI, KLAUS. "Heinrich Böll: Die Syntax des Humanen." In *Zeitkritische Romane des 20. Jahrhunderts: Die Gesellschaft in der Kritik der deutschen Literatur.* Edited by Hans Wagener. Stuttgart: Reclam, 1975, pp. 301–17.

——. *Rhythmus und Figur. Zur Technik der epischen Konstruktion in Heinrich Bölls "Der Wegwerfer" und "Billard um halbzehn."* Bad Homburg: Gehlen, 1968.

JURGENSEN, MANFRED, ed. *Böll: Untersuchung zum Werk.* Bern: Francke, 1975.

KAISER, JOACHIM. Review of Heinrich Böll's *Die verlorene Ehre der Katharina Blum. Süddeutsche Zeitung* 10–11 (August 1974): 76.

KALOW, GERT. "Heinrich Böll." In *Christliche Dichter der Gegenwart.* Edited by Hermann Friedmann and Otto Mann. Heidelberg: Rothe, 1955, pp. 426–35.

KAUFMANN, WALTER. *From Shakespeare to Existentialism.* New York: Doubleday, 1960.

KERNAN, ALVIN B. *The Plot of Satire.* New Haven: Yale University Press, 1965.

KURZ, PAUL KONRAD. "Heinrich Böll: Die Renunziation des Krieges und der Katholiken." *Stimmen der Zeit* 96 (1971): 17–30.

——. "Heinrich Böll: Nicht versöhnt." *Stimmen der Zeit* 96 (1971): 88–97.

LEISER, PETER. *Heinrich Böll: "Das Brot der frühen Jahre"/"Ansichten eines Clowns."* Hollfeld. Beyer, 1974.

LENGNING, WERNER, ed. *Der Schriftsteller Heinrich Böll: Ein biographisch-bibliographischer Abriss.* 5th ed. Munich: Deutscher Taschenbuch Verlag, 1977. Each edition of this work contains a different collection of essays on Böll.

LEY, RALPH. *Böll für Zeitgenossen: Ein kulturgeschichtliches Lesebuch.* New York: Harper & Row, 1970.

——. "Compassion, Catholicism, and Communism: Reflections on Böll's *Gruppenbild mit Dame.*" *UDR* 10, no. 2 (1973): 25–40.

MACPHERSON, ENID. *A Student's Guide to Böll.* London: Heinemann, 1972.

MARTIN, WERNER, ed. *Heinrich Böll: Eine Bibliographie seiner Werke.* Hildesheim: Georg Olms, 1975.

MURRAY, ANNE LOUISE. "Satirical Elements in the Narrative Prose of Heinrich Böll." Diss. Indiana University, 1972.

MYERS, DAVID. "Heinrich Böll's *Gruppenbild mit Dame*: Aesthetic Play and Ethical Seriousness." *Seminar* 13, no. 3 (1977): 190–98.

NÄGELE, RAINER. *Heinrich Böll: Einführung in das Werk und in die Forschung*. Frankfurt am Main: Athenäum Fischer Taschenbuch Verlag, 1976.

NICOLAI, RALF. "Zum historischen Gehalt in Bölls Erzählung 'Steh auf, steh doch auf.'" *Literatur in Wissenschaft und Unterricht* 8, no. 1 (1975):12–17.

PARENT, DAVID. "Böll's 'Wanderer kommst du nach Spa . . .': A Reply to Schiller's 'Der Spaziergang.'" *Essays in Literature* 1 (1974):109–17.

PICKAR, GERTRUD B. "The Impact of Narrative Perspective on Character Portrayal in Three Novels of Heinrich Böll." *UDR* 11, no. 2 (1974): 25–40.

————. "The Symbolic Use of Color in Heinrich Böll's *Billard um halbzehn*." *UDR* 12, no. 2 (1976): 41–50.

PLARD, HENRI. "Mut und Bescheidenheit: Krieg und Nachkrieg im Werk Heinrich Bölls." In *Der Schriftsteller Heinrich Böll: Ein biographisch-bibliographischer Abriss*. 5th ed. Edited by Werner Lengning. Munich: Deutscher Taschenbuch Verlag, 1977, pp. 51–74.

POSER, THERESE. "*Billard um halbzehn*." In *Möglichkeiten des deutschen Romans: Analysen und Interpretationsgrundlagen zu Romanen von Thomas Mann, Alfred Döblin, Hermann Broch, Gerd Gaiser, Max Frisch, Alfred Andersch und Heinrich Böll*. Edited by Rolf Geissler. Frankfurt: Diesterweg, 1962, pp. 232–55.

RASCH, WOLFDIETRICH. "Zum Stil des 'Irischen Tagebuchs.'" In *In Sachen Böll*. 3rd ed. Edited by Marcel Reich-Ranicki. Cologne: Kiepenheuer & Witsch, 1970, pp. 259–67.

REICH-RANICKI, MARCEL. *Deutsche Literatur in West und Ost*. Munich: Piper, 1963.

————, ed. *In Sachen Böll*. 3rd ed. Cologne: Kiepenheuer & Witsch, 1970.

————. "Nachdenken über Leni: Heinrich Bölls neuer Roman *Gruppenbild mit Dame*." *Die Zeit*, 10 August 1971.

REID, JAMES HENDERSON. "Böll's Names." *Modern Language Review* 69 (1974):575–83.

————. *Heinrich Böll; Withdrawal and Re-emergence*. London: Oswald, 1973.

ROSENTHAL, ERWIN THEODOR. "Böll in Brasilien." In *Böll: Untersuchung zum Werk*. Edited by Manfred Jurgensen. Bern: Francke Verlag, 1975, pp. 147–52.

ROSS, WERNER. "Heinrich Bölls hartnäckige Humanität." In *Der Schriftsteller Heinrich Böll: Ein biographisch-bibliographischer*

Abriss. 3rd ed. Edited by Werner Lengning. Munich: Deutscher Taschenbuch Verlag, 1972, pp. 84–89.

SCHWARZ, WILHELM JOHANNES. *Der Erzähler Heinrich Böll: Seine Werke und Gestalten.* 2nd ed. Bern: Francke Verlag, 1968.

————. "Heinrich Böll." In *Christliche Dichter im 20. Jahrhundert.* 2nd ed. Begründet von Hermann Friedmann und Otto Mann. Edited by Otto Mann. Bern: Francke Verlag, 1968, pp. 432–44.

STRESAU, HERMANN. *Heinrich Böll.* Berlin: Colloquium Verlag, 1964.

THOMAS, R. HINTON, and VAN DER WILL, WILFRED. *The German Novel and the Affluent Society.* Toronto: University of Toronto Press, 1968.

TROMMLER, FRANK. "Der 'Nullpunkt 1945' und seine Verbindlichkeit für die Literaturgeschichte." In *Basis: Jahrbuch für deutsche Gegenwartsliteratur.* Band I. Edited by Reinhold Grimm and Jost Hermand. Frankfurt: Athenäum Verlag, 1970, pp. 9–25.

WIRTH, GÜNTER. *Heinrich Böll. Essayistische Studie über religiöse und gesellschaftliche Motive im Prosawerk des Dichters.* Berlin: Union Verlag, 1967.

————. "Tradition 'im Futteral.'" In *Böll: Untersuchungen zum Werk.* Edited by Manfred Jurgensen. Bern: Francke Verlag, 1975, pp. 111–38.

ZIMMER, DIETER E. "Dr. Murkes gesammeltes Schweigen." In *In Sachen Böll.* 3rd ed. Edited by Marcel Reich-Ranicki. Cologne: Kiepenheuer & Witsch, 1970, pp. 268–72.

ZIOLKOWSKI, THEODORE. "Albert Camus and Heinrich Böll." *Modern Language Notes* 7 (1962): 282–91.

————. "Heinrich Böll: Conscience and Craft." *Books Abroad* 34 (1960): 213–22.

————. "The Author as *Advocatus Dei* in Heinrich Böll's *Group Portrait with Lady.*" UDR 12, no. 2 (1976): 7–18.

————. "Typologie und 'Einfache Form' in *Gruppenbild mit Dame.*" In *Die subversive Madonna: Ein Schlüssel zum Werk Heinrich Bölls.* Edited by Renate Matthaei. Cologne: Kiepenheuer & Witsch, 1975, pp. 123–40.

Index